FROM THE TOP OF A SECRET TREE

PEARL DOPP

J. PHUNN PUBLISHERS

Library of Congress Catalog Card Number: 79-89312

ISBN 0-931762-11-1

PRINTED IN THE
UNITED STATES OF AMERICA
BY ADAMS PRESS, CHICAGO

Dedication

To the memory of
four parents,
two who
gave me life,
two who
taught me to live,
and to George
with whom
life is love.

ACKNOWLEDGEMENTS

To Professor Robert Gard, Extension Arts, University of Wisconsin, for inspiring the writing of this story,

To the several persons who studied the manuscript, the drawings and cover painting, making constructive suggestions,

To Mildred White Wells, past president of the General Federation of Women's Clubs, for her book, "Unity in Diversity,"

To Jean Gordon for her books, "Immortal Roses," "Rose Recipes," and "Pageant of the Rose,"

To the rural midwestern village for the privilege of service,

To George for washing the dishes and sweeping the porch,

To parents and Ripon College for opening the doors to life more abundant,

I give my never-ending gratitude.

CONTENTS

Introduction vi

Footprints vii

Prologue viii

I Enveloped by Love 3

II Beyond the Horizon 55

III Miracle of Words 89

IV Nature's Handmaiden 99

V Stop and Shop with Dopp 119

VI Chosen Children 129

VII Oh, My Sister! 159

VIII Mustard Seeds and Wild Roses 165

IX Back to the Beginning 185

X Tomorrow's Yesterdays 193

XI Woman 217

XII Elva 231

XIII Paying the Piper 239

XIV The Gift 261

XV On the Eve of a Golden Wedding 269

Epilogue 273

INTRODUCTION

My desire in writing this book is not to relate the autobiographical story of one ordinary person, but to picture the people of a rural village in central Wisconsin as they experienced the period of most rapid social and technological change in the history of the world—the first three quarters of the twentieth century. The important thing here is not to spotlight the silhouette of a solitary figure, but to portray the backdrop against which its diminutive shadow passed briefly across the stage.

Footprints

My bare feet climbed a spring-lit tree
From limb to shadowed limb,
To brighter air and bluer skies.
The world stretched out before my eyes,
My world as far as I could see,
My world as close as breath to me!
My tree! My secret tree!

On surer feet in the swiftening years
I climbed the far blue hill.
In consuming thirst I drank my fill,
For the world was wide on the other side,
The world as far as mind could see,
The world as close as love to me,
Its ecstacy! Its tears!

Through frosted grass the slow feet pass
To the tree, the secret tree.
And standing there in the filtered sun,
The warp and woof of a lifetime spun,
Though the wind be chill the heart will sing,
For leaves drift down in a coral ring,
And some of them fall on me!

Prologue

A mountain stream
Was muted momently
By my first cry.
Liquid crystal,
It swirled past boulders,
Dashed itself to spray and spume
As it sang its irrevocable way
To the sea.

Laughing and glinting in summer,
Raging and hungry at flash flood,
It had stolen two little girls,
Sisters, scarcely older than I,
And a woman's crying
Was lost in its roar.

Born to Gustavus and Salina,
The last of their ten daughters,
Mt. Hood glinting white
On the mounded horizon,
Born, not in pioneer cabin,
But in the new house—
Upright and two wings—
Built by their hands.

Before casings were fitted
To windows on the second floor
Stealthily
Tuberculosis sentenced Gustavus,
And Salina, once as spirited
As the colt on which she rode
To fetch supplies,
Now bruised by travail of pioneering,
Birthing, menopause,
Ended her living.

Motherless girls tended fields,
Baby sister, dying father.
Gustavus, summoning strength,
Wrote a letter
Asking brother, Jerry
And wife Fannie, childless,
If they could give his baby,
Then newly three,
A home.

How slow the train that sped them West!
With aching throats they said goodbye,
Locked me in their hearts
And took me home,
While Martha and Florence
Sought hiding places for tears,
Elva by the river
Wept the day long,
And Gustavus
In peace at last
Was ready to die.

Enveloped by Love

I

The click clacking of wheels on the railroad track, the swaying coach, the crying whistle in the night were frightening to a three-year-old who had just lost the only world she knew. In the lower berth Aunt Fannie, now to be known forever to me as "Mama," tried to comfort me with her new love but finally had to release me to the soothing warmth of my new Papa's arms until all was quiet within me. This Papa who, until three days before, had been the Uncle Jerry I had never seen, bore no physical evidence that he and my father were brothers. His eyes were blue and he was tall, while my father was dark and of medium height. Yet, there must have been a likeness which eyes could not see, a way of speaking, a way of saying without saying it, "I love you. You are my precious child," for the bond between us was instantaneous. There must have been familiarity in the warmth of his body, the tenderness of his voice, the gentle manhood of him that soothed my anxieties until sleep came at last.

The train, arrowing through the night, was taking me, in 1905, from the native home in the State of Washington, a home shadowed by anguish, to a new home, a Wild Rose, Wisconsin, home of love, security and opportunity.

There is one other picture from early childhood that flashes again and again across my consciousness—a large black box in the parlor of the old home, and sisters crying. Our father was crying, too. He was wrapped in a blanket and sitting in a rocker. Why was he crying? I couldn't understand. I had just become three, surely too young to remember the death of our mother, but having been separated from everyone who was there, how else could this dim memory be stored in mind?

Children adjust quickly to a new environment, especially when it includes a rag doll, a sled, a rocking chair, tender care and, joy of joys, a collie puppy. We played hide and seek, and no matter where I hid he always found me, his wagging and lapping bringing forth shrieks of joy. Even more fun was sliding down hill, Foxie running beside the sled and, holding the rope in his mouth, helping pull it up the hill. But there was no sliding down hill on Sunday. That day was reserved for church and quieter pursuits.

A few months after coming to Wisconsin, I was standing at the dining room window watching the rain make little rivers across the glass, when Mama, an open letter in her hand, held me close to tell me that my father was dead. Rain, beating on the window, has been a lifelong reminder of that morning.

As the holidays approached, the house was a-bubble with excitement, for I was to be flower girl at the wedding of Ethel Smart and Fred Shepherd. Mama went to Smart's Store to thumb through the pattern catalogues for a pretty little dress. She bought white dimity and yards and yards of lace and ran the Singer treadle sewing machine late into the night making ruffles and tucks and sewing lace by hand with such tiny stitches that they could scarcely be seen.

It was the most elaborate wedding ever solemnized in the little Methodist Church, festive with candlelight and arches of evergreens. The bride was elegant in her white satin dress, and her skirts swished as she stepped slowly and sedately down the aisle behind me. By the time we reached the altar, where the groom was waiting, my little basket of rose buds was empty. I caught a glimpse of Mama and Papa, their eyes singing.

After the holidays there was no more sliding down hill, for whooping cough ravaged me until spring. The anxiety my new parents must have felt, the fear of my having contracted tuberculosis from my father always hanging over their heads like a cloud! Papa carried in armloads of wood to keep the house warm and brought milk, warm from the Jersey cow, and Mama made eggnog, chicken broth, catnip tea and everything she could think of that would make me strong.

Dr. Fuller came regularly, took me out of bed wrapped in a blanket and held me on his soft lap. He was something of a ventriloquist. There would be the sound of a baby chick peeping, and Dr. Fuller would ask, "Is there a little chick in the house?"

"No. We don't have chickens in the house!"

"Well, someone must have brought one in. (peep-peep) There it is again! Don't you hear it?"

"Yes, I hear it."

He would begin looking around the room. "Where do you suppose it is? (peep-peep-peep) It must be in this room somewhere."

His rotund figure shook with laughter when we could never find it.

He retired the next year and, before moving to Nebraska, brought me his concert roller organ to remember him by. We never saw him again, but many hours were spent turning the organ handle and listening to the accordian-like music produced by the wooden rollers and their brass pegs.

Papa never missed an opportunity to tease me. We both enjoyed these sessions. Often he would sing a little ditty, perhaps one his father had sung to him, "I love you. You don't love me, and we both love Mama." He would wait for my protest, "That's wrong, Papa! I do love you!"

"No you don't," he would tease.

"Yes, I do! I do!"—the answer he expected.

"Well," he would say, "I'll sing it over and try to get it right."

But again he would sing, "You don't love me" and enjoy the inevitable assertion that I did, too, love him.

"If you do, how much?"

"More than tongue can tell."

He would laugh and ask, "How much is that?" expecting the usual, "More than a bushel."

Squeezing me, "How much is a bushel?"

"One hug and two kisses," the proof of which ended that happy encounter.

One summer Mama and I went by train to Tacoma, Washington, to see her sister, Mary. I was seven then. Aunt Mary and Mama went visiting one afternoon and left me in charge of the granddaughter, who was four. She wanted her hair cut, so I obliged, snipping off the brown curls one by one. Oh, the look of dismay on Aunt Mary's face when they returned! Mama asked me who cut those curls. I said I didn't know. There was no scolding, but I was put directly to bed, and Mama left the room without kissing me goodnight. That was the most severe punishment she ever administered, leaving no doubt that honesty was the best policy.

We stayed a few days with my older sister, Mira, who had

children as old as I. We did not go to see my old home or other sisters. Perhaps Mama thought it would be a traumatic experience to part with them again.

That fall I entered school—seven and a half years old, but was passed along to fit the seats until I caught up with my peers.

Each morning Foxie walked with me the one half mile to the school door. He returned directly home, but with an unerring timing system, appeared at school at four o'clock to walk down the street ahead of me all the way home. A man we met one afternoon patted my head, and Foxie nipped his trouser leg.

On the way to school sometimes we saw Mr. Roberts in front of the last house on his milk route. The lady of the house would be holding a kettle while Mr. Roberts dipped milk into it from a large tin milk can. The milk wagon was big and black and had sliding doors on the side which he could close in bad weather. I stopped to pet old Dusty and to say to Mr. Roberts, "My! You must get up early to be all through delivering by school time." He said briefly, "Five o'clock."

"You must be sleepy, getting up at that time."

"Oh, sometimes." Old Dusty nodded his head. Mr. Roberts volunteered, "In summer, when I make two deliveries, I don't get home until nine o'clock at night. And after that, the milk cans and strainers have to be washed."

"I wish Mama would let me stay up that late. —Milk gets sour quick in hot weather, even on the cellar floor."

"That's right, girl."

As Foxie and I trotted along to school, I was thinking that old Dusty could go on the route all by himself, except that a horse couldn't measure out milk nor make change. Foxie nuzzled me as though he, too, thought that was why Mr. Roberts had to go along.

Mrs. Hotz must be an early bird, too, for every Monday morning she would be hanging out her wash, unless, of course, it was a rainy day. Mama said, "If Monday is wet, the whole week is all mixed up."

The school was made of yellow brick with a little tower on top for the bell. Cords of wood leaned against the outside wall to feed the furnace in the basement. Down there, too, was a "girls' basement" and a boys' basement" with little stalls of toilets over a pit under the cement floor.

Each morning the janitor carried drinking water from the pump outdoors to the covered crock in the hall. That was the best time to get the collapsible cup from the desk and have a really fresh drink.

There were four rooms on the first floor with two grades and one teacher in each room. As each pupil came to school he hung his coat and cap on a hook in the hall outside his room, and put his lunch pail on the floor underneath. We knew it was nearly nine o'clock when the janitor began looking at his pocket watch and started up the creaking wooden stairs to pull the rope that rang the bell in the belfry. Anybody who came after the bong-bong, bong-bong of the bell was marked tardy. He would be sorry when his folks saw his report card.

The steps that went to the second floor were wide and sort of hollowed out from so many feet using them. They squeaked and squawked and sounded like thunder at recess when high schoolers rushed down to go outdoors to the playground.

We never went upstairs to the high school rooms. When somebody was acting up, though, the teacher sent him up there to the principal's office. He left the room kind of slow, most likely because he was scared. That happened almost never.

We loved our teacher, the first one. She taught us to read. (I was so much older than the others that I already knew a little about it.) She played with us and comforted us when we got hurt, made it fun to learn, and felt we were her children. We loved the other teachers, too, as we passed to different rooms, but never loved them quite as much as we did the first one. Most parents invited teachers to supper, and she came to our house often. She walked and didn't get there until nearly six because she stayed a long time after four helping pupils who didn't understand something, washing the blackboards, cleaning erasers and getting things ready for the next day. Her home was in Chicago, but Wild Rose was her home as long as she taught there. She belonged to the Study Club and helped in the church.

The idyllic summer days of childhood! The expectant, glad days of wonder and surprise, of seeing and touching and listening! A wren's song! The velvet of Foxie's ears! An ant in the grass! The voice of a cricket! The discovery of God's world! The play house under an oak tree, a board resting on potato boxes, where mud pies were given a touch of elegance with curled dandelion stems! The pet hen, tagging along or being carried, clucking her approval of the attention given! The cat who didn't seem offended at the indignity of wearing doll clothes! The Jersey cow to pet and talk to! Colonel, the spirited driving horse, his chestnut coat shining, who whinnied when he saw me coming and nuzzled me at the pasture fence! (Nearly everyone had a horse anu a cow then.) The swing with notched board seat and new rope hanging from a high oak branch, the wind on my face, the sky in my eyes! The sun-warmed steps to the side porch with Foxie beside me sharing a piece of warm cinnamon-topped coffee cake! The straw stack to climb up and slide down! Tea parties when children came to play, little white dishes on a low table for cookies and cambric tea made of hot water, sugar and cream! And always Foxie and the warming love of Mama and Papa!

Grandma Pierce, Papa's mother, lived with Aunt Amanda, Uncle Jim and cousin Lelah about two miles West of our home. Often, Papa hitched up Colonel and took us with him to see her. At that time she had become old and was blind, her days of toil over, her work-worn hands idle in her lap. But when I greeted her, those idle hands would trace the outline of my face, stroke my hair and hug me to her as she whispered, "Gus's little girl, Gus's little girl."

Life had not been easy for Grandma Pierce, nor had it been easy for anyone who had endured the Civil War. At the beginning of the war, Grandpa had enlisted, thinking, as did President Lincoln, that the rebellion would last only a few weeks. When he went off to war, he left her and seven children, one only a baby. The oldest girl, 15, cared for the house, the baby and little girls, while Grandma and the three boys, 9, 11 and 14, worked in field and barn. They wanted everything to be in perfect condition when Grandpa returned.

The weary days dragged on, and nine months had passed when they received a letter notifying them that Grandpa was very ill with chronic dysentery, that nothing more could be done for him, and he was being sent home to Omro, Wisconsin. When he reached home, he weighed 87 pounds. He lingered on for several years, but was never able to work again. Those years were hard on him for he felt so useless at not be able to take care of his wife and children. Those years were hard on Grandma Pierce too, and the three young boys who continued to try to operate the farm as they had before; but in spite of their brave effort they lost the farm and moved to town where Grandma took in washings to support the family. By then, there was another baby, Jerry, who, years later, became my second father.

The Civil War was in its fourth year. President Lincoln had just issued another plea for 500,000 volunteers. Feeling was running high. The Oshkosh Northwestern carried a copy of a speech made in Knoxville by Andrew Johnson. The oldest boy, Albert, then 16, and

Gustavus, 14, read it over and over. They were determined to help win the war, but they kept it secret from their mother, who would have gone to battle herself to keep her boys from enlisting when they were so young.

The speech in part follows: "The time has come when treason must be made odious, when traitors must be punished—punished and their property taken away from them, whether it be their homes, their horses, their slaves, and given to the honest, loyal people who have suffered the calamity of this war. Make them suffer as you have suffered, as your wives and children have suffered, as your country has suffered!" The boys thought that was cruel, making the people of the South suffer, when they were just fighting for what they thought was right. Still—and they read on. "What has brought this upon us? Slavery! What right has any man to hold his fellow man in bondage, to use his labor without compensation, to separate a man from his wife and children and sell them, or him, like dumb beasts! We have had slave labor long enough! Let Him who is our Maker, break every yoke, loosen every shackle, open every prison door and set the slaves free! This is not a time for tears, but a time for blows! May I fire your hearts with bold indignation and nerve your arm for unconquerable fight! If liberty dies, let there be an inscription on yonder mountain, 'Here is the end of all that is dear to the heart and sacred to the memory of man!' "

The two boys helped their mother move from the farm and get settled in a little house in the village. When they drove the team to market in Oshkosh with the last load of potatoes, they wondered why there were great crowds of people lining the streets, yelling, dancing, and singing. A bystander told them that Company C of the 2nd Wisconsin Regiment was coming home and everybody was out to meet the train. The crowd was cheering, bands were playing and cannons booming. Church bells were ringing and everybody was waving a flag or handkerchief. When the soldiers got off the train, some were crying, seeing such a crowd of cheering welcome. Their faces glowed. They had served their country and now they were home! They all went in a procession to Arcade Hall, where the ladies had a banquet for them, then to Washington Hall for a dance in their honor.

Albert and Gustavus were so enthralled, watching it all, that they talked about it all the way home and concluded that the best way to help their mother was to enlist and send their wages, $26 every two months, to her. They tied the team to a hitching post when they reached Omro, and marched into the recruitment office and said, "We want to join up." The officer filled out the forms, asked their ages and did not question them when they said, "Eighteen." Without going home to say goodbye and face the vociferous, resistance of their mother, they left for camp and were off to the war leaving the team at the hitching post.

Twice as many Civil War soldiers, in both the Union and Confederate ranks, died of disease and starvation as were killed in battle. Many of them had to live off the land, sleep on the ground and drink contaminated water. Typhoid fever, diphtheria, tuberculosis and dysentery, the four pestilences, swept throughout the army camps.

With very little training, the two boys from the country, who had never been away from home, were thrown into battle. They had never heard a cannon boom nor seen anyone die before, nor heard the wounded crying for help that would never come.

Later that year, General Lee surrendered, President Lincoln was assassinated and Albert died of typhoid fever. Gustavus developed a double hernia as a result of unloading heavy military equipment from freight trains that supplied the Union Army, and was given a medical discharge. Still only fourteen years old, he returned without his beloved brother to a grieving family and a father who moaned, "Why Albert? Why couldn't it have been me?"

Ten years later Gustavus married Salina Lyon of Hixton, Wisconsin. How they met, one can only imagine, for in that day of walking or driving a horse, Hixton and Omro were far, far apart.

Salina's father was an adventuresome spirit, always looking for better opportunities farther West. He would buy land in a new area, erect a cabin and log barn, clear the acreage, then sell and move farther West, finally settling in Washington Territory in 1880. Of course his wife, Laurinda, went along, endured the hardships of pioneering and felt it was her "bounden duty."

They had been in the West two years when they wrote Salina and Gustavus urging them to come to the new wilderness, the land of opportunity. After a week's consideration, the young couple decided to go. They packed their belongings and, with their two little girls, boarded the train that now united the East and West of a vast continent. I was born out there, the last of their ten daughters. The tragedy that stalked their pathway sent me back to Wisconsin with Uncle Jerry and Aunt Fannie, my new Mama and Papa. And sightless Grandma Pierce, holding me close, always crooned "Gus's little girl, Gus's little girl."

Cousin Lelah, nineteen years older than I, was one of my favorite people. She enjoyed helping care for Grandma Pierce, making her comfortable and telling her stories. She loved me, and I loved my Cousin Lelan.

Lelah's father, indulgent and kind in his family, always went to school meeting where his appearance repeatedly spelled trouble for the school board, for he objected vociferously to every expenditure recommended in the budget. It was an embarrassment to Mama and Papa to whom education, regardless of cost, was of primary importance.

Two of Papa's sisters married and went to rural Oconto to live on adjacent farms. They did not often get to Wild Rose to see their mother and other relatives because the responsibilities at home were great, their children were many and the route by train through Fond du Lac was circuitous. When one of them did come, she had to bring the younger children.

On one such trip she carried a bag of apples to keep the children occupied. Finishing his apple, one of the boys, who had never been on a train before, began walking up and down the aisle of the coach with an apple core in his hand. The conductor, seeing him, asked, "What are you looking for, young man?" He chuckled on receiving the answer, "The swill pail." (Swill, for those born at a later time, was composed of vegetable peelings, table scraps, dish water and other tasty treats which were taken to the pig pen and poured in the wooden trough for squealing, slurping hogs.)

Once in my late teens, I was permitted to go alone to Oconto to spend a few days with relatives, a happy experience to be part of a large family for a change. The aunts' days were demanding, but they allowed themselves one luxury. As soon as the mail arrived, each sat in a rocker on her front porch and read "The Yellow Jacket," an anti-Catholic newspaper, from cover to cover.

Grandma Pierce had died before Aunt Mandy, Uncle Jim and Cousin Lelah moved to town, and Lelah's half-brother and his family settled on the family farm. His wife died when the last of their four children was born, and he raised the family alone. They went to town in a surrey to do their trading, passing our house en route. We could hear them coming at a distance, for usually they were singing. When the singing stopped, we knew they were telling jokes, for there would be an explosion of laughter, lighthearted, infectious laughter.

At the end of the school day, when the four children trooped from the building, they made a bee-line to get some of their Aunt

Lelah's doughnuts or try on some clothes she was making for them, or take their music lesson. Lelah gave other music lessons, too, and was the organist at church. She tithed. One tenth of every bit of money she earned from music lessons and quilting patchwork quilts, though meager, was put in a jar on the piano. She always had money for any charitable purpose. It was her joy to give.

Grandma and Grandpa Etheridge, Mama's parents, lived up the road half a mile. She and I walked to see them often, and sometimes I stayed over night in the little upstairs bedroom with sloping ceiling and narrow window under the eaves. A black stove pipe from the heater below ran through a circular register in the floor and entered the chimney near the ceiling, providing a bit of warmth in winter. Grandma, her gentle goodness shining in her face, enveloped me in her love, and at night the feather bed was soft and deep. It would have been pleasant, snuggled there, to lie awake awhile, but the instant sleep of childhood always claimed its own. If there were dreams, they did not foretell that someday this would be my very own room.

Breakfast consisted of fried salt pork, potatoes left from supper, home made bread (what other kind was there?) and apple butter, also home made.

Each morning after breakfast, Grandpa took the Bible from the shelf by his chair and read aloud a long chapter, or several short ones, while the family listened. Then everyone knelt on the well-scrubbed wood floor beside a chair while Grandpa in a long prayer implored the Lord to have mercy, to forgive our manifold sins and transgressions, to rescue backsliders and to claim for His own those who had not seen the light. Grace was besought for the faithful and gratitude expressed for the blessings bestowed upon us. (To bear aching knees was an attribute of faith.)

Rising from prayers, Grandpa sat back in his chair and sang hymns, one after the other, his resonant voice, too powerful for walls to contain, drifting out across the countryside.

During this period of the morning service, Grandma could rise quietly and clear the table. As she listened to Grandpa's singing long-loved hymns, sometimes she hummed along under her breath the expression of a faith that had sustained them through a lifetime of pioneering and incessant toil.

Grandma was 65 when she died, worn knitting needles protruding from unfinished mittens, a pieced quilt still on the quilting frame. Our whole life changed. Mama felt we must not leave Grandpa there alone, so we left our home and went to live with him until he could be persuaded to come to live with us. Our home was empty for a year, rented for two, and then, giving up ever being able to return, Mama and Papa sold it. Grandpa's refusal to leave his land, his insensitivity to the impact of that decision on Mama and Papa, is more understandable now, in retrospect.

Josiah Etheridge (Grandpa) and another nineteen-year-old—opportunists, as pioneers must be—had come to the new world from England in 1848, worked in Buffalo, N. Y., for two years and, with a little money in their pockets, headed west to Wisconsin, which had just become a state. When they reached Ripon, they set out into the wilderness with all their worldly goods in packs on their backs and walked thirty-five miles through woodland "that had never known the mark of an axe."

Facing an unknown future, they must have developed within themselves a security that defied fear and anxiety. They built a crude shelter of branches and pine boughs and for five months had nothing to eat but wild berries and corn meal mush, which they cooked over an open fire beside the shelter.

Tiring of their monotonous diet, they walked mile after mile until they found a settler who had a cow and from whom they could buy a little butter, rancid though it was. Later, near Wautoma, they discovered a pioneer who had butchered a hog. From him they bought a ham which, though the summer heat had not improved the flavor, they relished as though it were the best food they had ever tasted. Eventually they found a settler who would sell them a rifle, and from then on they never lacked meat. Deer roamed the woods and prairie chickens flew in droves that darkened the sun. As powder and balls for the gun were hard to come by, Josiah would wait until two prairie chickens were lined up on a roof or branch and shoot both with one blast. Eventually they bought a cow. Milk and butter at last! Days of hunger were over!

In 1851 the two young men walked forty miles to Stevens Point, a settlement on the Wisconsin River where there was a land grant office. Each bought land in the Town of Rose, Waushara County, forty acres for fifty dollars. Of prime importance in choosing land was the availability of water, wood and marsh hay.

Returning, each began the Herculean task of clearing his land, felling trees, grubbing stumps, and burning all the logs that were not needed for buildings and fences. As the fields were cleared, hand-split rail fences were built around them, protecting crops from cattle which roamed free, a cow bell telling of their location. Josiah split the rails for his own fences rather than pay someone $40 to split 4,600, the accepted wage.

He broadcast the first wheat by hand and worked it into the rough soil by dragging brush over it. He cut marsh hay with a scythe and gathered it up with hickory teeth of rakes he made by hand. Grinding toil was overshadowed by fierce pride in his land, his piece of God's earth.

Josiah built a little blacksmith shop beside the trail that ran past his land and made charcoal for the forge. There he made tools for building the shanty, a little log barn and implements for converting wild land into productive fields. He drove the tortoise-paced oxen five miles each day to Springwater for timbers to build his barn, cut a tamarack tree, hewed it out, twelve feet long and thirty-two by forty-eight inches thick, and hauled it home all in one day. His grandson said later he was a master with an axe. I added that he must have been a master at many things, as pioneers must be if they were to survive in the wilderness. He carved wooden lasts on which he made his shoes, crude perhaps, but better than none.

Wishing to marry and establish a family, Josiah built a house, which he rightly called "the shanty," of hand-hewn pine slabs, planed by hand. Doors were made by hand. Shingles were hand-split cedar. As an extra touch for gracious living, he plastered the downstairs walls.

Josiah chose as his wife Permelia Pease, who had come in 1850 with her parents from York State by boat through the Erie Canal, the Great Lakes and the Fox River to Strongs Landing, which is now Berlin, Wisconsin. From Strongs Landing, they walked forty miles through virgin forest to the Town of Rose. She was fifteen at the time of her marriage. Girls assumed adult responsibilities early in a pioneer community.

A daguerreotype, taken at the time of the wedding, shows Josiah's strong face and rugged physique, his steady eyes and dark hair, collar length; and Permelia, petite and delicate, her straight hair parted in the middle and smoothed down to a pug in the back, accentuating her pretty face.

In many cases marriage was a matter of convenience. A man needed a wife to help him carry the load of pioneering and bear his children, who, in a few years, would help him farm. Every girl needed a home. How else could she sustain herself? Personal attractiveness and affection did not necessarily motivate the arrangement.

Some men outlived several wives. Women bore large families, had no prenatal care, were worn out while still young in years. Because of their high mortality rate, there were not enough women to go around, and a would-be husband had to take what was available. One man married a woman who was so homely he made her wear a veil whenever she went with him to town to do the trading, and when he sent a daguerreotype of his wife to his relatives in Wales, it was a picture of a local beauty.

Josiah and Permelia lived on the Indian trail that ran along the East bank of Pine River and West, up over the bluffs, to the prairie. The red men never came to the shanty without being given a piece of meat or johnny cake or vegetables or melons, of which they were particularly fond. Indians never stole from their benefactors.

One day the chief, Menominee John, and several braves came to the shanty. The chief was seriously ill with a fever caused by a carbuncle on his side. Grandma made a sheepskin bed for him on the floor near the stove and spent the night applying wilted beetleaf poultices and in the morning the carbuncle broke, giving the chief relief. The guests stayed several days until Menominee John was able to travel. They thought the "white squaw" had done wonders.

On a bitter winter night the next year an Indian came to ask if he could sleep in the barn. Instead, Josiah made a sheepskin mat near the stove. In the spring the Indian returned with a quarter of venison.

On another occasion an Indian brought his speckled hen and asked them to keep it for him. They turned it loose, the only speckled hen in their flock. A year later he returned for it. By then, in addition to the speckled hen, he was given two speckled chicks.

Josiah had only two egotisms. He wore heavy woolen pants summer and winter, long after they were frayed at the cuff and patched at the knees, but he would not wear them if they were patched on the seat, for in the work ethic in which they lived, that would be an indication of laziness.

His other egotism was the amount of work he could physically accomplish. He enjoyed competing with neighbors to see who could scythe the most hay, husk the most corn, cut and shock the most grain. On one occasion he competed with a neighbor, Binan, each cutting and shocking eight rows of corn across the forty rods of a field. Binan, falling behind, dropped one row, so Josiah cut nine rows and, with glee, turned at the end of the field and made two shocks on Binan's rows.

Usually corn husking was done in the field, one man on each side of the shock, each using a sharp husking pin to tear off the dried husks, but occasionally shocks of corn were hauled to the barn floor for a husking bee. Neighbors were invited to this social event and competed for speed of husking. If a girl or young man found an ear of red corn, it was an omen of impending marriage and brought merriment to the festivities.

Josiah and Permelia were "close managers," never buying anything unless they had gold to pay for it. They lived without polluting the environment or destroying natural resources, except in burning logs to clear the land. When they could afford it, Josiah traded the slow-paced oxen for a team of horses, for which he paid three hundred dollars. He owned the first Easterly Reaper and later a McCormick reaper and a McCormick mower. The age of mechanized farming had begun.

In the pioneer area of central Wisconsin, where the village of Wild Rose would eventually be built on the Davies farm, there were three ethnic groups: Welsh, Norwegian and English. Each nationality settled in its own isolated area, built its own little church and a one-room school, which was used the few winter months when children did not need to work at home. In both the church and school the native language was spoken. There was no fraternization between the groups, the language barrier and the desire to preserve its own heritage keeping each settlement unto itself.

Norwegians, seeking in a new land a familiar landscape, settled in hilly areas of Mt. Morris and West Holden. They were honest, hard-working people, devoted to their church and school. Both the Mt. Morris and West Holden churches were the center of the settlement and, over 100 years later, are still used and loved.

English immigrants, of whom Josiah was one, and the English who, like Permelia, were native-born and came from York State, settled on Jeffers Prairie, at the South end of which a hill was capped by their little church and burying ground. The church was called "Standalone" after one by that name in which they had worshipped in Rose Township, York State, the only two Standalone churches in existence. They were not affiliated with any denomination. They stood alone.

In 1870 part of that congregation broke away and, with their own hands, built the Christian Church West of Etheridge Hill.

The Welsh settled in and around the area they called "Springwater." As they loved to sing, they had singing school each winter, the best musician leading the singing and another playing the reed organ. Welsh people came from near and far, walking through the snow. It has been said that where there are four Welshmen, there is a quartet.

One morning a Welsh settler walked ten miles to see Josiah. As neither could understand the other, and as their sign language proved inadequate, Josiah was in a quandary as to the reason for the visit until the farmer used a stick to draw a wagon on the ground, pacing off its length and width. Understanding! The following week he came before daylight, leading a team of oxen to pull the new wagon home. Both men were delighted. It was one small step in breaking the ethnic barriers that divided the community.

Sheep and flax were raised for the raw materials out of which woolen and linen fabrics were woven. The process of preparing flax for weaving was a tedious one. Plants were cut in the field with a sickle, soaked in a retting pond until the leaves and extraneous materials were rotted. leaving the bare stalks which encased the linen fibers. To free the fibers, the tough casing was broken away by throwing the stalks over a log and beating them with a wooden tool, one half inch thick and sharp at the edges. Then, after combing the flax fibers with a hetchel, a wooden board with long, sharp metal teeth, Permelia spun it and wove it into cloth from which she made shirts, sheets, towels and the bed ticks which were stuffed with fresh straw once a year at harvest time. From the home spun, hand woven wool. she made sheets and cloth for winter clothes. All the clothes that their son, Alanson, wore until he was 21 were home spun. Yarn was converted into mittens, hoods and stockings and mufflers.

Spinning was a slow, tedious process. It would take seven spinning wheels to keep one loom in operation, but it was an indispensable operation in a pioneer household. The young woman who never married spent her life spinning for the family needs and was thus called the spinster.

Perhaps the spinning wheel should have been the emblem of the United States. (Please, I'm not trying to downgrade the eagle!)

Because England raised many sheep, and one of her chief industries was the woolen mill, where fleece was converted into cloth, King George wanted the colonists to buy all their fabrics from the mother country. To make sure the colonists did not make their own cloth, he placed an embargo on spinning wheels. Time and again the colonists tried to get a spinning wheel out of England to use as a pattern for making their own, but each time the wheel was confiscated. Finally, a model was made of brass, cut into small pieces and each piece mailed separately from England through France. At last the pioneer housewife spun and wove her own worsteds! Long after American mills began producing their own fabrics, the colonists wore homespun in defiance of King George, another symbol of the determination to be free, which would one day bring independence to the young and struggling colonists clinging to the Eastern seaboard of a great and unexplored continent.

In 1866 baby Edward came into the lives of Josiah and Permelia. At last, a child! How they loved him! But when he was three years old he died, shattering their world. Their grief was understood by those who had experienced the same tragedy, for many children in a pioneer settlement did not reach adulthood.

The Lewis and Clark Expedition had given Americans a faint idea of the vastness of the continent. Permelia said, "This country needs PEOPLE! Lots of people!" But Alanson, Mary and Fannie, who became Mama to me, were all she and Josiah could provide.

Alanson became a robust, adventuresome little boy. On New Year's Day of his fourth year, when playing outdoors, he decided to go visiting. He trudged off down the snowy trail dragging behind him a piece of hog's liver on the end of a string, which he had taken from the hemlock tree where his mother had hung it to freeze.

It was half an hour before his parents missed him. Each had assumed he was with the other. They searched and called, but the only response was the crying of the wind, which had obliterated the prints of his little feet. Terror gripped Permelia. Josiah was more stoic, but his eyes revealed that he, too, feared that the child might be lost in the cold or devoured by wolves who roamed hungrily over the countryside in winter. Josiah ran East and Permelia West to ask neighbors to help them search.

In the meantime, a mile down the trail, Alanson came to the

door of Mr. and Mrs. John Davies, whose land lay along the East bank of Pine River. Mrs. Davies hustled him into the house and to the stove to get warm. When she took off the little boy's mittens and shoes, his hands and feet were frozen white. Hurriedly she scooped up snow in which to pack them until they were an aching pink.

Relaxing after her effort, she asked. "What is this on the end of a string?"

"Meat for my dog. He didn't come. I give it to you."

Mrs. Davies thanked him and went to the cupboard. A native of Scotland, she had brought to the new land a custom of her heritage. Coming back to Alanson, she said, "In Scotland anyone who comes to the door on New Year's Day with something in his hand must be given a sixpence and a piece of mince pie. Put the sixpence in your pocket and eat the pie quickly, lad, for we must be taking you home. Your folks will be worried."

Mr. Davies, who had gone to the barn to get a horse, rode up to the door and leaned down to take the little boy his wife lifted to him. Wrapping her apron around her arms, she watched them start down the trail, exhaling white fog that dispersed in the wind.

In the early darkness of a winter afternoon the searching party in front of the Etheridge shanty was ready to start out when one of them saw, riding toward them, a man with a child in his arms.

Josiah and Permelia had another child, Mary, by the time John, Josiah's brother, came from England to join him in America. He brought with him his wife, Christiana, and their three children, one an infant. Cornelius, another brother, had come earlier. They all lived together in the shanty while the three brothers spent the winter cutting logs for a cabin for John's family on land joining Josiah's on the West, where the fifth generation of that family now lives. One can only imagine the crowded conditions as ten people lived in a shanty too small for four. The children slept on the floor in the loft, where winter blizzards forced snow between the rough-hewn boards.

With the coming of summer and the cabin completed, John, Christiana and family moved to their new home. Years of toil lay ahead for them, too, but this was their land! Their land!

Eventually Josiah bought lumber at $8 a thousand (linear feet, that is) and replaced the shanty with a frame house. Permelia had gotten her wish of having an upstairs high enough to stand up in and a stairway instead of a ladder leading to it.

Alanson, as he grew, learned quickly the skills of blacksmithing and farming. Each Sunday the family walked to church and Josiah conducted them down the aisle to the familiar pew. Alanson was not a conformist. Eventually he confronted his father. "I want to tell you, Pa, before we start for meeting, that I intend to sit in the back of the church with the boys. You have marched me down the aisle to the front pew for the last time. I'm most grown up, Pa."

There was a long silence. Permelia looked apprehensive. Josiah spoke, trying to control his anger. "Well—I reckon the Lord won't give no mind to where you sit as long as you are there. But mind you this! There will be no carrying on back there! If I don't march you out, Elder Burnap will! Remember how he laid those young bucks in the aisle when they were disturbing meeting at Standalone?"

"Yes, Pa. And one more thing, while we're on the subject. I may decide I'm not going to meeting every single Sunday. Once in a while I may decide to stay home."

"We'll see about that!" In anger and disbelief, Josiah called after Alanson as he left the room, "You're so uppity lately I can't make you out! I don't know what this world is coming to."

Mary, in contrast, was like her mother—passive, submissive, always helpful, and little Fannie, precocious and pretty, was the joy of the household and would one day be my Mama.

One cold Sunday afternoon in 1873, Mr. and Mrs. Davies walked over to the Etheridge farm to "visit a spell." On seeing Alanson they recalled the New Year's Day when he had walked to their home. They reminisced, too, about the growth of the country and about their passage to the new world. Josiah said, "When I came over, I thought that sailing ship would never get here. It took us eight weeks for the crossing from England and we had fair weather and good winds."

Mrs. Davies remembered, "When I came over from Scotland, there was a big storm at sea. The wind blew so hard I looked for the sails to be ripped right off the boat, but it weathered the storm, and here we are."

Josiah turned to Mr. Davies and remarked, "A lot of things have been happening over your way with a mill going up and the millpond ready to fill and the Grange Hall ready to use."

Mr. Davies confided, "That's what's fretting me. Now Ceyon Lincoln wants to buy a lot for a blacksmith shop and Dr. Briggs wants a couple lots for a hotel, and the Methodists want to build a church.

"You know, it's funny. Most everybody that wants to buy a lot wants one along the river."

"Well," Josiah observed, "I guess that's where most settlements were built—along the rivers—good water supply without having to dig wells. Folks had enough to do getting a shanty built and fields cleared without taking time to dig wells."

"And folks along a river can have a millpond to power a grist mill."

Josiah nodded in agreement. "There are lots of advantages. And they don't have to take time to dig a pit for an outhouse. They just build the outhouse over the water, and the river washes everything away—no smell, everything nice and clean."

"But I wish I had never sold that first lot."

Josiah wanted to know why. "Don't you fancy having the money roll in?"

He understood the reply, "Not when it means losing my farm. If I sell to them, somebody else will want a lot and then somebody else. There'll be no end! That's my farm, and I want to till those fields! I spent the last twenty years grubbing out the stumps, driving an eight-team hitch of oxen on the breaking plow. I don't want to give it up now that it's just beginning to produce!"

Josiah leaned forward. "I understand how you feel. I have the same love for this land from the day twenty-odd year ago when I walked into the wilderness with all I owned in a pack on my back. I spied this land and walked to Stevens Point to buy it and have poured my life into it, as you have done on your place, and I'm not going to part with it until the day I die. NOTHING—no matter what happens—NOTHING can get me off this land!"

There was silence for a few minutes as the two kindred spirits remembered the years of struggle. Mr. Davies broke the reverie.

"I've decided what to do. I'll sell the lots along the river, as I said I would do, just saving a piece where the cattle can go down to drink. After I'm dead and gone, they can divide the whole farm into lots if they want to. But while I'm here I'm going to farm it. I love those fields!"

"That's just what I would do," responded Josiah. "And, as the Good Book says, 'Your seed will fall on good soil and will yield one hundredfold.' "

The two men had sat in contented silence a moment when Mr. Davies remarked, "You knew that J. H. Jones was fixin' to build a store and post office."

Yes, Josiah had heard, but he hadn't been over that way lately. Too busy.

Mr. Davies chuckled. "Yesterday, when they were hauling lumber for the store, the whole load tipped over when they forded the crick—the ox cart on its side and all the boards and kegs of nails in the water."

The room reverberated with Josiah's laughter, but Permelia interjected, "They had to get in that icy crick and fish all that out of the water?"

Mr. Davies nodded.

"Oh, those poor men! It's February!"

Permelia's sympathy for the men did not dampen Josiah's merriment. "Funniest thing I ever heard," he said.

When the room was quiet again, Permelia mused, "I wonder what they will name the new village they're starting to build on your farm, Mr. Davies? I know what I wish they would call it— Wild Rose. It would make us think of our nice homes in Rose, York State, and how we have worked to make homes in this wild land."

Mrs. Davies agreed, "That would be nice. We didn't come from York State, but when we got here there were wild roses blooming everywhere. Pretty little pink things."

Mr. Davies said, "Well, I presume that would be as good a name as any. But there may not be any village. That's my land!"

A few days later Alanson, with his mouth pressed in a straight line, came to his father. "Pa, at the Grange Hall a week from Saturday night there's going to be a dance, and I want to go!"

Josiah, in disbelief, could hardly speak. "A dance! A dance! Dancing is an instrument of the Devil, and you know it! It's a scheme of the Devil to lead young folks astray. Go to a dance? I forbid it!"

Alanson insisted, "I want to go, Pa," and almost expected his father's reply, "The answer is NO!"

Alanson threw back his shoulders and faced his father. "I'm going—to—go!"

Josiah's pent-up breath exploded. "If you go to that dance, don't come home! And that's final!"

There was a long silence, each standing firm, until Alanson stalked out the door. Josiah stood in silence, his head erect. Permelia turned to face him. "Josiah, you are the head of this house. In all these years I have never stood up to you. Sometimes I felt like it, but I never did. Now I have to say you are wrong!"

"Wrong," Josiah exploded. "You know yourself that dancing is an abomination unto the Lord!"

"Yes, I know," she answered. "I don't sanction it any more than you do. But Alanson is our son! Our only son! You can't send him away like that!"

Josiah, once his mind was set, didn't change it. "But he's not going to that dance! I will not permit it!"

Permelia pleaded, "Alanson is a man now. You cannot tell him all his life what he can do and what he can't do! He has been a man for a long time! He has worked and worked with us since he was a toddler. He was only twelve when he cradled forty acres of wheat all alone. Don't you realize he is a man grown?"

Josiah banged his fist on the table and concluded the argument as he stalked out. "He may be a man grown, but I'm still the head of this house, and while he lives under this roof, he is not going to a dance! That's all there is to it!"

Before daylight the day after the dance, Permelia tip-toed from the bedroom, buttoning her dress, threw a shawl over her shoulders and started toward the door. The door opened and Alanson, shoes in hand, confronted his mother.

"Ma! What are you doing, up so early?"

Permelia put her finger on her lips. "Shh—your father is still asleep. I was going to the barn to see if you were there."

Alanson explained, "I rested in the barn after getting home from the dance and have come to get my clothes and leave home."

He moved toward the ladder to the loft, Permelia trying to stop him. "No! No! You can't do this! We love you! I can't let you go like this!"

"But Pa said—." She wouldn't let him finish. "Your Pa thinks you gave up going, thinks you are asleep in the loft as always. You go up and change into your work clothes, and when he calls you for chores, come down all ready for work," She pushed him toward the ladder, though he resisted. "Go on! Hurry! Get up there before your father wakes up! Hurry!"

She watched him go and heaved a sigh of relief, her hands and body limp. She built a fire in the fireplace and was cooking breakfast over it when Josiah came out and called Alanson.

Alanson descended the ladder slowly and faced his father.

"Pa, I'll help you do chores this morning and then I'll leave home as you said I must. I went to the dance last night."

Permelia could not suppress a wail, "Oh, Alanson!"

Josiah paced up and down the room trying to control his emotions, then faced Alanson. "I am a man of my word. I don't make promises that I don't keep.—This is no longer your home."

Wordlessly, the boy left the house, and his father, with head erect, said, "The Lord giveth. The Lord taketh away. Blessed be the name of the Lord."

By the time I was in school, children of all three original ethnic groups were in attendance and, although they spoke their native languages at home and church, English was spoken in school.

Saturday nights were social occasions when villagers and country people alike went to town to do their trading and walked from store to store, stopping along the board walk to visit with friends. Horses were tied to hitching posts along the unpaved streets. Stores were lit with kerosene wall lamps and a few with bright gas lights.

On one such evening I met Mary Roberts in front of the drug store and invited her to go in and have an ice cream sundae with me. Mary was a pretty Welsh girl with dark hair and sparkling brown eyes. Though she was two years older than I, she was a girl I wished to have for a friend. We sat at a table on little white wrought iron chairs and enjoyed our pineapple sundaes with salted soda crackers. They cost ten cents each. When I opened my purse to pay for them, I wanted to die for I found I had only fifteen cents and had to ask Mary to pay the other five.

In spite of this inauspicious beginning, she invited me home with her occasionally for the weekend. They lived on a farm, as most people did at that time. It was hard for me to understand the English her parents spoke in my behalf, but they smiled warmly and I loved them.

On Sunday most of the day was spent in their little Caersalem church. Sermons were preached and hymns sung in Welsh. Oh, how they could sing the loved hymns of their homeland! The church service was preceded by Sunday School with a class for everyone. After the morning service and a sack lunch under the trees, there was an afternoon service at the close of which everyone went home to do chores. In the evening the young people returned for a service of their own.

With the building of the Horeb Presbyterian Church in Wild Rose, the little rural Welsh churches were closed, their members joining the church in town. For many years the minister in the new church preached in Welsh, and Welsh hymns were sung. Now, though, English is spoken, and other nationalities are welcome as members.

At the beginning of the twentieth century there was an influx of immigrants to the United States. In 1907 alone one and a half million came. Among them were Polish immigrants who were met in Chicago by a man named Heffron and sent to a virgin area about six miles Northwest of Wild Rose. They built a large Catholic church in the settlement they called Heffron, but when they began tilling the land they had bought they discovered it was pure sand. They worked and toiled to try to make their farms produce but, after a few years, many of them left and returned to Chicago. Those who remained, those hardy few who refused to give up, were the forebears of the Polish who still live near and worship at the Heffron Church. They now speak English and are an integral part of the Wild Rose area.

When we went to live with Grandpa, Andrew Etheridge, son of John and Christiana, was operating their adjacent farm. John had died, and Christiana occupied the parlor and two bedrooms of their new frame house. Andrew, Louise and their ten children lived in the all-purpose kitchen, a downstairs bedroom and bedrooms on the second floor.

When, occasionally, I went home with the girls to spend the night, we talked in whispers after going upstairs to bed lest Christiana's cane should knock against the ceiling, demanding quiet.

Nothing could prevent Andrew from going "up North" with his friends for the deer-hunting season. He would tell Papa, who was not a hunter, "First I thought I wouldn't go this year, but Louise said I better, so I guess I will." The venison he brought home was a welcome addition to the winter food supply. I don't recall that Louise ever went anywhere. With ten children, a petulant mother-in-law and all the duties of a farm wife, how could she?

Andrew was a kind father and a good neighbor. When there was a blizzard or sub-zero weather, he would say to the children, "Bundle up good. It's too cold for you to walk this morning. I'll go hitch up the team and take you to school."

We knew he would come. He always did, and gave a ride to all the children along the road. When the sleigh bells announced his coming, I was bundled and ready, and ran to the road to climb in beside his children. There was a cushion of clean straw on the floor of the sleigh box. We sat in two rows, facing each other and snuggled together for warmth, blankets stretched across our laps. Horse blankets made a canopy over our heads and shielded us from wind and snow. Merriment filled the sleigh, the laughter of children mingling with the jingle of bells.

Many children from the country drove to school in a horse-drawn cutter or buggy, and the horse was sheltered during the day in a rented stall in one of the many small barns in the village.

For the most part, though, children walked to school, carrying lunch pail and book bag. In the spring and fall, roads were dusty, and in winter they were packed deep in snow. Walking was especially difficult in the early spring when the packed snow, "breaking up," was no longer solid enough to support our weight, and our feet sank with each step through the winter accumulation of snow to the still-frozen road bed below. After the snow was gone, we walked in mud until the sun dried the roads.

We had never heard of trampolines, jogging, push-ups, organized athletics or any of the trappings of physical fitness. We were in "spring training" all year round.

Winter clothing was cumbersome. Long drawers, though folded tightly at the ankle, were baggy under long black stockings topped with black buttoned-up-the-side leggings. Rubbers or buckled boots kept the feet dry. A heavy coat, scarf, mittens, crocheted hood or knitted fascinator were essential, and, for the lucky ones, a fur muff warmed the hands and shielded the face from wind. I disliked most the fascinator, a long knitted wool scarf wrapped around the head and neck. "Girls in town don't have to wear them," I protested, but always yielded to Mama's insistence.

If we were cold when we reached the village, we walked the full length of the lumber yard, protected from the wind, and stopped in the little office to warm hands and feet at Mr. Holt's wood-burning stove. He was a tall, kindly man who seemed to enjoy the morning visits of his young friends. Often I hid my fascinator between piles of lumber and donned it dutifully on the way home.

In the evening, after Mama and I had washed the supper dishes on the kitchen table and emptied the dish water in the slop pail, we joined Papa at the dining table, where an oil lamp lighted our winter evenings. Grandpa had already wound the clock and retired. After my school assignments were finished, Papa read aloud while Mama and I crocheted blocks for a bedspread. (Wouldn't today's girl consider that "square"!?) Lamp light, warmth from the wood-burning stove, serenity and love filled the room and insulated us from the cold. There was no intrusion of telephone, radio, television. This was our world, our special world, the lovely, gentle close of the day, the link of shared pleasure that binds parent and child.

When Papa's voice tired, Mama would lay aside her crocheting, take her turn at reading from the book, which transported us to other times and other places. She would skillfully skip romantic passages, lest they contaminate my young mind, but never so skillfully that I could not find and read them for myself the next day when she was otherwise occupied.

A lifelong love of literature was incubated in that lamp-lit room. Hearing it read aloud gave me an acquaintance with sentence structure and an appreciation of the music or words. The most cherished of Christmas gifts was a book.

Children had few toys and took care of them, knowing that if they were lost or broken they would not be replaced. I told Papa I wanted a set of jacks. He said I could have it as soon as I saved enough from my allowance to pay for it. That took forever. My allowance was a penny a week. But I still have the jacks and the little red rubber ball, hardened with age, in the original red cloth bag with a draw string.

Each morning one of my jobs was to wash the lamp chimneys so they would be bright when the evening lamps were lit, while Mama went to the bedrooms to fluff up the feather beds and empty the chamber pots into the slop pail. She always carried a kettle of hot water for rinsing.

As I left for school one morning Mama said, "I need a spool of white thread, size 60. Will you go to the store at the noon hour and get it for me? Here's a nickle for the thread and a penny for candy." She called after me, "Be sure to hurry back from the store so you won't be late for school."

I ate my buttered bread and hard-boiled egg quickly that noon, excited at the prospect. Skipping along to town, I passed Mrs. Sage's millinery shop and wondered for whom she was making a hat today, and if it would be trimmed with silk flowers or an ostrich plume. It was sure to have ribbons.

Mrs. Williams made dresses for folks at her house. I had been there lots of times because her girls were my friends. Their papa had died. It must be hard not having a papa.

Horses were tied to hitching posts in front of the stores. Some looked as though they were asleep and others didn't seem to like waiting, for they had pawed hollows with their front hooves in the sandy street.

Patterson's Store was the nearest, so I ran up the steps and to the candy case to choose which to buy for a penny. Oh, so many kinds! Horehound, gum drops, wintergreen, peppermint, stick candy, licorice ropes! Should I take some of each? No, maybe the penny would buy more if I spent it all on gum drops.

As the clerk was busy, I sat on one of the round stools in front of the counter where she was fitting a customer with a pair of black kid gloves. The customer was sitting on a stool, too, with her elbow on a little cushion on the counter. It seemed as though the gloves were too small, but the clerk smoothed the glove over each finger, just so, for she said, "The seams must be straight the first time or the glove will always look crooked." The hand that was already wearing a glove looked about half the size of the one that was being fitted.

While waiting, I could hear the ring of the blacksmith's hammer on the anvil down the street. Maybe he was making shoes for somebody's horse or putting a new metal tire on a wagon wheel. Must be Dr. Stevens was going home for dinner, for I could hear footsteps on the iron stairway that reached along the outside of the building from his office above the store to the street. In one corner of the store was the post office. Folks were coming for their mail.

Clerks who worked in Smart's store were going to the house across the street where Mrs. Smart fed them their noon meal. She was a special friend of Mama's. They had pretty things in their house. She and Mr. Smart worked harder in our church than almost anybody, and Mama said, "They always try to do whatever is best for Wild Rose."

I wished I had time to go down the street to Stevens' drug store to look at the pretty dolls and teddy bears and to stop at Keppler's harness shop. The shop smelled of leather, kind of a nice smell, from the harnesses or the shoes Mr. Keppler made.

When the clerk finally waited on me, I ran all the way back to school, chewing on gum drops, and got there just as the bell bong-bonged.

Sometimes neighbor children and I slid down hill in the evening, down the middle of the empty road. (Even after the coming of the automobile, winter roads were empty, for cars were jacked up and rested on wooden blocks for the winter. (It was assumed that rubber tires would deteriorate if the weight of the car rested on them in cold weather.) It was a long climb to the top of Etheridge hill, but the exhilarating ride down, two on a sled, down, down into the hollow and up the other side nearly as far as our house! Sometimes a belly-flopper, with a running start, would shout in triumph as his solo sled slid past the others. Returning home, laughing, red-cheeked and breathless, I kissed Mama and Papa goodnight. Cradled in the feather bed with a warm soapstone at my feet, morning came instantly.

There was nothing in the world as cold as the seat of an outhouse in the winter. In summer, though, it was a rather interesting place to go, for the walls were papered with newspapers whose advertising slogans could be memorized, and there was the Montgomery Ward catalog to dream through until a page was needed. Before leaving, a scoop of white, powdery lime from the pail in the corner was sprinkled down the hole to keep the air fresh.

A Saturday night ritual was the bath. Water was pumped from the well and carried to the foot-tub on the stove. When the water was warm, newspapers were spread on the floor in front of the parlor stove. The little tub was placed in the center and the door to the parlor closed to give the bather privacy. Then the bath water was carried outdoors to empty.

It was impossible to carry in wood for the range and Round Oak heater without littering the floor, nor to carry out ashes without scattering some of the silver dust. In spite of the work involved, a cast iron stove was a comforting thing when days were cold and the wind was chilly.

"Round Oak" was the trade name of an iron, wood-burning heater. The stove itself, about the size of a barrel, stood on four legs, some six inches above the floor. Circling the base of the heater was an ornate chrome ledge on which to warm cold feet, and at the top of the heater was a similar, though narrower, chrome ring whose sole function was ornamentation. On top was an ornamental dome which could be swung aside if the housewife wished to heat a kettle of water. The chunks of wood were fed to the fire through a door in front, and ashes removed and ventilation provided by a narrower door below. The stove stood on a square of zinc as protection against burning the floor.

One advantage of the cook stove was that the oven was always hot for baking bread or a day-long pot of beans or the cake, cookies, pies or puddings, one of which must always grace the end of each meal. Well-water in the tea kettle was always hot for a cup of tea, should a neighbor stop by. Cistern water in the reservoir at the opposite end of the stove from the fire box was always warm, too.

On cold mornings and evenings the open oven door doubled the amount of heat the stove could radiate to the room. A decorative iron shelf above the stove surface kept food warm if "men folk" were late for a meal. But the cook stove was most appreciated by children when a chair was pulled up in front of the open oven to warm hands and feet chilled by the trek home from school, sliding down hill or making angels in the snow. There was an ornamental chrome ledge, level with the bottom of the oven, on which to rest cold feet, and a rod at the top of the oven for drying snow-ball mittens or stockings wet from winter snow or spring puddles.

On Saturday afternoons in winter, village children amused themselves by catching and riding on bob sleds. There was a long row of potato warehouses at the South end of Main Street where companies bought potatoes from farmers, who hauled them to town on horse-drawn sleighs. Children ran to catch a sleigh, jumped on the runners and rode to the warehouse, then caught an empty sleigh for a ride back, back and forth, back and forth from one end of the village to the other.

In March, frogs in the hollow nightly announced the coming of spring. It was time to pick pussy willows, put the stems in water and watch the buds develop into full-blown velvet catkins. Later, the edge of the hollow was fringed with wild blue flags interspersed with marsh violets and cowslips. Hepatica, blood root, ladyslipper, jack-in-the-pulpit sprang into bloom and, at the top of the bluff, where someone in search of gravel had excavated a small crater, pasque flowers on velvet stems cupped the sun in their gray-blue throats.

A few weeks later in the pasture and at the edge of the woods, birdfoot violets gave themselves to spring and to the hands of children who took them home to their mothers (always hoping their bouquet would include a "velvet one."). Red-winged blackbirds hovered around the hollow, shrilly discussing building materials; sparrows chirped in excited monotone as they searched for bits of straw; a pair of robins wove a nest in the old hemlock tree by the back door, plastered it with mud and lined it with feathers in the age-old ritual of spring, and squirrels, freed from winter's prison, chased each other across the tree tops. For one hushed week a gnarled wild crabapple tree became a perfumed pink cloud. In the spring, time is not marked by days and hours but by miracles.

With the coming of May, it was time to make May baskets, fanciful creations of ingenuity and left-over wall paper. The most common design was a cone shape with a paper loop for a handle, just large enough to hang over a doorknob. On a prearranged evening, usually May 1, the baskets were filled with wild flowers, and groups of children ran from house to house, leaving a May basket, knocking on the door and expecting to be caught in the wild chase that followed. Sometimes, in the excitement of the chase, we traveled far, and it grew dark. If a boy asked to take me home in his buggy, Papa was waiting at the driveway, and I wondered as I went dutifully to the house if all fathers were as protective of their daughters.

Summers fled by. In town, adventuresome boys crawled along under the board sidewalk, hunting for money that had fallen through the cracks, and emerged with hands full of treasures to be counted, compared and gloated over. At home, the barn offered unlimited interesting things to do, either alone or with friends. When a neighbor boy or girl came to play, we headed for the barn to slide down the hay mow to the barn floor, to pet a little calf, hunt for eggs, feed chickens, check mouse traps in the granary corner of the barn (Papa paid me a penny for every mouse I caught), give hay to the horses, spear by spear, play hide and seek.

One day we met a mother skunk and three little ones in the alley in front of the stanchions and though they were the most beautiful babies we had ever seen, we didn't stay long to admire them. On another day we saw a snake swallow a frog and watched the hapless bulge travel down the snake's interior. Mama brought us cookies and, when the guest was a boy she looked in on us often.

George Jeffers was about the age of my parents although, come to think of it, he was ageless. I never saw him read or write, but it was scarcely necessary that he should for he had no need for mail and no business to transact. He did odd jobs here and there, enough to supply his few physical needs. People gave him things, and he often appeared at our house just in time for a meal. When Mama saw him coming, she would say, "Set the table for Georgie." Often he came with a present—some posies or hickory nuts he had found along the way, or he might tell us of a "purty leetle tree" and ask, "Want I should fetch it to ye?" Several of the trees in our yard were planted there by Georgie.

Horses have personality, likes and dislikes. Colonel, who liked most people, did have a consuming dislike for two men. Georgie, who was one of them, was taking a short cut across the barnyard one day when Colonel, who had been sleepily sunning himself, sprang into action, rearing, snorting, showing his teeth and pawing the air. Georgie fled in panic across the barnyard and scrambled up and over the wooden gate, Colonel right behind him. As Georgie picked himself up and looked back from a safe distance, Colonel's teeth were still bared in what looked like a laugh.

We did not go to see Mama's cousin as often as we might have because Colonel had such a dislike for her husband, who put him in the barn while we visited. When it was time to go home and the man hitched Colonel to the buggy, the horse was plunging and screaming. Finally we were able to climb into the buggy and Colonel ran in a frenzy all the way home.

There is something elemental about man's love for the hills, their majestic beauty, their permanence, man's awe of them, his desire to explore them, to climb them, to build altars to God on top of them. When David sang, "I will lift mine eyes unto the hills from whence cometh my help" he was speaking not only for himself, but for all mankind.

At the back of Grandpa's farm was a ridge of hills we called the bluffs, their wooded beauty dominated by one ancient pine that towered above the oaks along the ridge. One of the joys of childhood and youth was to walk down the lane, following a cow path, across the pasture and up into the hills to sit under that special pine tree.

Foxie went with me, racing a joyous circle, his long golden fur rippling in the wind, circle after circle, always returning to me panting and wagging. Then he ran away again, his nose to the ground, on the trail of a creature of his imagining.

When Colonel was in the pasture, I tried to catch him. Often he teased me, let me get nearly close enough to touch him, then galloped away to wait at a short distance to repeat the game. Eventually he let me lead him to the fence where I could climb on his back for a ride around the pasture, a ride which he seemed to enjoy as much as I.

Sliding to the ground I patted his velvet nose and promised him, "Someday we are going to have a saddle. Just you wait and see!"

The Sears Roebuck catalog was a book of dreams, and the pages of saddles were worn with study, anticipating the day when I would have saved fifteen dollars to buy one. That day came, and for years, even after Colonel was but a precious memory, I couldn't bring myself to part with that saddle.

Foxie and I climbed the bluff to the pine tree. To me, the top of a huge boulder near the pine tree was the top of the world. I could see the pasture below, the hollow where the cows and horses went to drink and, at the edge of the fields, the lane leading home to love, understanding and encouragement. The ridge surrounding the valley was the boundary of my world, my loved and lovely world! Someday I would see beyond the valley, but wherever life took me, I must give my best effort to whatever I attempted, for Mama and Papa must be proud of me and glad I was their child.

Under the tree, brown needles were deep and air was sweet. Scattered around the bluff were hundreds of little pines, children of the ancient tree that would not always stand alone. There, too, were velvet green mosses, gray lichens with their miniature red cups, and the lavender-pink of wild geraniums.

Halloween was a time of pranks and escapades, of exciting, giggling fun, when a friend would spend the night with me or I with her. On one such occasion, Esther came home with me from school, and after supper we walked down the dirt road to the neighbors with the express purpose of tying the pump handle to its base. The next morning, when Papa drove the team to the field, the plow he had left at the end of the furrow the night before, had been spirited to the far end of the field.

Esther and I had an exciting plan for the next Halloween. I would stay over night with her and after supper we would go down the road half a mile to scare the Sherman kids. The day of Halloween dawned gray, and rain fell chillingly. Disappointed, she and I went to the basement at school, closeted ourselves and knelt by the stool to pray that the weather would clear so we could go Halloweening. Surprisingly, God didn't choose to answer our prayer.

A few days later, the autumn sun shone brightly and we decided that, although the ghostly eve was past, we would carry out our scheme. After supper, draped in old white sheets, we trudged down the sandy road in the dark, stopped at the next farm to ask Marvin to go with us, and continued on our way. When we reached Sherman's lamp-lit house, we raced around it shrieking the repertoire of terrifying sounds that ghosts and goblins shriek. Satisfied that the household was sufficiently frightened, we started for home, took off the sheets and became three children again, chattering in self-satisfaction at the success of the mission.

Suddenly, a howling man jumped at us from the side of the road. There was no time to rationalize that Mr. Sherman had run across the field to lie in ambush. We streaked down the dark road like three scared rabbits, expecting any minute to be lunged at again. Panting, we paused in front of Marvin's house to catch our breath. Esther and I wanted him to go the rest of the way with us, but he was afraid to come back alone, so she and I raced down the road as fast as our feet could carry us.

Our hearts pounding, we stumbled up the porch steps and ran into her father who, before going to bed, always went out there "to spit."

Esther's sister was entertaining a beau in the parlor. When we went upstairs to bed we tiptoed into the best bedroom above the parlor and crouched to the floor with our ears to the circular register around the stove pipe, hoping to hear what they said. They weren't talking, so we went to bed.

Each fall, when children earned money by going to farms to pick potatoes, school closed for a two-week vacation. Papa gave me a penny a bushel, the accepted wage. He dug the potatoes with a six-tined fork, row after row, across the field. I followed him, tossing them into wooden bushel boxes on a stone boat, which a horse dragged along the rows until the boxes were filled.

The stone boat was made of two long, heavy planks, side by side, and sawed in such a manner as to curve up at the front end. A strip of wood along each side and a cleat across the back kept the boxes from sliding off. Primarily, the stone boat, as the name implies, was used to haul stones which were always cropping up as the land was cultivated. The stones were picked by hand or loosened by crow-bar, loaded on the stone boat and dragged to a pile in the far corner of the field. Stone picking, to most farmers and their children, was one of the most distasteful tasks of agriculture.

Papa would lay aside his fork long enough to lift the filled boxes into the wagon and place empty ones on the stone boat and, when the wagon was full, drive the team to the house and carry the boxes down the cellar stairs for storage. It was a rushing season, for the crop, which had been left as long as possible for maximum growth, must be gotten into the cellar quickly before the first hard frost.

Oh, how my back ached the first two or three days of the potato harvest! Undoubtedly Papa's did, too, although he didn't say so. I knew by the way he looked how tired he was.

Farming was not Papa's chosen means of livelihood, but living on Grandpa's farm there seemed to be no alternative. He had the usual eighth grade education in the country school, but when he became a man he went to a business college in Oshkosh for training in real estate and insurance, the endeavors he pursued successfully until fate made him a farmer. Though self-educated, he was well-informed and an interesting conversationalist, civic-minded and high-principled. But to me he was just Papa, my loving and loved Papa.

There was a vacation from school, too, on the first day of trout fishing. Few would have been in school anyway. We took sack lunches and stayed all day, but few trout were caught. The wily trout, with children cavorting along the bank of the stream, instantly lost their appetite for worms.

Papa's brother Frank lived about four miles west. The children went to the Chain O'Lakes School, a one-room building typical of the period. For some reason, life was not kind to Uncle Frank, or perhaps he couldn't receive what life had to give. At any rate, he was always "hard up." Aunt Sarah, kind, serene and good, was such a poor housekeeper that Mama dreaded going there. However, we went often. The children would see us at a distance, race to the buggy and receive with joy whatever we brought—little surprises their father couldn't afford, or never thought to give.

Aunt Sarah always met us at the stoop with a broom in her hand, perhaps the first time it had been used since our last visit. When the two boys, Ray and Carl, reached the age of 21, Papa gave each of them a horse and shiny new buggy.

One fall, to "help them out," Papa agreed to buy a quarter of beef when Uncle Frank butchered. When he brought it, the meat was lying on the dirty floor of the wagon, unprotected from the dust of the road. At Mama's cry of dismay, Uncle Frank said. "That's nothing that won't just blow right off," which was almost too much for Mama, but she held her temper for the sake of Papa.

Mama had ne'er-do-well relatives too. A cousin of hers, with husband and children, lived about seven miles north. We went occasionally, though dutifully, to see them and Mama was always dismayed at the conditions there. The husband would cut a tree, drag it to the house and saw off one stick of wood at a time as needed. Their supply was never more than two sticks ahead. Farming the sandy soil did not appeal to him, so he did odd jobs, and they lived "from hand to mouth." Mama said disapprovingly as we climbed into the buggy, "Such works!"

It was rumored that the telephone was coming to Wild Rose, and we children talked about it excitedly, not knowing just what "telephone" meant. Then, one afternoon on the way home from school, we saw some men digging holes along the side of the road and erecting long wooden poles in them. Mama told me, when I described what was happening, that, yes, the telephone line was being laid. A few days later, along the cross pieces at the top of the poles, other strangers were stringing shining silver wires through pretty green glass things that looked about the size of water tumblers. We sat down on the grass at the side of the road to watch, fascinated, then ran home to tell our folks what was happening.

We counted the poles from the depot to our house, seventeen of them, the new way to measure distance. Instead of saying to a friend, "I'll walk a piece with you as far as Sage's," I could say, "I'll walk a piece with you to the fourth telephone pole." If, by the time we reached the fourth pole, we were having an especially good time, and if Mama hadn't told me to hurry back, I could say I would go one more pole.

When I reached home from school about a month later, two men were stringing a wire from the pole in front, right to our house. I ran in. Another man was fastening a big brown wooden box to the wall of the dining room. It had a handle on the side, something like the handle that turned the roller organ that Dr. Fuller had given me, and a cup-shaped thing sticking out of the front of the box and a long black tube hanging on the side with a cord attached to it. Near the top of the box were two silver domes that looked a little like the bell the teacher tapped when she wanted silence.

When the man turned the handle on the side of the box, a bell rang. He lifted what he called the receiver to his ear and said into the cup-shaped thing, "Central, did that ring come through all right?" Apparently it did, for he turned to me and said, "Is there someone you would like to talk to?" I said excitedly, "You mean I can talk to anybody, just anybody?" He assured me that I could as long as that person, too, had a phone. "You mean I could talk to Mary or Evelyn, way down town, and they could hear me without my yelling?" He nodded, smiling, and handed me a little flat book and said, "Look up the name of someone you would like to talk to. Look up the last name first. That's it. Now, turn the handle and when Central says. 'Number please,' tell her this number."

Following his directions I listened, my heart pounding. There was a long buzzing sound and two short ones, then a voice said, "Hello." I could hear it just so plain! I turned to the telephone man pleadingly, not knowing what to do next. He prompted, "Say something. Ask to talk to your friend." I was embarrassed, for he seemed amused, but he swiveled the mouthpiece down and told me to talk into it. I yelled, "Hello. Is Mary there?" He told me not to talk so loud. Mary answered. I said, "Hello," but couldn't think of anything else to say, so hung the receiver back on the hook.

After the telephone men were gone, I sat on the front steps and gazed at the shining wires in disbelief. How could a voice be squeezed into that thin little wire? And even if it could, how could it travel all the way down town? The wind wasn't even blowing in that direction!

In April, 1912, the newspapers headlined the tragedy of the Titanic, which sank with the loss of 1500 lives. The largest passenger ship, the most elegant that ever put out to sea, the pride of the British naval service, was on its maiden voyage from Southampton to New York. It was doing 22½ knots in an effort to reach New York harbor ahead of schedule, when it hit an iceberg off the coast of Newfoundland. Because of Marconi's invention of wireless telegraphy and the discovery of the short wave, which could follow the contour of the earth and travel at the speed of light, 770 passengers in lifeboats were saved by other ships which were called by wireless to the rescue.

We read of the Panama Canal, that it was one of the greatest engineering feats in the world, that it required the work of a half million men. Supplying workers with food and machines was a test of logistical skill; and cutting the canal through mountains, jungles and swamps was a task other countries had dreamed of doing—France had tried in 1881—but only the United States was technically able to accomplish. Before the work began in 1904 Colonel William G. Gorgas used his professional skill to rid the zone of the rats and mosquitoes which had infected the French force with bubonic plague, malaria and yellow fever; and Colonel George W. Goethals, U. S. Army engineer, perfected the plans that would conquer the formidable terrain. Both men were promoted to Major General.

The Panama Canal cost 387 million dollars. When the first ship went through in 1914, it traveled only fifty miles to make the canal transit from the Atlantic to the Pacific Ocean instead of the previous 8000 miles around South America.

In 1918 the influenza epidemic swept its cruel way around the world, killing 30 million people. Doctors and nurses worked valiently but helplessly. They had no experience, no vaccine with which to fight the epidemic. In little Wild Rose the people were terrified, as they were everywhere. The black horse-drawn hearse made its mournful way, again and again, to the cemetery. The grim reaper was indiscriminate. It swept along Main Street, taking business men with it, and entered the sealed doors of dwellings to take young mothers with babes at their breasts. The sound of weeping encircled the earth.

We had heard a little about a war going on in Europe between England, France and Russia, on one side, and Germany, Turkey and Austria on the other, but Europe was a long way off. The United States was a fortress, protected by the moats of the Atlantic and Pacific Oceans. Senator LaFollette in Wisconsin, and other leaders across the country preached isolationism.

Woodrow Wilson, an idealist and pacifist, was president in 1917 when a German submarine sank four United States ships. America seethed with anti-German fervor. German textbooks were burned in the streets. Citizens with German names were suspected of disloyalty. President Wilson called on Americans to "make the world safe for democracy." Congress declared war. Over two million boys came from the farms and villages to enlist in what an aroused American public considered a holy war against tyranny. German soldiers, at the same time, wore belt buckles with the inscription, "Gott mit uns." Each side prayed God for victory against the other.

The Americans tipped the scales in favor of the Allies and came home to a jubilant nation. Some of them came home, that is. Some would never walk again or talk again or think again, and 112,000 were dead trying to save the world for democracy.

On that first Armistice Day there was only jubilation. School children were dismissed. The populace of excited Wild Rose and the surrounding area gathered on the "village lot" to hear the band play in the bandstand, to sing, to listen to patriotic speeches and to ring the fire bell which sounded across the countryside from the top of its wind-mill elevation. The bell rang and rang and rang until it cracked, and the clear belltone was no more than a thud, thud, thud, but it continued to ring. Evelyn, who was standing beside me, nudged her elbow into my side and said, "What do you suppose is the matter with Mr. Storm? He's walking crooked."

"He is, isn't he? I hadn't noticed. And he's talking funny, too. Is he sick, do you think?"

We watched a minute and she said, "Dr. Fisher is right over there. Let's go tell him."

Dr. Fisher smiled at us and told us, "Mr. Storm will be all right after a while. He was so happy about the war ending that he must have drunk some home brew, but thank you, girls, for telling me."

We were shocked. We had never seen anyone drunk before.

At home, the tasks of homemaking were never-ending. Each spring, the maple trees which Grandpa had planted when he built the shanty were tapped by drilling a hole in each tree and inserting a wooden spout which conducted sap to pails hung below. Every morning Papa donned a wooden yoke which fitted across his shoulders. At each end of the yoke there was an arm-length wire with a hook on the end from which a pail was suspended. He went from tree to tree, pouring into the pails the night's accumulation of sap. The yoke distributed the weight of the pails of sap more evenly for the walk back to the house. Mama had scrubbed the copper wash boiler and placed it on the cook stove to receive the sap, which then bubbled away until evaporation produced syrup. One pail of sap made one cup of syrup. It was a delight to come home from school to a house full of sweet-smelling steam and the realization that dessert for supper would be baking powder biscuits and sauce dishes of warm maple syrup.

In season I went with Mama, each of us carrying two baskets (mine smaller than hers) to gather mulberries, cherries, grapes and plums from the trees Grandpa had planted, and then helped her make fruit butters, jellies, sauces and juices for use in winter when no fresh fruits were available. The apple orchard he had planted still bore Wealthies, Russets, Snow apples, Greenings. Every other day we went to the orchard to pick up the apples that had fallen to the ground, leaving the perfect fruit to store in the cellar for the cold winter. Frequently she went to the cellar in winter to sort apples and pick out spotted fruit for immediate use. She said, "One rotten apple will spoil a whole bushel." In her thrift, we seldom used apples that were not spotted. It was sometimes called "rotten apple economy."

Grandma's method of drying apples that she had peeled, cored and quartered had been to string the wedges on heavy thread and hang them over the stove, but she had fussed so often about the flies that roosted on them that Grandpa had made an apple drier of galvanized tin to fit on top of the cookstove in the summer kitchen. We still used the drier, spreading the apple wedges on the wire trays, one above the other, where heated air from a slow fire circulated through the trays until the wedges were crinkled and golden brown.

We picked sweet corn from the garden, husked it and, with a sharp knife, cut off rows of yellow kernels and scraped the milky pulp from the cob, drying it in the same way as the apples. The resulting flavor was quite different from that of fresh sweet corn and perhaps excelled it. Carrots and beets were packed in sand to prevent shriveling, and cabbage was preserved in large earthen crocks in the form of sauerkraut. The odor of sauerkraut permeated the whole house as it cured behind the cookstove. I was ashamed to bring friends home when the house reeked with curing sauerkraut.

In the fall pigs were butchered. Mama placed hams, shoulders and bacon strips in a large earthen crock and covered them with a brine made of salt, saltpeter and brown sugar. In three or four weeks, when the meat was sufficiently cured, it was smoked in the small smokehouse beside the woodshed where the fire, tended week after week, must not blaze or the meat would cook instead of cure. On windy days the vents were stuffed with rags. On still days, to increase circulation of air, rags were removed lest the fire suffocate. The smoked meat was hung from the cellar ceiling.

Pig's feet were pickled, side pork was kept in a crock of brine "strong enough to support an egg," and pork chops were fried, placed in a crock and covered with grease to keep out the air. Thus sealed and placed on the cellar floor with a white cloth tied over the top, they would keep all winter. Fat was "tried" in the oven, and the lard, thus produced, was used for all cooking needs.

In Grandma's day, suet from beef and tallow from sheep were "tried" and used for making candles which gave off an unpleasant odor when burned, but with the coming of oil lamps just after the Civil War, this task was no longer a necessary part of homemaking. However, ground suet was always the shortening that Mama—and later I—used for the festive English plum pudding which was steamed in a cloth bag and, (at a later time, steamed in tin vegetable cans) for Thanksgiving and the holidays.

In the winter when venison and beef were available, Mama placed selected pieces in a spiced brine and labeled the crock "corned beef." Other pieces were hung high on the hemlock tree to freeze, out of the reach of animals.

Another duty of the farmer's wife was to care for the chickens, ducks and geese. The feathers were needed for stuffing pillows and feather beds, and the meat for food for the family. She needed the eggs to do her "trading" at the store, bringing home in their stead the things not produced on the farm—sugar, calico, thread, salt, spices, flour, pins and needles. Chickens roamed free, and found much of their own food including strawberries and tomatoes. When Mama went out to feed them late in the afternoon, they came running to meet her. She gathered eggs from nests in the hen house and searched the yard for eggs in "stolen nests."

In the spring, when hens began to cluck and peck at hands that tried to remove them from their nests, they were ready to set. Then Mama would make a nest of straw in each of several little A-shaped coops, place a dozen eggs in each nest to give the hen the idea, then confine the hens in their individual coops to incubate the eggs. After she was sure a hen was dependably setting, Mama would open the coop and let her come and go at will. Occasionally an irresponsible hen became bored with the responsibility and left the eggs to get cold, and Mama, burying the eggs, would sputter about the shiftless biddy that didn't want to raise a family. (The "shiftless biddy" usually ended up in an iron kettle surrounded by bubbling gravy and topped with dumplings.) For the most part, though, hens accepted the task of incubating the eggs and sheltering the chicks. When they left the coop to forage, the chicks stayed close to their mother, but if one strayed, a cluck brought it scurrying to her side.

All the chickens were raised, hens providing the eggs and roosters Sunday dinners. A few roosters were kept to make sure the eggs were fertile for next spring's nesting. My introduction to the secrets of reproduction came in seeing a rooster chase and overtake a hen. As far as I knew, cows produced calves all by themselves. The annual visitation must have been planned for a day when I was in school.

Mama had little respect for a minister's wife who came to church as usual, though pregnant. Mama would say indignantly, "She should go into seclusion and stay there! Such works!"

In the winter Mama sewed, often of used materials, everything that she and I wore; and she knitted mittens, scarves and socks for Papa and Grandpa. The weekly schedule was unswerving—Monday wash, Tuesday iron, Wednesday mend, Friday clean, Saturday bake, Sunday church.

Doing the laundry was perhaps the most arduous. Early Monday morning a roaring fire heated cistern water in the copper wash boiler. If the supply of homemade soap was exhausted, a bar of "Fels" or "P and G" soap was shaved into the boiler and dissolved before the white clothes were added to boil until the dirt was removed.

Papa pumped and carried pails of water from the well and emptied them in the two tubs, one for washing, one for rinsing. After spots were soaped out on a scrub board, white clothes were placed in the copper boiler to bubble until they were a whiter white, then a long, clean "pot stick" removed them from the boiler and deposited them in the tub. A hand-wringer transferred the clothes from the tub of suds to a tub of rinse water and out of the rinse to the wicker clothes basket. In summer the steaming kitchen was nearly insufferable, but in winter, hands that hung the clothes on the line and later removed them, frozen stiff, became numb with cold. Drawers, union suits and petticoats, blown up as though stuffed with balloons, looked like grotesque gnomes dancing in the wind.

Everything was starched and ironed—linens, long ruffled petticoats, drawers, dresses, shirts, skirts and shirtwaists. Regardless of the heat of the day, an intense fire must burn in the cookstove to keep the flatirons hot. By the time the washed, ironed and mended laundry was put away, Monday, Tuesday and Wednesday were gone.

Cleanliness, to Mama, was "next to Godliness." Making conversation at the supper table she said, "After I did the trading this afternoon, I went to see Mrs. Doe about having Ladies Aid. She was reading. She reads a lot. Good books, too. Well, I like to read as well as anybody, but *she* was reading by a dirty window! Such works!"

Spring housecleaning and fall housecleaning were as integral a part of the season as washing was the purpose of Monday. As soon as the weather was warm enough in the spring, the sooty parlor stove pipe was taken outdoors to clean, and the cast iron heater was removed to the woodshed for the summer. It did take up a lot of room in the parlor.

All the furniture was carried outdoors to be washed and polished and, if it was upholstered, to be beaten with the wire carpet whip until no more dust came forth. Carpet tacks, which secured the woven carpet to the perimeter of the room, were removed and the carpet was dragged out on the grass or suspended over the clothes line to be pounded with the same wire beater. It was considered a good housecleaning day if there was enough breeze to carry the cloud of dust away as it rose.

Back in the parlor, Mama tied a clean white rag around a broom to brush down walls and ceilings. Lace curtains were laundered, starched and dried on a wooden stretcher, while the windows, pictures, woodwork and knick-knacks were washed and polished.

After the floor was scrubbed and dried, we spread fresh straw or newspapers for rug-padding before bringing in the rug—smelling like sunshine—to be stretched and tacked along the mop boards. If it had been a good cleaning day and the work had progressed as planned, the room was ready for furniture when the men folks came in for supper. However, if walls had to be papered and woodwork painted, the room might not be ready for use for several days.

I shall never forget one housecleaning session. After learning to print, I had written some little verses about being lonely for my sisters and old home and wishing to go back to them. (What brought that on I cannot guess, for I remember only happiness with my lot.) Not wanting Mama to see the verses I had hidden them in my little umbrella hanging in the closet and forgotten them. When Mama was housecleaning that spring, she opened the umbrella to dust it, and a sheet of folded paper fluttered to the floor. She read it! With anguish she said, "Don't you love us? Don't you like it here?" "Oh, Mama, I do! I do! I do!" There was no way to erase those words and no way to explain them!

Spring and fall cleaning continued, room after room, from the attic to the cellar, leaving the most distasteful until last.

Men were unanimous in their opinion that housecleaning was foolishness, but their grumblings fell on deaf ears until, with the advent of the vacuum cleaner, they were rescued from their spring and fall aggravation.

Mama was an intellectual woman, having gone to York State to stay with relatives while attending normal school and having attended Evansville Seminary in Wisconsin for a term. During the years before her marriage, she had taught in country schools and had gone regularly to teachers' institutes.

It had not been easy to keep informed. With no radio, television, telephone or daily paper, news of the outside world was slow in reaching remote rural communities. In 1910 Mama and twelve friends had organized the Thirteen Club which met every two weeks to study and discuss the world beyond their horizon, using the "Bay View" and "Mentor" magazines for sources of information.

They spent a year studying Shakespeare, other times studying Browning and the American poets, a year or more familiarizing themselves with English history and the royal family tree. They refused to let the arduous tasks of everyday imprison their minds. The Thirteen Club finally expanded its membership to twenty-five and changed its name to the Wild Rose Study Club, which now is the Woman's Club with open membership.

Mama and two friends had driven a horse fifteen miles to Plainfield to join the Order of the Eastern Star for the purpose of instituting a chapter in Wild Rose. Papa was active in Masonry and in Eastern Star. The Methodist Church, Study Club and fraternal orders were the social, intellectual and spiritual respite from daily toil.

Though Mama and her friends were among the literates of the community, vestiges of old superstitions still clung to them. Mama felt it was bad luck to kill a spider. If she found one in the house, she picked it up with a cloth and released it outdoors. She would never walk under a ladder. If, in dressing, she got a piece of clothing on wrong side out, she wore it that way or put on something else in its place. It was bad luck to turn it. If, after leaving the house to go somewhere, she discovered she had forgotten something, it was bad luck to go back in the house after it without observing this adage: "Sit down, count ten and spit."

She and her friends were formal in their salutation, always addressing each other as "Mrs. Clark," "Mrs. Hoaglin," "Mrs. Darling," never by their first names. Decorum was at all times "proper." There were certain things that "ladies" did not discuss.

In getting dressed in the morning, Mama's voluminous outing flannel nightgown served as a tent to preserve her modesty and in winter a circle of warmth when Papa's wood fires had not yet had time to take the chill from the air.

There was no generation gap. In our intimate talks, though Mama skirted subjects too personal to discuss, she would advise, "Never do anything you would be ashamed to tell Mama and Papa and "Take nothing in your mind or body that would make it unclean." Ruled out were contaminants such as tobacco and alcohol, profanity and dirty jokes, dishonesty and immorality.

As regularly as Sunday morning came, I put on my best dress and walked the mile to Sunday School. As my class was such a close-knit group, the teacher passed along with us from grade to grade. Years later, teaching in that same Sunday School for 25 years, I realized how much, how very much, of herself she had given us. By then, as is so often the case, it was too late to tell her how much her life had meant to me.

Mama and Papa arrived in time for church. Usually they walked, but if they drove Colonel, he waited in one of the stalls of the long horse-shed that stretched across the back of the church yard.

Each summer the Sunday School had a picnic at Silver Lake to which all the church constituents were welcome. They gathered at the church and climbed into as many horse-drawn wagons and buggies as were necessary to transport the assemblage. Skirts were full and ankle length, which made the ascent to the wagon and the descent therefrom a bit precarious and seldom graceful.

Those who went "bathing" changed clothes in a tent, one by one, of course. The swim suit consisted of a calf-length skirt over black stockings and long, full bloomers. A white blouse with long sleeves and ruffles in strategic places completed the costume. Some wore sun hats, as well, for "ladies" must retain their peaches and cream complexion. For that reason, even doll carriages had parasols.

After a dinner, served on a long table constructed of boards on saw horses, there were games—three-legged races, pom-pom-pull-away, drop the handkerchief, relay races, tug of war. And there was lemonade! The only other day in the year when we had lemonade was the Fourth of July.

Christmas Eve was always spent at church. Children provided recitations, dialogues, music and simple dramatization of the nativity, listening the while for the jingling of sleigh bells announcing the coming of Santa with a bag of candy for each child.

Walking home in the clear, cold night, the air clean and tingling in the throat, breath rising in white fog, footsteps squeaking in the snow, and the moon, always the moon, gleaming white across the fields, I would look up at the myriad stars and wonder if one of them was the star of Bethlehem. There was no other light anywhere except for an occasional yellow square of lamplight in a house we passed. Arriving home, we briefly lit the candles on the Christmas tree that Papa and I had brought home from the woods and then went to bed, anticipating Christmas morning.

In the gray light before dawn, the stair steps cold against my feet, I crept down the stairs to see what Santa had left, and there under the tree, on one such morning, was a doll—the most beautiful doll I had ever seen! As I sat on the floor hugging her, I knew that the babies I would have some day would be as beautiful. I hummed a little song, loving her and visualizing them.

I was ten years old when an evangelist came to the church for a series of evening services. Though crowds flocked to the church, we stayed home until the last evening when, yielding to my coaxing, we went. The evangelist described in detail the terrors of hell and the glories of heaven where there were gates of pearl through which golden streets led to the throne of God. Pointing his finger at the congregation, his voice trembling with emotion, he cried, "Are you saved? Are you washed in the blood of the Lamb? Do you want to walk the golden streets and sing praises to God, or do you want to spend eternity in the torment of the fires of hell? Come forward! Come forward and be saved!" I rose, as in a trance, and walked down the aisle and knelt with others at the chancel rail. My sins were forgiven! I was saved!

One night Foxie did not come home from his after-supper run in the snow. We waited for him anxiously and hunted for him four days before a neighbor came in the evening to tell us he had found our dog burrowed in his straw stack for protection against the cold. He was alive but very weak.

Papa and I took a lighted lantern and the big wooden sled Grandpa had built to haul stove wood to the house and went to bring Foxie home. He was so glad to see us! His great plume of a tail wagged weakly and he tried to lick Papa's hand as we lifted him gently onto the sled. We carried him in the house to lie on a rug Mama had placed in front of the stove. As she patted his head and talked to him soothingly, he feebly wagged his tail.

There was no veterinarian, so Papa called Dr. Fisher, who had been our family doctor since his graduation from medical school years earlier. One of the horses in the doctor's barn was always harnessed and ready to go. Dr. Fisher arrived quickly, examined the dog and found a gunshot wound, which he dressed as gently as though he were treating a human patient. He gave the dog medication to make him comfortable, patted me on the head and left.

Dr. Fisher lived across the street from school and practiced in a small office back of the house. At recess the next day he saw me playing in the school yard and came over to put his arms around me and tell me my dog was dead. Although I didn't know it until years later, he had driven back to the farm that morning to put Foxie to sleep, for he had not wanted to do it when I was there the night before. Such was the dedication and compassion of a country doctor, who often took his pay in chickens or potatoes or had no pay at all.

In current events periods at school we began to hear about motion pictures—"movies," as they were called. We heard that people, watching a big picture, could actually see actors moving around! How that could be possible, no one could imagine.

Then a famous movie, "The Birth of a Nation," was to be shown in Wild Rose! We could hardly wait! An empty store building became a temporary motion picture theater with a big white screen hanging in the back of the room; a big box that looked something like a giant camera pointed toward it; and bow-backed chairs lined up in neat rows. Oh, it was exciting, all about the story of our country—and the pictures really did show the actors walking and motioning! We read on the screen the words the actors were saying while a piano player set the mood of each scene.

Many scientists had used their skill to make motion pictures possible. We didn't know at the time the price a little-known Belgian, Joseph Plateau, had paid. People had thought he was queer because he stared at the sun. In trying to determine the effect of light on the eye, he discovered that the picture remained on the retina one-sixth of a second after it had disappeared, making movement in a series of pictures appear continuous. Joseph Plateau worked on the experiment over a period of years, even though sun-gazing was impairing his vision and he knew the retinas of his eyes were being destroyed. In the darkness of his permanent blindness, he had the satisfaction of knowing he had brought motion pictures one more step toward reality.

In 1928 there would be sound as well as pictures at the movies, when Al Jolson starred in "The Jazz Singer," and five years later movies would be in color—as lifelike as life!—in Walt Disney's "Flowers and Trees."

A cousin of Mama's and her man-of-the-world husband came one September in their shiny new black Pierce Arrow touring car to take us to the county fair. We watched as it flashed down the road and into our driveway and rushed outside when it stopped at the back door. It was as long as two buggies! We scarcely greeted the occupants in our excitement over the car, its brass lanterns in front and back, the gleaming brass strip around the radiator, the bulb horn that said "a-oooo-ah" when it was squeezed, the tool box in the middle of the long running board, a wooden trunk on the back. Mama's cousin said the Pierce Arrow had won an 870 mile round-trip race between New York City and the White Mountains in New Hampshire. My! What a car!

It was our first experience riding in an automobile. Meeting a car on the road was the first experience for most of the horses we met, too. They reared, plunged, and took to the ditch, their buggies or wagons swaying precariously as drivers held the reins tight and swore under their breath at the new-fangled contraption. We bumped up and down on the back seat as the car put-putted along on the rough road.

Halfway to Wautoma it started to rain the equinoctial rain of September, and the car plowed along in mud, the shiny body splashed with it. We would have been splashed, too, except for the side curtains, which rattled in the wind but kept out most of the rain. Occupants of the horse-drawn vehicles were less fortunate, those in wagons wholly unprotected from the mud and rain.

It took several years for horses to become accustomed to the roar and speed of motorized transportation, but for them, too, the technological age was fast approaching. With the advent of the tractor, the truck and the automobile, horses no longer pulled the plow and hauled the load. They were to be used almost exclusively for pleasure riding and racing.

The first motorcars were toys for the rich, but Henry Ford's ingenious mind developed assembly line production which increased output and wages, enabling workmen themselves to become customers. Motorized transportation came to the common man.

Eventually Papa bought one of those little black Ford touring cars with a running board and narrow fenders on each side, a crank at the base of the radiator and side curtains to button on in case of rain. The dealer told him how to start the motor with the crank, how to shift, where the brake was, and Papa drove it home, beep-beeping to Mama and me as he reached the driveway. We rushed out to see it, and after brief instructions, she and I took turns driving it a mile down the dusty road. It was so simple to operate that no one took driver training. We just cranked it up and drove.

Cranking was not always easy. Sometimes one twist stimulated the motor to coughing, sputtering life. Sometimes the crank backfired, straining the shoulder or bruising the shin or even breaking the arm. Sometimes more profane men than Papa used language children were not supposed to hear.

Everyone who drove had to learn to change tires, which at that time were short-lived. When there was a blowout, the axle had to be raised with a hand-operated jack until the wheel was free, then the wheel removed and the tire pried from the rim. After the inner tube was removed and the hole patched, it was reinserted in the tire, the tire remounted and filled with air by the use of a hand pump.

I was delirious with joy at having a car, but Grandpa's disapproving comment was, "That's an instrument of the Devil!" I use a capital "D" advisedly, for to Grandpa the Devil was utterly real, always hatching schemes to trick folks into sin.

Clarence Corning, a neighbor, the father of two of my school friends, was a rural mail carrier. With the coming of the motorcycle, he bought one and turned his horses out to pasture for the summer. He roared into our yard after supper one summer evening and said to me, "Would you like a ride?"

"Of course I would!" It was the first motorcycle I had ever seen.

"Well then, climb on behind me and hang onto my belt."

I did, my heart pounding. He took us West on the sandy road, up and up to the top of Etheridge hill. There he turned the machine around, stepped on the accelerator and roared down the hill, slicing the wind. I thought I would suffocate—the excitement, the wind, the noise, the world flashing by! It was my introduction to speed, the obsession of modern man.

At Christmas time in 1919, Papa brought home two big crates and a smaller one and placed them under the tree in the parlor. I was consumed with curiosity and when no one was looking, lifted the boxes (one of them almost too heavy for me to get off the floor), and shook them for a clue to the contents. There was no hint. I could not guess. Mama smiled as though she knew, but why ask her for she wouldn't tell me, not before Christmas anyway. The happy, expectant days passed slowly. I thought Christmas would never come, but it did!

On Christmas morning, sitting close to the tree, Papa pushed the packages toward Mama and me and told us to open them. Fumblingly, I loosened the string from the smallest package and pulled out half a dozen black cylinders about six inches long and two across. What in the world? Mama used a hammer to pry open the heaviest crate and lifted out a strange looking wooden box with a crank on the side and a horizontal post suspended over the top. What a mystery! Together we pried open the last carton. (Mama so deliberately!) and out came a big wooden bell-shaped horn. What was all this? Did it belong together?

Papa laughed at my confusion as he inserted the horn at the back of the wooden box, and slipped one of the black cylinders over the post. As he turned the crank, music came out! Music! Out of that box! "Yankee Doodle" and "Old Black Joe!" Papa said it was a graphophone. Most of the day one of us was in the parlor turning the crank while music filled the house. We played the cylinders, one after the other, over and over while Christmas Day passed.

In the summer of 1920 the Etheridge girls, who had an aunt living in Portage, invited me to go with them in the family Model T Ford to spend the weekend with her.

For girls like us, whose horizons had been limited, a journey of 60 miles was an expedition! We sang as we rode along the dusty road. There was exuberance and laughter.

In the middle of a hay field, to our disbelief, was a small aeroplane, the first we had ever seen, a young pilot standing beside it.

Amy, who was driving, stepped on the brake, and we scrambled out of the car and ran across the field to get a closer look at the wondrous one-seated craft.

The handsome pilot was friendly, probably amused. At any rate, he allowed us to climb into the open cockpit, one by one, and imagine clouds and sky and flight. In retrospect, the remainder of the weekend is a blur. Nothing else made a lasting impression, for we had seen an aeroplane! We had touched it! What's more, we had sat in it!

There were only four teachers in the Wild Rose High School. They taught basic subjects—math, geography, English, history, not much different from the three R's of a generation earlier. There was no music other than assembly singing; no gymnasium, no art, Latin, football, hot lunch or laboratory equipment. There was also no smoking or drinking, and although there was undoubtedly sexual curiosity, I know of only one girl who had to leave school in disgrace to get married. The only sex education was in surreptitiously reading the family doctor book or exchanging information (often misinformation) with one's peers.

Teachers, without extra pay, coached basketball after school hours, and forensics, drama and glee club. They were dedicated to their students and their profession and in return, the students admired and often loved them. Rapport between faculty and students made the learning experience natural and enjoyable. Perhaps teachers could give of themselves so freely and happily because their energy and enthusiasm were not sapped by disciplinary problems and disrespect, nor their originality and time drained by administrative bureaucracy.

By today's standards we would have been considered educationally disadvantaged, but not knowing what we were missing in not having an expanded program, we did not feel deprived of opportunity. My mental capacity was only average, but I studied diligently and was rewarded by my parents' pride in me. More than anything else I wanted them to be glad I was their daughter, and they were.

At school parties which were held in the third floor attic, we danced the Virginia reel and had to be out of the building before eleven o'clock when electric lights were turned off. The old water-powered mill, which had ground the grain for the pioneers, now generated electricity for the village and did not operate after eleven o'clock. (In the country we still used oil lamps.)

Class plays, musical programs and graduation were held in Patterson's Hall, a large room above the general store. Basketball practices and games were held in an empty building or the town hall. Out-of-town games, in those days of little travel, were exciting events. The players and chaperones went in a horse-drawn sleigh to the neighboring village where, after the game, there was no opportunity to shower or otherwise cool off before the blanketed ride home through the winter night.

In 1921, high school days were over for our class of twelve, six boys and six girls. In such a small class my valedictory was of no significance except that Mama and Papa were as pleased as though it were a class of a thousand.

They gave me a camera for graduation, a folding Eastman camera. When closed, it was about 7x3x1½ inches. For the picture-taking position, the front of the camera opened and the nested mechanism telescoped along a track until it was the right length for the distance from the object to be photographed. The folding camera evolved from the simple box camera which George Eastman, who was previously a bank clerk, had developed to bring photography to the people.

Instead of the cumbersome technical equipment which Matthew Brady, the famous photographer of the horrors of the Civil War, had used, with glass plates which had to be developed immediately, Eastman cameras were simple, light-weight, could be held in the hand, and used rolled film which was sent to one of the Eastman factories for development.

That camera, given to me as a graduation gift, recorded life's experiences for 46 years until we replaced it by another Eastman, an Instamatic, that photographed in color.

Thus were the early years of my life spent in the sheltering love of a home where mutual trust and understanding warmed each happy day and wrapped the nights in security and dreamless sleep.

Patterns

If will of mine could chisel out
The pattern of my scope of days,
I think that I would have it show
A great expanse of untrod ways.

But, in the lonely afterglow
When sailors weary of the foam
And mothers murmur lullabies
I know my dreams would build a home.

Beyond the Horizon

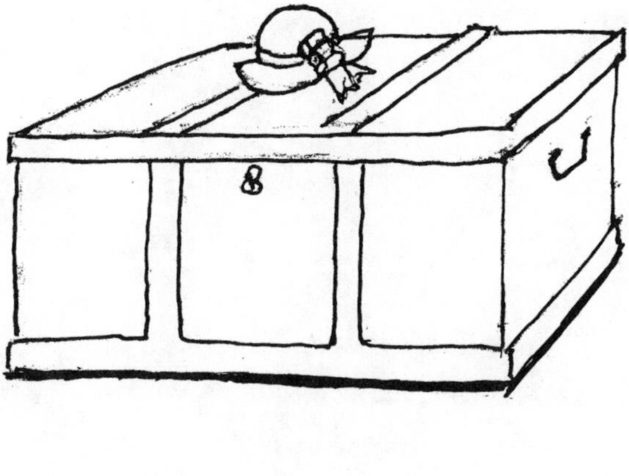

II

The Central and Northwestern Railroad was completed and had begun service between Fond du Lac and Marshfield in 1901, with freight service and four passenger trains daily. There was a depot agent-telegraph operator in each village along the way, including Wild Rose.

Previously, Plainfield, fifteen miles west, had been the shipping center for the Wild Rose area. Farm produce was hauled by team to Plainfield and shipped from there, and incoming merchandise was unloaded there and hauled by dray to Wild Rose. Salesmen, serving other parts of the county, detrained in Plainfield, rented a livery wagon and drove with their merchandise from store to store and village to village.

Then railroads, following the historic linking of the steel rails at Promontory Point, Utah, in 1869, began carrying passengers, mail and freight from coast to coast. The long trek by covered wagon across the prairie and over the mountains was no longer necessary nor the passage by steamboat up the Missouri River and thence overland to the Pacific.

A vivacious cousin of Mama's said, "When the railroad cars were hauled through Plainfield (where she lived) enroute to the new Northwestern Line, I went to the depot and spit on every car as it passed! I knew they'd ruin Plainfield."

The villages the railroad bypassed were diminished, too. Pine River, for instance, was the early county seat and a progressive village with two large mercantile stores. The County aristocracy was there. A. M. Kimball was a member of Congress. But the railroad bypassed Pine River, which is now residential, with no place to buy a loaf of bread or a package of pins.

The new depot in Wild Rose had an iron pot-bellied, wood-burning heater in the center of the passenger waiting room, wooden seats along three walls and a ticket window, open to the telegraph office, in the fourth. Beyond the office was the freight end of the depot.

The telegraph keys clickety click clicked the dots and dashes of the Morse code along the battery-operated relay system, sending and receiving messages that once were delivered by runner, by boat, by pony express, by stage coach.

When the whistle blew, and the steam engine puffed around the bend, the waiting room emptied onto the station platform as the brakes hissed and the engine chugged to a stop. Some passengers got off, others climbed aboard, while those on the platform either waved goodbye or welcome.

Mail bags were tossed aboard. The brakeman signaled, the whistle tooted, the engine hissed and chugged, and the train moved lumberingly down the tracks to stop at the coal chutes for fuel and at the water tower to fill the steam boilers which were the source of power.

Horses bore their passengers away in buggies, wagons, livery vehicles, and the dray horses plodded toward the Post Office with mail. Except for the clicking of the telegraph keys, the depot was quiet again.

In 1905 Mama and Papa (then, Aunt Fannie and Uncle Jerry) had boarded the new train in Wild Rose, Wisconsin, and alighted in Amboy, Washington, to be taken by team and wagon to the farm to see their three-year-old daughter for the first time and take her home with them.

Now that daughter was ready for college, the goal toward which they had been working and economizing, and the railroad would be the chief means of transportation to and from Ripon, an old and respected liberal arts college. Any convenient weekend could be spent at home by taking the Friday evening train to Wild Rose, returning on the 6 o'clock train Monday morning, and walking across the city of Ripon to the campus in time for the first class.

To attend college! What a privilege! "Behold I set before you an open door which no man is able to shut."

The most priceless gifts of Ripon, that small, private, liberal arts college where I spent the four most stimulating years of my life, were the personal nature of the educational process, the warmth of relationship between student and student, the rapport between student and faculty. During the summer each prospective freshman girl received a personal ietter from a member of the college Y. W. C. A., who was to serve as her "big sister," to meet her at the depot, show her around the campus and the city, and introduce her to fellow students. The college Y. M. C. A. had a similar program for feshman men.

A few days after registration there was, annually, a gala evening called "the walk around" to which upper class students escorted freshmen. Before the dancing began, the orchestra played while freshmen filed past and were introduced to faculty and upperclassmen, who had arranged themselves in a large circle around the gymnasium.

When I was a sophomore there was a freshman who was black, the only one in college. There were noncaucasians from other lands, but only this one American black. Lest he not have another invitation, I asked Don, my roommate's friend, to invite him to be my escort to the walk around. He proved to be courteous, intelligent, a graceful dancer and an enjoyable companion. Perhaps fear of being rebuffed prevented him from asking any of the other girls to dance, and after that one evening he never pursued our acquaintance other than to be friendly when we chanced to meet. Although there was no evidence of prejudice against him, he always walked alone. He was ahead of his time in attending a white college in 1922.

It was considered proper for college girls to go in groups of two or three to make a hat-and-glove call on the wife of President Evans. She and Dr. Evans, in turn, invited small groups of students to their home, with Mrs. Evans preparing and serving the evening meal. On one such evening in 1923, Dr. Evans invited us to his study after dinner to take turns wearing a pair of earphones and listening to his radio. It was our first experience with radio. It seemed incredible that we could hear a human voice all the way from Pittsburgh! And no wires? No wires! There was gentle amusement in Dr. Evans' eyes.

Other professors invited us singly or in groups to their homes to listen to classical recordings, look at books of art or just discuss this subject or that.

Once when I was ill for a few days and couldn't go to the commons to meals, Mrs. Boody, a professor's wife, and Mrs. Inghram, the Congregational minister's wife, brought a complete chicken dinner on fine China, and on the two previous evenings Mrs. Inghram had brought me home-made celery soup and oyster stew. The small college of the early 1920's!

Miss Finch, young, pretty and vivacious, taught freshman English, and insisted on perfection in grammar and spelling. The first week, she asked us to write a composition, each of which she read aloud to the class the next day, criticizing the weak points, praising the good ones and making suggestions for improvement. Only the student whose theme was being read knew the author. She opened one which she said was a "pitiful tragedy." She read it aloud, praising it for imagination, choice of words and general technique, concluding with "That girl can write. She has talent and imagination, *but* she can't spell!" The theme was mine! she said, "There are two mispelled words! She would have gotten this D if there had been only one!"

The next objective of Miss Finch was to increase our vocabulary by 100 new words in as many days, usable vocabulary both in meaning and spelling, climaxed by three old-fashioned spell-downs. By then, my dictionary was dog-eared but my composition was acceptable.

For some strange, inscrutable reason, Professor Boody would say at the beginning of each Public Speaking class, "Miss Pierce, let us hear from you." Knowing what to expect, I entered the classroom each morning with cold hands and pounding heart at the prospect of getting up on the stage and delivering a speech without notes. How I worked for that course, writing a new speech the night before and going to the dormitory basement to practice it aloud!

Thomas Edison is reputed to have said that invention is one percent inspiration and ninety-nine percent perspiration. I had been told, too: "Writing is one percent inspiration and ninety-nine percent perspiration." But when the one percent inspiration did not come, no matter how much perspiration was poured forth, the pencil refused to function and the page remained blank. I must get my inspiration! Let's see . . .

At that moment my roommate rushed in and breathlessly exclaimed, "Oh, I've had the most marvelous time! You ought to have been there! All our bunch went! Dode played the most thrilling number on the piano, and Dot! What a bird voice she has! We had refreshments, too—angel cake . . ."

An hour later everything was quiet, and I went reluctantly in search of my inspiration. The point is—Oh, I have it! How easy everything is when you have your inspiration! This is a peach!

My buzzer rang. I went into the hall to lean over the banister and ask what was wanted.

"Telephone," came the reply.

I ran down the stairs and into the booth.

"Hello!—Hello!—Yes, it is I. Am I what? President of Latin Club? Oh no, Peter Nelson is president. You're welcome. Goodbye."

Seated once more at the desk, I tried desperately to think of what I should write. Just as that telephone rang I had had the best inspiration, but now it was gone! An inspiration is as fleet as an elf, and is no sooner come than it disappears, leaving behind only an impression of something elusively beautiful that smiled and beckoned. No matter how long you call, no matter how sweetly you implore, no matter how diligently you search, the same inspiration never returns. It is gone, and gone forever!

I set myself in the mood to receive another inspiration. Finally I felt the beat of tiny wings against my forehead. "Here it comes," I thought. "Let me grasp it while I may!" A wee voice whispered in my ear, "—The idea is . . ."

Someone rapped. Jane came in and asked, "May I borrow your red beads? Fred is taking me to the Grand View to dinner tomorrow night—"

Jane was standing in the door with the beads in her hand when the proctor peeked in and said, "It's 10:15. Lights out."

Writing a speech wasn't always easy but, as the weeks passed, the anxiety and tension which at first tormented its delivery disappeared forever.

Spencer Tracy was also a member of that class. He would amble into the room and sit loose as though he had not one nerve in his big frame. Why make preparation? He probably wouldn't be called on anyway to give a speech, and if he were, he could always ad lib about something or other. His luck was with him, for he heard "Mr. Tracy" only a few times during the year. Probably Professor Boody didn't think he needed the experience.

The loved roommate of my freshman year, the little Welsh Mary, whom I had invited to the drug store for ice cream years before, didn't make preparation either. She was called on only twice, and each time she smiled demurely and said without repercussion, "I'm sorry, Professor Boody, I'm not prepared today."

Professor Boody, in spite of this regrettable imbalance in student training, was a remarkable man. It was his drama coaching that pointed Spencer Tracy toward stardom. It was his speech and debating techniques that cured John Davies of the stuttering that had plagued his days, and enabled him to teach speech and debating in Kenosha High School for all of his notable professional career.

How happy I was! How filled with promise the future! How excitingly challenging the experiences of each day! How grateful I was!

I wondered why it seemed so difficult for most persons to express gratitude. I thought about those poor wretches at the time of Jesus, who had the maiming, disfiguring disease of leprosy, which made them outcasts, "unclean," not allowed to approach another person nearer than fifty yards.

As Jesus entered a village, he was met by ten lepers, who stood at a distance and lifted up their voices and said, "Jesus, Master, have mercy on us." He told them to go show themselves to the priests. And as they went they were cleansed. One of them turned back, fell on his face at Jesus' feet, giving him thanks. Then said Jesus, "Were not ten cleansed? Where are the other nine? Your faith has made you whole." Only the grateful person has the possibility of abiding wholeness.

If gratitude would make one whole, I, too, was whole. Over and over again I told my parents how much I appreciated them. It made them happy, and as a by-product, it made me joyous, expectant, glad to give, anxious to do—whole!

But across the sunlight of my gratitude there was always the shadowed awareness of three desolate young girls who had stood huddled together to watch a lumber wagon, bearing their baby sister and her new parents, drive out of sight on the way to the railroad station. They were motherless, soon would be fatherless. The future for them was bleak—little education, no home, few opportunities, no parents to give them love and security and purpose. Oh that they could have been aboard the wagon that August day in 1905, traveling down the road to a new home! How could life have been so harsh to them and so beneficent to me? Why were they there and I here? Why me, God? Why me? Why me? Why was I lifted out of misery and desolation to these opportunities? Over and over I said, "Thank you, God, for the challenge of this day!" Over and over I asked to be made worthy, to be given a task equal to my gifts. The world was large. Surely there must be a place, a special place, where I could repay my debt!

I dove into college with everything I had, always carrying more work than required, seeking extra curricular opportunities, trying to extract every priceless drop from the Ripon experience. College would not come again. "To whom much is given, from him much shall be expected." I must be ready!

Having been brought up as an only child, dormitory life was a joy—the camaraderie, talking together, studying together, dancing in the parlor after supper, singing, laughing, sharing clothes and ideas and dreams.

Frequently someone would receive a box of home-made food from her mother. Today it would be called a "Care Package." Such a package from home called for a "spread" in the room of the recipient for a few most intimate friends or all the girls on her dormitory floor. If it was on a Friday or Saturday night, the party could be hilarious until lights must be turned off at 11. But on other nights, after eight o'clock we talked in whispers lest Mrs. Gardner, the preceptress, ring the buzzer to end the festivities.

Occasionally some girl would make the brash remark that she was going to stay out late and get back in the dorm by way of the fire escape, but I knew of none who actually tried it.

A college friend had given me a Hawaiian guitar. Though I didn't know one string from another, its chords made good background for group singing, and the guitar (and a ukulele, if someone had one) was in demand for spreads, picnics, boat outings on Green Lake, and house parties.

The discussions at the spreads were lively and covered every conceivable subject including religion and philosophy.

Somehow it had never occurred to me that there were others within the Christian faith who did not believe as I did. I had never been exposed to any other theological thought than that taught at home and in our little Methodist church. Of course there were "poor heathens" in dark corners of the world who didn't even know about the Bible—but Christians, didn't they all think alike?

After a few "spreads," which might now be termed "rap sessions," my unquestioning certainties faded under the barrage of diverse thought. I had to unscramble all these things in my mind.

There were so many things in the Bible I could not understand, and not being able to understand, could not believe. How was it possible that Mary could conceive by God? How could Jesus call Lazarus from the dead or make the blind see or the lame walk? Wasn't it impossible to break the laws of God? How could He be crucified and live again? How could He ascend into heaven? Some said that heaven was not a place but universal good. Hadn't Jesus said, "The kingdom of heaven is within you?" This I wanted to believe. Heaven was in you, yes, in me and all living things, a bond that encircles all life. And yet Luke said, "He ascended into heaven."

Each Sunday in the little church in Wild Rose I had repeated by rote the Apostles' Creed but now I no longer could say it because it made so many statements about which I was intellectually unsure. How can one say, "I believe," when not sure one does believe? I was tormented with doubt. I felt like a blind person surrounded by beauty. It was as though there were a telephone ringing in an empty house with no one there to answer. I wanted to go forward from cocksure ignorance to thoughtful surety or even to thoughtful uncertainty if sureness was not altogether possible.

Each morning at ten the students trooped down the hill to the Congregational Church for one half hour of chapel. Attendance was required, as it was at Vespers one Sunday afternoon each month. At Chapel we sang the great hymns of the church and listened to a thought-inspiring talk by a guest speaker or a member of the faculty, usually by Dr. Silas Evans, the admired and loved President of Ripon College. This warm, gracious Christian gentleman was one of the country's intellectual and spiritual greats of that period.

Seeking answers, I joined the Congregational Church, which many years before had founded Ripon College, and I joined the Christian Endeavor and Y. W. C. A. and became a leader in both because I was earnestly seeking. We were all seeking—"the blind leading the blind."

Later, what a privilege it was to serve as fellow in the Religion course of Dr. William Mutch and the Bible course of Dr. Silas Evans! In essence, they taught that there are many things about the mind of God that finite mind cannot understand. We study earnestly, take our minds as far toward the God-mind as we can, but need not expect to understand it all intellectually. Do we understand the cause of gravity? Do we know how the planets are held in orbit or why spring follows winter? We see more with the heart than with the eyes. We "walk by faith, not by sight."

"Your creed is not your religion," Dr. Mutch said, "but a statement of your religion. Religion is an attitude."

We live by things we cannot understand. There are robins in the nest—we don't know how or why, but we assume an intelligence over all, which must have existed always. We trust the whole thing and go ahead. That faith is worth all the knowledge in the world.

I went back to the New Testament again trying to penetrate the high purpose of Christianity, this time keeping in mind that it was not necessary to intellectualize. In searching the life and teachings of Jesus, one concept dominated everything, and that concept was love. He gave only one commandment: that one who tries to follow Him must love God and man, must respect himself as a child of God. Everything He said, everything He did had love at its core.

Love lightens the heart and illuminates the face.. It heals, radiates, harmonizes and attracts. It draws people together, magnetizes minds and needs no language to be understood. Just as the sun continues to shine though we can or cannot see it, so love is the unifying force of the universe, whether or not we are aware of it. It extends beyond the family, the community, humankind, to all the intricate patterns of life that comprise the universe. It is a frame of mind.

Beyond this, a life motivated by love will give of itself and give and give. It will "feed my lambs."

Doesn't the quibbling between one sect and another over one dogma or another miss the whole essence of Christianity? Holding a pebble close to the eye can blot out the view of a mountain.

Yet since time began, every human being has searched for God, and if he searched long enough he found that which, to him, was most satisfying. Whatever it was, it was his—his faith, his pattern to live by. And there are as many patterns as there are human beings who have searched for them. No one can live on someone else's faith. Each must seek out his own fulfillment for the deepest desires of the human spirit and the universal longing for spiritual renewal. For me, the intellectual struggle between doubt and faith was over. For me the answer was love and service. Peace at last descended on my soul.

There are still, and probably always will be, periods of perception and new insight, and periods of looking "through a glass darkly," but music is sweeter when it contains both high and low notes. What would vision be without light and dark, the seen and the unseen? To those who live among them, the wooded, rolling hills of Wisconsin are more beautiful than the plains.

In Latin class there was a young man from Armenia by the name of Khacker Tutunjian. He sat in the rear corner of the room, spoke English with difficulty and wore shabby clothes that might have been purchased at an army surplus store. He had the swarthy complexion, full lips and large brown eyes of his race and the sturdy frame of one accustomed to toil.

As he always seemed to be alone, one day I waited a moment in the hall and walked along with him when he came out of class. He seemed to appreciate having someone to talk to and, as the weeks went by, told me of his life in Armenia and of the Turkish pogroms which had executed his father and brothers before his own eyes and destroyed their home. Twice he had rebuilt the business, only to have it destroyed, so he decided to come to America and get an education which no one could take from him. Penniless, he was working his way through college.

I became fascinated with his description of life in that anguished part of the world and the inhumanity of the Turks toward these earliest of Christianized people.

As our acquaintance grew, I found Khacker Tutunjian to be one of the noblest men I had ever known. He was studying to be a medical missionary to help alleviate the miseries of the sick and persecuted. His singleness of purpose was as much an inspiration to me as sharing it was to him.

In the 1970's with its preoccupation with sex, when it is assumed that any relationship between two people, whether or not of the same gender, indicates sexual involvement, it is cleansing to remember that there are warm, enduring Platonic friendships that influence and enrich.

South Woods, about 2½ miles from the Ripon campus, was a favorite destination for hikers. The terrain was diverse and beautiful; a little stream meandered through the valley; nearby was a high bluff with a perpendicular cliff, a flower-strewn meadow at its base, and virgin trees—maples, birch, basswood and spruce. Students hiked out there to enjoy every season as it came, often carrying supplies for a picnic to prepare over an open fire. Even in winter, the base of the cliff and a blanket hung to the wind made a sheltered spot for a picnic fire.

On Saturdays or after school, couples—singly or in groups—

would cross-country ski and stream down the slopes of the woods while those of us who were novices sat on the skiis, using them as toboggans.

One early spring, a friend and I wandering through the woods, came on a muddy curve in the stream where perhaps seventy-five snakes, too intertwined to count, were coming out of hibernation on the mud flat. A long stick, with which we curiously disturbed them, failed to arouse them from their stupor. Though we returned to the spot on other occasions, we never saw them again.

In the spring we went to South Woods to see the chartreuse buds unfolding and to enjoy the varieties of wild flowers that carpeted each type of terrain; in the fall to revel in the beauty of red maples, yellow birches, interspersed with spruce, and the swishing sibilation of footsteps through their showering leaves; in the winter to marvel during ice storms at a forest turned to crystal.

En route to South Woods there was a small house whose yard was always strewn with litter and swarming with little children. One Saturday afternoon two other Bartlett Hall girls and I, with more humanitarian spirit than judgment, picked our way across the yard and knocked. A bedraggled, disspirited woman opened the door. "We have no special plans for this afternoon," I said. "Is there something we could do to help you?" She looked at us guardedly and with suspicion, yet, after a moment, stepped aside, waved toward the room and said, "Do what you want."

Everything was filthy—more dirt than we had ever seen anywhere, especially on the faces of nine otherwise beautiful children under eight years of age. (There were three sets of twins.) Though each of us questioned our sanity, we set to work picking up litter and scrubbing the floor with water we had pumped, carried in and heated on the wood-burning stove, while the drooping woman and shy children looked on in bewilderment. The floors clean, we washed the children's faces and hands and brushed their matted hair. Before we left, Mrs. Doe had warmed to us, and everything was transformed, at least superficially. In spite of the fact that the children's faces were pink and shining, several of them begged, "Wash my face again," or "Comb my hairs some more."

Reaching Bartlett, we rushed for the showers, feeling the need for external purification, but inside there was a warm elation at having brightened the faces of nine little children and a desolate woman.

When I was twenty-one, it was a stirring experience to go to the polls to vote. Just three years before, in 1920, the Woman's Suffrage Act had become the nineteenth amendment to the Constitution. After a generation of the suffrage movement, Susan B. Anthony had become furious when, after the Civil War, black men, newly freed, had been given the vote which women, not being considered intelligent, were still denied.

The feminist effort had intensified with marches and demonstrations until a reluctant Congress passed the amendment which would make women full citizens. As I held the ballot in my hand for the first time, I said a silent "Thank you, Lucretia Mott, Susan B. Anthony and all you other women who have made this day possible."

Carl Sandburg, the folk-singing poet, came to the Ripon campus to lecture, though one could scarcely call it a lecture in the usual sense of the word. His clothes and hair were rumpled, his guitar accompanied the folk songs he sang, his talk was folksy and spiced with biting humor. But his poetic genius, his sympathy for the oppressed, his dedication to promoting legislation that would benefit the working poor, stamped him as not only one of America's poets, but also as one of the leaders in social reform.

Mama wrote that Cousin Lelah was going to marry Will Knights. "Why! He's old enough to be her father!" Mr. Knights was a distinguished citizen of Wild Rose, one of the three founders of the Gideons. When he and two other traveling salesmen had signed in at a hotel in Boscobel, Wisconsin, they met for the first time and spent the evening discussing enthusiastically the idea, born then, of placing Bibles in every hotel and hospital room in the country and, eventually, around the world. Their idea caught fire in the minds of other Christian business men, and the dream materialized.

Cousin Lelah and Mr. Knights had much in common and did marry. They had taught for years in the Methodist Sunday School, were devoted to the church in all its facets of work and to the Gideon organization. Their greatest pleasure, aside from the church, was in going to Gideon conventions, which were held in parts of this country and Canada that they would not otherwise have seen.

It was that hushed, fruition time of year, the sky its deepest blue, each tree vying with the next in saying, "Look at me! Look at me!" I visualized our maple grove and decided to go home for the weekend. Beside the pleasure that going home always brought, there was another reason this time. I wanted to see Dr. Fisher about an uncomfortable bulge in my side. He diagnosed a large internal cyst which should be removed without delay lest it burst and produce others through the abdominal cavity.

In two days I had surgery in the nearest hospital, St. Mary's in Oshkosh. Mama was with me through the crisis. After three weeks in the hospital and three weeks of recuperation at home, I went back to Ripon.

Several months later, when Mama thought I had sufficiently recovered, she told me about the day of the surgery. "After they wheeled you away for surgery I waited hours and hours—or maybe it just seemed that long. Then an intern in a white outfit came hurrying to me in the waiting room and said the surgeon wanted to see me. I was never so scared. Wanted to see me! Something must be awfully wrong! I hustled along after the intern to the operating room. The surgeon said he had to have my permission to go ahead. He said if he finished the operation—and he had to finish—you could never have children. Well, of course I signed, but I hated to, knowing how you wanted a family someday. They thanked me and said I could go. I was so shaken by it all that I wandered around, couldn't find the waiting room."

Now I knew! The blow, though gently given, was not a gentle one, for ever since the childhood days of playing with dolls I had wanted more than anything else to be a mama when I grew up.

But facts that cannot be changed must be accepted. I would have to take a new look at the future. One thing was certain: I would never marry. A home without children would be only half a home, and I could not care for a man who would be willing to marry me because he did not care for children.

That Saturday I felt strong enough to walk out to help Mrs. Doe. Marian and Lucille went with me. For the first time there was a light in her eyes when she came to the door. She had washed the curtains, the house was less dirty, and when we gave the children their baths, one by one, in a little foot tub, there were clean clothes to put on them. The children's hair was snarled but not matted, and after a series of shampoos there was a clean brush and towel. The children clung to us when the afternoon was over.

Going out into the fresh, cold air, the lavender light of approaching evening tinting the snow, suddenly I knew! I would be a missionary! I would be a foreign missionary! In so many countries children were doomed before they were born by malnutrition, poverty, disease and illiteracy. They would all be my children! To them would I pour out my love! The ache which had tightened my throat ever since Mama broke the news was gone. I felt like singing.

The children of the whole world plead,
Imploring hands reach out in need,
For care, for love, they call.
Oh, to them I must turn my face!
Among them might I find my place!
Mother of them all!

The Saturday afternoons at Doe's continued, except when we went home for the weekend, and at Christmas time the Bartlett girls invited the children to a party. We went with sleds to get those too young to walk. There was a lighted Christmas tree, games, toys and refreshments. Who enjoyed the party more, the little guests or their hostesses?

Dr. Mutch, as faculty advisor for the Ripon College segment of the Student Volunteer Organization, was glad to let his son Warren take the family car and a group of student members to a rally in Oshkosh. Khacker Tutunjian, Meta, Frona and I were the other delegates.

It was early March. The snow, which had packed the roads deep during the winter months, had melted, leaving mud—fine, deep, black mud—which sprayed centrifugally as the wheels turned. We were shielded from it by the side curtains Warren had snapped in place.

Student Volunteers were idealistic, compassionate college students interested in becoming missionaries. The plight of so many of the world's children inspired in these students the desire to spend their lives caring for them, educating them, loving them. With no prospect of having children of my own, this was the way I wanted to spend my love! It was no romantic impulse, but a thoughtful, realistic decision. My heart sang.

The day's sessions gave information concerning the places and types of most urgent need and suggested practical methods for alleviating misery and bringing hope to the hopeless.

At the close of the evening session we started back to Ripon by way of Picket. After the day's additional thaw, the mud in the road was deeper than ever. Warren tried to keep the wheels running in the ruts previously made, but they ground deeper and deeper until the car was resting on the running boards. It could go no further.

The night was ebony. Not a star shone. Not a lighted window glowed. Warren walked back, ankle deep in mud, hoping to find a farmer with a team to haul us out, but he could find no human habitation.

There was no alternative to settling down in the car for the night. Though the side curtains were protection against the wind, they could not ward off the cold. We clung together to conserve body heat, but cold penetrated to the very marrow. It was a matter of teeth-chattering determination to endure until morning. We did!

The cold, colorless dawn, inching its way up the sky, outlined a cluster of farm buildings in the distance. Again Warren started out, this time returning with a farmer and a team of heavy draft horses who pulled and plunged until the car was on higher ground.

It was daylight when we reached Ripon, and students were hurrying along the walks to Ingram Hall and the classes of the day. We, who had stayed out all night, would have been expelled for a lesser reason. Except on Friday and Saturday nights when the dormitory doors were not locked until eleven o'clock, all girls must be in their rooms before eight. There were no exceptions.

Mrs. Gardner, Bartlett Hall's preceptress, had undoubtedly spread the alarm that three girls were missing and was prepared to tell them, when they returned, to pack their trunks for home.

Before thawing out or changing my clothes, I went to Dean Graham, explained the circumstances and received the understanding I was sure would be forthcoming. He already knew we were out all night but assured me he had been confident it was unavoidable.

Grandpa, though he had hardening of the arteries and became a problem to care for, retained his rugged physique nearly to the end of his ninety-three years, hoeing in the garden in summer, splitting kindling, kneeling on his rheumatic knee every morning for family prayer. He read without glasses, believing his good eyes were the result of putting a grain of salt in them each day. He would shake his head while tears ran down his cheeks, then smile in triumph at his fortitude.

Gypsies roamed the country in caravans of horse-drawn, enclosed wagons in which they lived and traveled, stopping at one isolated farm after another to scrounge. Their technique was to divide their forces when they stopped in a dooryard, some going in the house, some in the barn and hen house, looking for money and provisions. One day, while one group kept Mama busy in the house, another surrounded Grandpa in the garden, thinking an old man with flowing white hair would be easy prey. Grandpa always carried his money on his person, and, not intending to be separated from it, he flailed at the gypsies with his hoe until they gave up and went their way, defeated.

Often Grandpa became confused and demanded, though he was at home, to be taken home. The only way to ease the situation was for Papa to harness the horse and take him for a long ride, telling him repeatedly, "We're getting closer" or "It won't be long now," calling his attention to familiar landmarks they passed, and finally pointing out the home buildings in the distance. "There's the house! Won't it seem good to get home!" Probably Papa had two objectives in these excursions: to bring Grandpa "home," and to give Mama respite.

They never could go anywhere together because Grandpa could not be left alone, lest he wander off and get lost. Some of the time they took turns staying up with him at night, trying to keep him calm so the other could rest.

Roads were unplowed at that time, and each spring there was a period when the roads were "breaking up" and their winter's accumulation of deeply-packed snow could not support a horse's weight. Such was the case one day when, in need of supplies, Papa decided to walk the mile to town rather than risk driving a horse. He discovered, though, that the snow would not bear his weight either. Walking was laborious.

Soon after he had gone, Grandpa, with the nearly superhuman strength he received at such times, became violent, and Mama phoned the store to ask Papa to come home as quickly as possible. It was a plea she regretted the rest of her life, for the anxious struggle to hurry home, each step a battle with deteriorating snow, damaged his heart. Dr. Fisher advised him not to try to operate the farm the next summer, so he rented the land to neighbors and sold the cows.

As that harrowing winter ebbed away, so did Grandpa's life. He was ninety-three when he died, the last of the rugged pioneers who had come into the wilderness of the Town of Rose in 1851 and conquered it. The land, as we know it, was the result of their courage and incessant toil, their hardships and privations, a gift to all future generations.

Though we were concerned about Papa's health, it was a tranquil, happy summer. Freed of stress and strenuous physical labor, his health improved.

We drove to Camp Cleghorn several times to hear a speaker in whom we were particularly interested. Camp Cleghorn was a campground on the Chain O'Lakes, not far from Waupaca. Hundreds of people flocked there on Sunday afternoons during the summer season to the open air pavilion to hear famous orators of the day—William Jennings Bryan, college presidents, outstanding clergymen, senators. Public address systems were unknown, but those orators needed none.

Agnes Hanson, a college friend, came to spend the weekend with me in late summer. As something interesting to do we took our little Ford and drove to Camp Cleghorn. The pavilion was nearly full when we got there, but we were fortunate to find two seats near the back where a breath of air was circulating on that sultry afternoon.

At the end of the speech, someone sitting back of us put a daddy long legs on me which, of course, I returned. It was George Dopp, whom I knew only slightly. He had finished Wild Rose High School before I entered, and, as we lived in different rural areas, we did not see each other socially.

That week there was a party at the Methodist Church to bid farewell to one parsonage family and welcome to another and as the little Dopp Church was part of the parish, several came from that community, among them George, who slipped into the seat beside me. We shared a hymn book for congregational singing and he slid his thumb along the page until it pressed against mine. Such impertinence! My face felt hot! Driving me home, he tried to put his arm around me, which of course I would not allow, for nice girls kept young men in their place!

George and his brother Walter operated the farm five miles

north of Wild Rose, which at that time had been in the family for three generations.

His grandfather and three brothers had come from Waukesha into the southeast corner of Portage County where they settled and developed farms on adjacent land. George's parents started their married life in a one-room home on the farm where their children were born, the house growing as the family increased. As George and I got to know each other better, he told me about his family.

"Dad never was much of a farmer—should have been a preacher or professor. He read a lot, memorized poetry by the yard (guess he knew all of Scott's 'Lady of the Lake') and recited it for his kids and later for the grandchildren. Walt and I run the farm, pretty good farmers, if I do say so myself. Dad is secretary of an insurance company and of the Wild Rose Creamery Company, which is more to his liking than working on the land.

"Mother is an angel of a woman, want you to get to know her. She always goes to church to make it spic and span for Sunday, and Walt and I go early to build and tend the fire in the wood-burning furnace. Our house is a haven for the aimless, the shiftless, and mother always sends them on their way well fed and with a lighter step.

"Dud Carr lives in a shack in the woods a few miles away, drinks like a fish, and when he's drunk he heads for our place, and Mother takes care of him until he is on his feet again. He comes, too, when he wants a good meal. Once in a while he earns a little money doing painting around the farm, but for the most part he lives from hand to mouth. He's an expert trout fisherman. Only claim to glory is that he won a fly-casting contest at the Wisconsin State Fair.

"Sometimes Dud brings trout for our Sunday dinner and stays to have some. Mother most always invites the minister to Sunday dinner. One Sunday when serving Dud's trout, Mother asked the reverend if he would eat trout that was caught on Sunday. He said, 'Yes, but I wish you hadn't told me until after dinner!' "

George chuckled.

"I have twin sisters, you know—Grace and Pearl. They're married and gone now, but they used to be milk carriers for the neighborhood. They'd take a team and wagon and pick up cans of milk from our place and the neighbors.' The farmers hauled their cans of milk with team and stone boat to a platform near the road. The girls could slide the cans from the platform onto their wagon and deliver them to the cheese factory three and one half miles away.

You know there used to be a cheese factory at the top of cheese factory hill. Grace was quite a mimic, had fun at home repeating the conversations she heard at the cheese factory. She had the Welsh brogue down pat."

The one-room rural school of the Dopp neighborhood was the educational and social center of the community. It was in a lovely wooded area with large playground across a field from the meandering little trout stream known as "Dopp Crick." Church services were held in the school house on Sundays, the Methodist minister from Wild Rose driving out to officiate. Often there were testimony meetings at which members of the congregation rose to testify to their religious experience and belief. George laughed, "One old fellow had bushy red hair and beard, his ears stuck out, and he had the type of face usually associated with the Devil. He would get up and give a long testimony, always ending with, 'Ladies and gentlemen, beware! The Devil stands before you.' We kids thought it was so funny that we mimicked him for days, never within the hearing of Mother and Dad. They would have scolded us for laughing at folks."

In 1906 a rural Methodist Church was built across the road from the farm home and, because George's father gave the land and because it was built in the Dopp community, it was named the "Dopp Church." Neighborhood farmers worked on the building and gave of their savings to buy lumber and materials. A long wooden horse shed with stalls to shelter horses completed the building program.

Fall came and I went back to Ripon. There was a classmate who provided social and intellectual companionship during all the years at college. I told him I had a friend at home with whom I was corresponding. As I was going to be a missionary I didn't want either of them to take me for granted. Our association must end with college. I dreaded the hurt.

On weekends when I was home, George came over for an evening and the four of us, Mama, Papa, George and I, visited like old friends. Bit by bit, the events of his life unfolded. When George's sister, Genevieve, had finished the country school and then drove a horse to Wild Rose High School, George, 12 years old, went with her and entered the sixth grade. To earn spending money he got up at five o'clock, jumped on a horse and rode to the Dopp school to build a fire for the teacher, rode home, helped with the barn chores, had breakfast, cleaned up for school and drove with Genevieve five miles to Wild Rose. The trip took about an hour.

Rural children who lived too far from school to walk, drove a horse and housed it for the day in a barn in the village. Most people at that time had a small barn in the back yard for a horse and cow. Country children never had time to participate in athletics because they had to hurry home to help with farm work and chores.

The big event of the year was the Waushara County Fair in Wautoma, thirteen miles from the Dopp farm. The family would drive a team pulling a double buggy "with the fringe on top," the buggy big enough for everyone if the littlest sat on someone's lap. They would be gone all day, getting home in time to do chores.

George's three sisters had college educations and taught before their marriages. Walter, who wanted to be a knowledgeable farmer, took the short course in Agriculture at the University of Wisconsin. George, the youngest, had completed his freshman year at Ripon College when tragedy struck the family.

On a day when their father was away on insurance business and their mother had gone to Wild Rose with a neighbor to do the "trading," George and Walter were working at home with a wood-sawing crew to provide stove wood for the winter. Walter was "throwing away" each block of wood as it came through the saw, when a protruding set screw caught his mitten and pulled his right arm into the saw, mangling it. Fortunately the telephone had come to the community. George ran to the house, phoned Dr. Wilcox in Wild Rose, whose little driving horses covered the five miles in fifteen minutes, their coats white with lather. Dr. Fisher, who was to give the anesthetic, drove his steaming horses into the yard minutes later. They carried Walter to the kitchen, laid him on the table, and amputated his arm above the elbow.

Through the dark, painful days that followed, Walter never gave up his determination to be a farmer. "The only way that dream could be realized," George said, "was for me to stay home to help him, which I did."

I asked, "Didn't you hate to give up college?"

He admitted, "Yes, but there wasn't time to think about it. (Pause) I always thought I'd like to be a doctor, but I guess I wasn't studious enough anyway."

Walter, with courage and determination, learned to do everything a two-handed person could do except tie his shoe laces.

The farm prospered. they bought more land, developed a large herd of Holstein cattle, built a big barn and a commodious brick house.

Walter married Florence Frost, a teacher in Wild Rose. They had four children whom George loved as his own. George, his mother and father, and Walter, and his family lived together in the new home, the two men operating the farm together and sharing a common purse.

"A common purse?" Papa asked. "That's a bit unusual, isn't it? You are only one and Walter's family is six—six times the groceries, six times the clothing, six times the doctor bills. Is that quite fair?"

George showed not a moment's hesitation, "It's fair enough for me! I love those children just as much as Walt does, and I have just as much fun with them as he does. I don't regret one minute of it.—I have two arms, and Walter has only one."

George's mother and Walter's wife belonged to the Wild Rose Study Club, of which my mother was one of the founders. It met every two weeks in the home of one of the members, usually in town, for that was where most of the members lived. The two Dopp women drove a horse and buggy in summer or a cutter in winter, rain or shine, to the educational meetings of the club. No more than two could sit comfortably in either vehicle. The children were left in the care of their Grandpa Dopp who, when he became immersed in a book or other intellectual pursuit, was oblivious to what the children were doing. A neighbor asked the children, "Who takes care of you when your Mama and Grandma are at Study Club?" Buffy, the oldest, without hesitation, replied, "God takes care of us on Study Club day."

Winter ended and I was home for spring vacation. These days were warm with quiet joy—a whole week for Mama, Papa and me to be together! Papa's health had improved. He was like his old self again. There was the prospect of carefree years ahead for these two precious people whose love for each other had never dimmed.

Mama and I, returning from town one day, saw Papa cross in front of the window, probably coming to greet us as we stepped up on the porch. When we entered, he was lying on the kitchen floor. While Mama pillowed his head in her arms, I rushed to phone Dr. Fisher. He came quickly, but there was nothing he could do. Mama was a widow at fifty-five.

We drifted like sleepwalkers through the days that followed, automatically doing the things that had to be done. Neighbors came and went, helping wherever they saw the need. How else could they express the sympathy and ease the sorrow they, too, felt? Letters of condolence, sent to console, tore at our hearts.

There were eulogies. One by Rev. H. E. Mansfield of the local Baptist Church is quoted in part:

"Such minds, such men, are born to leadership, and to leadership this man marched inevitably. He would have stood out from the crowd in any company. He had the mysterious quality called "personality." He was not an orator but when he spoke men listened. He never sidestepped nor evaded issues. Forthright, plain-speaking, sometimes almost painfully direct, his target average was high. He got to the mark. His judgment was sound. His foresight was prophetic. And more and more, as the years ripened his acumen, his associates learned to trust the one and to respect the other.

"The problems before him were seldom his own. They were the problems of his business associates, his friends, his community. For these, his keen business ability and his public spirit were always on duty. Such service he never refused to render and he never betrayed confidence. He did not know how to lay his burdens down and so at last he died beneath them, died in harness, died as strong men always die with a thousand things still to do, a multitude of demands still waiting for his firm and wise disposal, and what we shall do without him, we scarcely dare to think.

"One will go far to find a man to whom public office was more truly a personal trust than it was to J. C. Pierce. Office as an honor would beckon to him in vain, but office as an opportunity for public service seemed to him a perfectly honorable ambition and he discharged its duties with a single-minded devotion that has set a standard for years to come.

"No catering to sectional interest was responsible for his unanimous election to the Chairmanship of the County Board at its late session. It was simply a recognition on the part of his colleagues, that here was a man, impartial to preside, fairminded to adjudicate conflicting interests, broad enough to compass the problems of the County as a legislative unit, outstanding enough to add dignity to its deliberations and prestige to its findings.

"This is not the time to enlarge upon a theme so sacred, so tender as his marriage to Fannie Etheridge. But it is fitting that this testimony be borne. Her vivacious intelligence, her comprehension of his aims, her sharing of his ideals was the great experience whose wonder never faded."

The officers and directors of the Wild Rose State Bank distributed a card edged in black, announcing the death of their president, Mr. J. C. Pierce. Mama was stoic through it all.

I received a letter from Dr. William Mutch, Professor of Philosophy and Religion at Ripon College, written on March 18, 1924, the day of Papa's funeral, in which he said, "I am pained to hear this morning of the passing of your father and hasten to send you this brief word of sympathy. I recall your mention of his critical state of health but did not realize the imminent seriousness of the situation and the mental stress which you have been under and which is still upon you. I trust that you and your kindred will be sustained in your troubles by the everlasting arms in which you have learned to trust.

"I am speaking for the whole faculty in offering our common sympathy and such encouragement as may be possible, and also in advising you to take such time as may seem needful to be at home without feeling any need whatever of returning promptly to your college work. Your work here has been of such a nature that you are free to take any liberties you wish at this time.

Most sincerely yours,
W. J. Mutch"

Postponing the day of decision, though I appreciated the kind suggestion, did not make the decision easier. Days passed into weeks, the future fogged in uncertainty. How could I leave Mama there alone? I was all she had. I enumerated the things she had done for me. Yet I knew Papa would want me to finish college. He had worked so long with that one objective in mind. The night-and-day turmoil of indecision, part of me saying, "Stay," and part saying "Go," added to the anguish I felt for Mama and my own aching loneliness without Papa.

Friends urged me to return. A letter from Rev. Mark Inghram, with whom I worked closely in the Christian Endeavor of Ripon's First Congregational Church, concluded thus, "You mustn't think of dropping out of school—you're making too good use of it, and you'll need it all the way. I know how easy it is in the midst of trouble to wonder if school is worth while. I know by experience. I'm awfully glad some good friend made me see that I couldn't afford to sacrifice my better life for the sake of a temporary sacrifice—even when it seemed advisable. Go on!

Most sincerely,
Mark Inghram"

Finally, after missing a month of school, I decided to return—not knowing, even then, if it was the right decision.

With the livestock gone, Mama was free to come and go as she liked. We arranged for her brother Alanson to stay there nights as long as she felt she wanted someone, and I planned to come home every weekend. I left her standing in that desolate doorway as I walked to the depot.

Faculty and friends at Ripon College were so kind! Mama's friends at home were, too, inviting her to visit them for several days or a week at a time.

After Papa's death, George was so thoughtful of Mama! Often when he went to town he drove a mile West to see her and do little tasks that he thought were too difficult for her. It was another outcropping of the innate, whole-hearted kindness he had always given to his own mother, to Walter and his family, and anyone else who needed him. The result was that Mama gave him her unqualified loyalty to the end of her days.

In one of her letters she wrote, "George came into the store, while I was doing the trading this afternoon, and asked if I had to walk home and *insisted* on bringing me, as he was *sure* his folks weren't ready. (George always drove his mother and father to town.) He apologized for not asking me if I had a way to get home from O. E. S. and I told him I was with E." "Well, *I* didn't know it!" he said, 'and *I* should have found out! I came near turning the horse around after I was half way home!' "

Her letter went on: "He asked when you were coming home. I told him in two weeks, that next Sunday was Vespers. I also told him you called up Friday evening to see if I wanted you to come and I thought it was best for you not to. As he was leaving he said, 'Now don't you discourage Pearl from coming in two weeks. *I* want her to *come.*' Now isn't he the limit? *Lovely man I say!* He said if roads kept good he wants to drive to Ripon Sunday, and I can go, too. I asked if he wouldn't rather go alone and he said *no,* he wanted company.

So—if the roads and weather stay good, he'll probably take a fit to go—although I think it's kind of foolish. Mama"

Added to the anxiety for Mama was the new realization that I would have to change my plans for the future. I would have to give up serving in foreign missions, for how could I leave her alone while I worked in the far corners of the earth? I couldn't! Doors seemed to be closing, one after the other—no children, no marriage, no service to the children of the world.

Why am I here, Lord?
Plans lie unfulfilled.
The path grows dark.

Where does my service lie?
What is the gift
That only I can give?

I cannot find the paths I chose,
Nor, finding them,
Follow where they lead.

I beg Thee, God,
Light my dark lantern
And show the way!

As the galaxies spun in space, as the seasons moved inexorably, one into the other, tomorrow followed yesterday's today, and my Junior year of college ended. I was home for the summer.

George and I had pleasant times together that summer. On some Sunday afternoons we walked across to the Upper Pine and sat with our backs against a large oak, watching the eddying stream flow by and an occasional trout rise for a fly or nymph. We could tell a bit about the size of the trout by the way he captured the floating prey. Young trout, in exuberance, often jumped in a complete arc out of the water. A mature one scarcely disturbed the surface, rising quietly from below and leaving only a circular, widening ripple as evidence that he had fed.

We sat motionless as little creatures, a rabbit, a chipmunk, looked at us a moment, unafraid, and then scurried away.

These were tranquil, sylvan hours of sunlight, respite from the shadow of concern over Mama's brave efforts to adjust to her aloneness and from the blindness with which I tried to look beyond the closed doors of the future.

One Sunday afternoon, as we often did, we followed the cow path down the lane across the pasture, empty now, to the hills where I had always loved to go.

Breathless but exhilarated, we reached the ancient pine and looked out over the valley of home. The verdure of spring had changed, chameleon-like, to yellow and bronze, the sunlit colors of late summer, the fruition of spring's promise. The dome of the vast blue sky was a bluer blue, and oak trees, etched against it, a deeper green. The air that soughed through the branches of the old tree was sweet with the familiar fragrance of pine.

We had been silent, enjoying the view, when he looked at me intently and asked, "Is there any reason we should not continue to see each other?" I drew a sharp breath. When the words finally came, they sounded calm, far off, as though someone else were speaking. "Yes, there is. I do not intend to marry, for there could never be any children."

I can't forget his stricken face.

As we came out of Christian Endeavor one Sunday evening near the end of his Senior year, Khacker Tutunjian asked me to be his guest at a League house party at Green Lake. (The League was a group of college men who did not belong to a fraternity.) It was customary for each club or fraternity to have a weekend house party once a year at Green Lake, to which each fellow invited his girl, and members of the faculty went as chaperones. Khacker was working so hard to get through school that I was sure he couldn't afford to go, but we were both conscious that after graduation we would probably never see each other again.

When I wrote home about going, Mama's reply was stamped with misgivings. I still have her letter. She said in part, "I hardly know what to say about your going to Green Lake next weekend. Probably it would be all right for you to go. I don't know on how familiar terms a fellow and girl are supposed to be to go on such an affair together. Of course, I think very highly of Mr. T. and know you do, but I should not want you to get to think too much of him. You have been nice to him because you respected and admired him as he deserved, but remember he is a foreigner, and they are apt to take too much for granted. This is a thing I have learned from observation, so it is best to be *very* careful.

"If it would not appear that you have too many on the string, I suppose it would be all right.

"Now you do as any *nice* girl would do and as would be thought proper for you to do. I'm sure you *would* like to go with Mr. T. before he goes away perhaps never to come back, and you'd feel richer for it maybe.

"We love you *dearly* and want you always to do right and have as good a time as you can in so doing. Love, Mama"

(And I had been serene in the assumption that I had never given my parents any worry!)

In replying I tried to reassure her. "Do not think that it is not perfectly proper to go on a mixed house party, for they are well chaperoned by faculty couples. All the clubs have them, and some of the finest girls in the dorm are going.

"Please don't worry about my getting to think too much of Khacker. I could not consider him in any light other than that of a fine friend, nor does he have any other thought of me. He has chosen me as a friend because I am interested in his experiences. His least serious thought is that of girls.

"I don't feel I can afford to lose the opportunity to spend a couple of days in the influence of such a genuine and unusual person, but if you would rather I wouldn't go, just say so and I'll be glad to give it up. Love, Pearl."

The house party was delightful. The sun shone unceasingly, and the young people reveled in it, swimming, boating, hiking, picnicking, singing, comaraderie. In describing it in detail in a letter home as soon as we returned to campus, I expressed pleasure that Mr. Tutunjian had gone, for everyone present learned to know him better and to admire him more. He said he enjoyed every minute of his first and last experience of its kind in America. And so did I.

Education increases awareness, understanding of our environment, and our place in the ecological system. It helps us choose values by which we want to live, a sense of purpose, of mission which can lift us above the mundane preoccupation with making a living to the sublime challenge of making a life. It gives us an appreciation for the persons and institutions of past centuries that cleared the trail for us, and developed the social and intellectual concepts of the modern world.

As a fledgling at the edge of the nest flaps his wings, testing them for flight, so I was anxious to graduate from receiving to giving, from preparation to action.

In the Senior year of college, choices must be made. All of one's future would depend on whether or not the choice was wise.

One of the soldiers of Alexander the Great was searching for treasures in the palace of Darius. He found a leather bag containing the priceless crown jewels of Persia, but the soldier was ignorant of the value of jewels. In fact he didn't know a jewel when he saw one, so he shook the little glittering stones into the rubbish heap and saved the leather bag. He went around boasting of the fine bag he had found for carrying his food.

Would I be any wiser? In a dream, I was not.

Carnival

1925

At night
I mingled with the pulsing throng
In the heat, red light and dust
Of a carnival,
Seething up and down
The street of booths
Where petty gamblers
Were hazarding lamps, Navajo blankets,
Candy, and honor
On chance.

Out of the mob
A boy pushed his way to my side.
His blouse was grey
With wear.
His face was dusky
And hollow.
His two eyes mirrored
A dream.
In his hands he carried
A rose—
A white rose.
(How did it live
in the air
That was pungent with fraud?)

The boy's voice pleaded:
"Lady, won't you buy
A rose?
Only five cents!"
"There are plenty of roses
At home," I said.

And I bought
A balloon
From a sleek swindler—
A round, red balloon
That burst
In an hour.

The Senior year was a joyous year, filled with subjects and experiences that were stimulating. The required subjects for a Bachelor of Arts degree were over. Education classes had been boring and foreign languages difficult.

The most rewarding course of the previous year had been Advanced Composition under Professor Allen of the English Department. He prodded our minds, taught us to think, to see, to listen, to perceive and to express the resulting concepts in writing. He encouraged me in poetry and had written at the end of the year, "You have a gift of song, which you must cultivate. Remember the Sandburg poem about the man with a furled sail monument? Don't be afraid to let joy and grief and isolation and pain play on your lute."

During the Senior year he initiated a course in advanced Advanced Composition just for me, concentrating on writing poetry. He and I met once a week after school, the only time it could be worked into our schedule. What a privilege! No one could have been more grateful!

But the Senior year was so full! It would not come again! There were not enough hours to hold everything that must be packed in it. It would have been wiser, in retrospect, to prune away all the extra curricular activities that at the time seemed so valuable. Wiser, perhaps, to have resigned from the editorial staff of college publications, the duties associated with the fellowships, organizational and social activities, South Woods, picnics and "spreads," as important, perhaps, as the academic work, which was my primary privilege in the process of personal growth. It must have been disappointing to Professor Allen that his generous gift of himself was not received with singleness of purpose.

Intriguing prospects were presenting themselves. A letter from Rev. Nickless, pastor of a Presbyterian Church in Nebraska, said that Dr. Evans had recommended me as director of education and the choir of his church.

In a few days a letter came from Dr. Evans, in which he said, in part, "I have written to Rev. Nickless after having talked to him at some length in reference to you and my letter strongly reinforces the recommendation I have given him orally.

"I hope the matter comes out all right. Both you and the church will be very happy in the type of work he outlines. I would so much rather see you in this kind of work than in public school teaching. Yours very cordially, Silas Evans."

The prospect was intriguing. It was work that would be satisfying. But, Nebraska! Thinking of Mama, Nebraska was the end of the earth! If it were near, she and I could have an apartment and go home often to see her friends. Could she be content in so different an environment as Nebraska?

Teaching, too, was a possibility.

For every youth dozens of paths lead into the future, but only one can be taken. Which should it be? They all looked equally alluring.

If a tree, sending its roots into the earth, can choose, among all the myriad elements available, only those that will make it strong and beautiful, why is it so difficult for a human being to choose, among all the paths that beckon, the one that leads to service and fulfillment?

George wrote as usual and, when I went home for the weekend, he came over to say hello. He was seeing other girls, too, and that was good! I knew what he wanted. After years of caring for Walter's family, as much as he loved them, he wanted a home of his own, a wife and children—his own family at last! "No one," I thought, "deserves it more."

After all the years of preparation, I was anxious to put the experiences to constructive use, and wondered where that desire might lead. As spring approached the answer came in the form of a letter from the Ripon High School Board of Education asking me to teach Freshman and Junior English at a starting salary of $1200. Dr. Mutch, a member of the school board, had recommended me. To teach in Ripon! It was too good to be true! Close to friends, faculty and college activities! Close enough to Wild Rose to go home often to keep Mama company! And my heart said, "Close enough to see George often!"

The reply was an immediate yes. One seldom telephoned home. A two-cent stamp was so much less expensive, but this deserved instant transmission! There were wings in Mama's voice when she heard the news. The excitement of the prospects for fall only intensified the compulsion to drain the last drop of goodness from the college experience.

In the meantime, George had done his searching and was reconciled to my limitations. As the compass points north, only north, so each of us was north to the other.

The mind's eye had led down each of the enticing paths to the future, and on each path I was alone. Life without George, however challenging, would be incomplete. So, we joined hands and decided to walk together along the path leading north, the eternal north of our at-oneness.

Though he had waited long, George understood my desire to try my wings for a year after graduation before marrying.

At the last class session with Professor Allen, he mentioned again his desire to have me choose poetry as my life way. He was disappointed when he learned I planned to marry. He said, "You realize that if you marry, life will be too full for you to develop your own potential." Of course that was true, but it would take years of concentrated effort to arrive at a personal literary style, and as far as the welfare of mankind was concerned, it would not make a bit of difference whether I wrote or didn't write. Giving up the life George and I had planned together was a greater sacrifice than I was willing to make.

At that time the price of being a woman was self denial. A man married as part of his life work and went on with his profession or business, the only difference being that his wife, instead of his mother, cooked his meals, cared for his house and kept his clothes clean and mended.

A woman left everything behind when she married, and marriage was all she had. She dropped her own ambitions and assumed his. She sublimated her own talents to promote his.

In our case, George was making a sacrifice too. I was just as sure that he would never mention his as I was that I would never mention mine.

Came the glad day—commencement! Caps and gowns, pageantry, processional, culmination, commitment! Then goodbyes, ache in the throat, wordless embrace. Bartlett halls grew quiet as, one by one, girls left for home. "Four years gone forever," I thought, tears dripping into the trunk as it was packed for the last time.

But one day realization would come that no experience is lost. It becomes part of the warp on which the rest of life is woven.

Miracle of words

III

In the summer there were quiet times to think of the challenge of the fall. The quality of life of many future adults would depend on whether I did my work well.

The importance of words in the transmission of ideas from mind to mind! Man, the only living entity capable of using them, was privileged indeed. He had dominion over other living things because of his ability to think, to use his superior brain to formulate ideas and to use his unique tongue to express those ideas to other human beings. It was God's gift to man.

It would be simple if thought could be exchanged directly from one mind to another, directly from thinker to receiver, without the use of words. There are a few who claim to be psychic and able to do just that, but for everyone else, words are necessary. Many, though, use them poorly or are afraid to use them at all. I had felt sympathy for the chairman of a business meeting who tried to get a consensus and faced silent women who never express themselves in public; and the program chairman who asked a member, "Will you introduce the speaker at the next meeting?" and heard, "You must be joking! You know I can't talk before a group. I'd be speechless!" A publicity chairman got a similar response when asked to write a news release.

This attitude is not new. Hundreds of years before recorded history, when the knowledge of the race was passed from father to son by the gift of speech, an uneducated shepherd, called Moses, was tending his father-in-law's sheep when God spoke to him, the Bible tells us, from a burning bush. When God instructed Moses to go to

Egypt to free the Israelites and lead them hundreds of miles across the desert to the promised land, Moses protested, "But I am slow of speech and slow of tongue . . . oh, my Lord, send I pray some other person." He seemed a most unlikely choice!

But God made Moses a promise: "I will be with your mouth and teach you what you will speak."

So Moses left his flock and went to find his brother Aaron, to tell him about the burning bush that was not burned, about the staff that had been turned into a serpent and back again, about being stricken with leprosy and instantly cured, about the task God had given him. Moses must have done an effective bit of speaking for, amazingly, Aaron believed this fantastic story and agreed to go with him.

Then Moses went to Jethro, his father-in-law, and told him this unbelievable tale and said that he and Aaron would no longer be tending the sheep, that they were going to Egypt to free their people from slavery. Instead of saying, "Cut out the foolishness, Moses, and get back to those sheep," Jethro said, "Go in peace."

That was quite an accomplishment for a man who was slow of speech, but Moses was able to translate the message convincingly because he, himself, was convinced of the truth and importance of what he had to say. That is the essence of self expression that can make anyone articulate.

There is the story of Jesus and his disciples taking a short cut across Samaria on their way from Judea to Galilee, a route seldom used by Jews because they despised Samaritans. Resting by Jacob's well while the disciples went for provisions, Jesus spoke to a woman who had come to draw water. Spoke to a Samaritan! That was not done! Spoke to a woman! No Jew could speak to a woman in public, not his wife, not even his girl child! Few in her own country spoke to this woman because she was a moral outcast, but here was a man! Jew! Speaking to her! She listened and was changed.

Leaving her water jar at the well, she ran to the village to tell the people to come to see this man who told her all she ever did! They listened to this woman whom they had known too well, and they believed her because she had a message to deliver, a service to render, and that had made her convincing. They followed to see Jesus. They were so impressed that their lives, too, were changed. They invited him to spend two days with them. Incredible! A Jew, the guest of Samaritans!

This all happened because of a brief conversation between two strangers at a well.

Throughout the ages, the pattern of human lives and the history of nations have been redirected by the exchange of ideas through the use of words.

Man is a social animal. People need each other. The chief way to reach out to people is through the use of written or spoken words. Scientists have discovered that talking with people is not only good for the listener but good for the talker. Psychiatrists encourage patients to exchange ideas, and often find that when a mentally disturbed person begins to talk, the healing process has begun. Heart to heart talks are encouraged by marriage counselors as one of the bases on which a happy marriage is built. Why do these exchanges of ideas enrich lives? To be real to himself, man must be real to another human being. Minds must touch to stay alive.

I read of a British soldier who was captured by the Germans and put in a windowless cell. The isolation, the weeks of utter silence, the dread of what might lie ahead, preyed on his mind. He feared he would go insane. Then one day he heard a tapping on the other side of the wall. It was the rhythm of the old jingle, "Shave and a hair cut—bay rum." He and the stranger on the other side of the wall took turns tapping out the first part of the rhythm and then waiting for the answering double beat. The aloneness was gone. They knew they could endure together.

I had a cousin who was a deaf mute. As soon as I learned to spell a few words, Mama taught me the alphabet for the deaf, and I began visiting with my cousin. These visits brought pleasure to both of us. She is long since gone, but even now, when I see a deaf mute, I talk with him and his face lights up and his eyes shine. Into his silent world has come another person. He is not alone.

Most people are not as isolated as the man in the solitary cell or the deaf mute, but everyone has need to touch other human beings. The chief way for minds to touch each other is through the God-given gift of speech. Though using words would be easier for some than for others, I was sure that every intelligent, physically capable human being could learn to use words effectively.

There was a man, so the story goes, who trapped wild monkeys in Africa and sold them to a zoo. He used large glass jars, the mouth just large enough to admit a monkey's paw when it was open, but too small for him to withdraw his closed fist. The hunter put a lump of sugar in the trap and waited. A monkey saw the sugar, wanted it, thrust his paw into the jar and closed his fist over the prize. He couldn't withdraw his paw. He wouldn't release the sugar and was captured.

Some unfortunate people hug to themselves their abilities, their possessions, their ideas. It is impossible to use the miracle of speech without opening the hand and the heart to people. I resolved to try to train all the students—not just the gifted who enter declamatory and essay contests, but all of them—to use words fluently and convincingly for "their voice goes out through all the earth and their words to the end of the world." That would mean spending evenings correcting student themes, and extra curricular hours training students to speak effectively, but unless it were done, those young people, when they became secretaries or salesmen or college students, would still be slow of tongue, unable to communicate ideas either orally or on the written page. All their lives they would miss their full potential. It would be up to me!

I went to Ripon and rented an apartment so Mama could come for the winter, and the morning dawned of the first day of school. Elms arched over the street as I walked the two blocks to the High School. The sun never seemed brighter nor the world more beautiful. The years of education had led to this!

My room was bright with sunlight when the buzzer rang and a class of Freshmen trooped into the room and looked me over inquiringly as they took their seats. The class had scarcely begun when, from a section of the room where some boys were sitting, a bat winged up and circled the room. Students' heads swiveled as they watched the bat fly round and round until it settled on top of a high window casing. The boys, though, were watching me, probably hoping this new teacher would run screaming from the room. Instead, we talked about what interesting little creatures bats were, and the assignment for the next day was a theme on the subject. When class was dismissed, an empty shoe box was visible under one of the boys' desks.

Teaching was as enjoyable as anticipated. There were no disciplinary problems. And Mama seemed quite content as she settled in for the winter. When we did not go home for the weekend, George drove to Ripon on Sunday.

Christmas approached. Mama and I always made all the Christmas gifts for relatives and friends—crocheted doilies, tidies, aprons, embroidered dresser scarves, knitted mufflers and mittens—but this was the first year of my betrothal to George. No homemade gift for him!

One Saturday in December Mama and I drove her little two-passenger Ford to Oshkosh to find the prettiest, softest sweater in the city. The streets and stores were abubble with holiday spirit, the glow of the season, of glad expectancy, marred only by an overwrought, irate mother yanking her bawling toddler behind her through the Fair Store aisles.

I found the perfect sweater and paid the clerk, who put the money in a little tin box which traveled along an elevated track to the cashier's station at the end of the store. By the time the package was wrapped, the box had returned with the change, and we left.

Outside the sidewalks had become glazed with ice. Pellets of rain were freezing as they fell. Realizing what lay ahead, we skidded along to the car and started back to Ripon. The roads were precarious and, what was worse, we couldn't see through the windshield without stopping every half mile to scrape off the ice. There was no way to heat the car nor to defrost the windshield. Finally I gave up scraping and drove the rest of the way back to Ripon with my hooded head out the window, sleet stinging my face and frosting my eyelids.

As the year progressed, teaching became more and more rewarding. It was a thrilling experience to watch young people develop self-awareness through self-expression. At high moments of response, I was not sure I wanted to get married.

Dust of Stars

My will has bound me to the dust
Of stars. My heartstrings hum
The echo of your calling voice.
But, Love, I can not come.

If fading light will make me free
Perhaps I may redeem
The dear contentment of your arms.
Oh, dreams, I dare not dream!

I'm sure there were times when George had his doubts, too. Doesn't everyone? But there was Mama to consider, she who had given of herself to make this choice possible. There were months of indecision, but it was inevitable that I chose George.

Walter grumbled at the outlandish idea of a sunrise wedding. Outdoors! On Green Lake! "Sam Hill! Why couldn't they get married in a church, right at home, like anybody else?" But, in spite of his dark view of the time and location, he did the milking early and drove his family to Green Lake by eight o'clock that Wednesday morning in June.

Except for inviting Walter and his family and George's sister Genevieve, who was coming anyway from Kansas with her children to spend the summer at the farm, we hugged to ourselves the plans for our wedding. It was our unshared secret! In retrospect, we might agree with Walter, but in 1926 it was exciting, romantic and natural, for our marriage was always going to be uniquely beautiful!

We had planned to have a house party at the close of school with two other couples of whom we were fond. I was finishing teaching, Marian and Harold were graduating from Ripon College, and Justine and Adam were coming back for commencement. Our widowed mothers, who came as chaperones, knew how the house party would end, but it wasn't until the evening before that we told the others and asked them to be our attendants.

George and I drove back to Ripon that evening to bring Genevieve and her children out to Sandstone Camp. On the way back we stopped to pick the wild roses which were to be my bridal bouquet.

Marian and Harold stayed up most of the night picking wild white daisies and tying them on the curved branch of an oak—a bower for the ceremony. I might as well have stayed up too, for who could sleep on the eve of one's wedding? At five o'clock I heard someone walking around downstairs so I got up quietly, slipped into some clothes and tip-toed down the stairs with the intention of seeing who was there, then watching the sun rise over the lake. It was George. He couldn't sleep either.

We went out in the before-dawn dimness, walked along the lake and said our own personal vows as the sun crescented over the horizon between lake and sky.

Back at the lodge everyone was stirring. After hurriedly dressing for the wedding, I went to get the bridal bouquet only to find that every petal had fallen from every rose. Not one pink petal left! So—the bride carried green, thrifty, thorny foliage, wild roses nonetheless. Any pink blooms or roseate fragrance were solely in the eyes and nose of the bearer.

Dr. William Mutch drove out from Ripon to perform at eight

o'clock the ancient sacrament of the church for two people whose vows had already been said, whose lifetime commitment to each other had already been solemnized.

The day was spent at the lake, and in the late afternoon we took Mama home. The dimness of twilight crept into the kitchen as we ate supper there before leaving on a three-day wedding trip. The sunset, as we drove toward it, is still painted on my mind with brushes dipped in saffron, mauve and flame. This was our Genesis, the sunrise and sunset of the first day, and it was good.

Nature's Handmaiden

IV

Before forsaking a career to become a farmer's wife, I made myself two promises. The countless mundane tasks which would, of necessity, consume the days, must not exclude all else, and I would not permit myself to dislike any of them! Life was too short to drag oneself from one distasteful job to another, day after day, resisting, resenting, complaining. He who dreads a task doubles the energy required to do it.

Youth sees great visions and is well on the way to capturing their reality when youth dies and the dreams grow dim. The momentum of the commonplace carries him along, rebelling at first, then complacent to be commonplace. Somewhere along the way too many adults lose the enthusiasm they had as children, enthusiasm that took them from one delight to another—an ant in the grass, a new hair ribbon, a wallpaper May basket, a secret, a hand-over-the-eyes surprise. They become disinterested in anything outside themselves, lose purpose, fail to see the lovely opportunities that each day brings.

There must be a middle ground between childhood's flitting from one yellow dandelion to another, like a bee collecting nectar, and the listlessness of age—a mature, purposeful approach to life, adult enthusiasm.

Enthusiasm gives purpose. It sharpens vision, not only for the simple beauties of the day, but in a larger sense for the challenge of the future. It means being aware of the voice of a cricket, the cry of need from a human being, or a deteriorating condition. It means understanding and the gentle voice of encouragement. Most of all it means the willingness to give of one's self freely, selflessly, without reservation, to the betterment of people and community—to give and give and give.

The greatest of all teachers said it best: that one who tries to save his life will lose it, that one who loses himself in something greater than self will find it. These things I believed. Could a farm wife make practical application of these tenets? Could she? She would try! Yes, she would try!

The old farm house, which had been vacated when the new one was built, had been used for many things in the intervening years—a brooder house for little chicks, a storage place for extra grain and everything else they didn't know what to do with. In it George's mother and father had begun their married life. There the children had been born. There we would live.

Mama and I began cleaning. We shoveled, scraped, scoured, and peeled off layer after layer of wallpaper until the building was hospital-clean. By mid-summer she and I had painted, varnished or papered every square inch of the old house and furnished it with whatever either family could spare. The only things we bought were a wicker settee, an Axminster rug for the parlor, and a wood-burning range. The kitchen-dining room had a "sink" made from an old commode with a pail under it to catch the waste water. Beside it was a work table with water pail and drinking dipper.

And there was an ice box! Every few days George lifted into the top of it a cake of crystal ice which he had dug out of the sawdust in the back yard ice house. Every morning I emptied the brimming drip pan. An ice box was a luxury.

Years later, George expressed regret that they hadn't hired someone to make the old house livable, but at the time, no one had considered that a possibility. The work ethic in which we were reared taught that whatever needed to be done, we would do ourselves.

As there was no electricity, we had two oil lamps and the added luxury of a gasoline-burning Aladdin lamp which, when the pressure was pumped up in the evening, gave an intense white light from a delicate mantle.

We used the old summer kitchen for a woodshed and a place for George to hang barn clothes when he cleaned up for supper. One night, after he had gone to the barn to do the milking, there was the sound of a rat in the summer kitchen. They had had the old house to themselves during the years it was vacant, but we had made it rat-proof except for the summer kitchen where a hole in the mop board gave them access from the unpaved cellar. A rat anywhere was unwelcome, and I decided to do away with this one.

Carrying the Aladdin lamp, I went out there, closed the door behind me and placed the lamp on a chair in the middle of the room. I covered the rat hole so he could not escape, took a broom and did battle with him, flailing at him as he ran across the room. But instead of hitting him, the broom struck the delicate mantle of the lamp and we were left in the dark, just the two of us. There was no other light in the house but after fumbling for the door, I slipped through, closed it quickly behind me, and felt along the wall to the match safe and an oil lamp. The rat had won the battle, but it was little consolation to know that he was probably as frightened as I. When George came in, his spontaneous laughter ignited mine and suddenly the house was warm. He had a more practical method for rat extermination. He nailed a piece of tin over the escape hatch and set a trap. That was that.

George was always kind and considerate, but I appreciated, especially, his patience as his novice mate learned the routine obligations of being a farmer's wife. My ineptness in many areas must have been amusing to him.

One day that first summer we played hooky and went to Adams County blueberrying. Either the crop was poor or we didn't know where to pick, for we came home with only enough blueberries to make one pie, my first. The next morning I didn't work in the garden as long as usual but came to the house to clean the blueberries. More wood was added to the firebox of the new range, and by the time the crust was made, the oven was just the right temperature. The pie looked delicious, even in its unbaked stage, and the fragrance as it baked activated salivary glands. When it had finished baking, George and the hired man had already come in for the noon meal. I took the pie from the oven, the crust golden, and thick blueberry juice bubbling through the slits in the top. The men leaned over my shoulder. This was an event! As I carried the pie across the makeshift sink to the work table, it slid from my hands into the dishpan of suds I had saved for washing baking dishes. As tears won't unspill milk, neither will they make edible a pie soaked in dishwater, but there were tears nonetheless—mine, for men are too big to cry.

Bread had to be baked several times a week, for the hired man (who was so big he could have lived indefinitely without any food at all) fairly inhaled it. Farm hands received $25 a month then, and room and board.

Sometimes after supper he and George "rassled" on the parlor rug. Wrestling had never been one of my favorite sports, but I sighed and realized that to farmers, who spend long arduous days in the field, sport in any form would be a welcome diversion.

One of the new responsibilities was to wash the milk pails and cream separator. Each morning I heated two large kettles of water to the boiling point and carried them to the barn's milkroom. This, too, was a new experience, for the small herd we had when I was growing up would not have warranted the expense of a cream separator. The most time-consuming part of the operation was washing the dozens of cone-shaped disks which fitted closely, one on the other, and through which the milk swirled in the separation process, leaving a gummy coating on both sides of each disk.

Cream was stored in large covered cans in a tank of cold running water until the truck from the Wild Rose Creamery Company gathered it twice a week in winter and three times in summer. Though whole milk was fed to the calves, skimmed milk was fed to the pigs and chickens and barn cats. There was always a goodly amount of thick cream in the bottom of the cans that were brought to the house to be washed, so we had whipped cream on cakes, salads, desserts, and sour cream for making cakes, bread and doughnuts. Who knew about cholesterol then?

It had been late in the season to plant a garden that first spring, but a garden was a necessity. George had plowed and dragged a piece of ground back of the house and presented it to me with a quizzical look, wondering, I suppose, what his novice gardener would do with it. Well, in a nutshell, what she did was struggle. The garden was about as successful as he expected it to be. It was an everlasting, often losing, battle with weeds. As it had been an unused piece of ground for several years, the weeds had claimed it as their own and instead of surrendering, they called up reinforcements from the new-cultivated, seed-saturated soil. Though red-faced and perspiring, and with blackened hands, I found it exhilarating, later in the summer, to bring fresh, runted vegetables to the house for each day's meals.

And in the fall, filling jars with the harvest, I was at one with squirrels and chipmunks and all the other creatures who felt the instinct to prepare for winter. As tomato juice has as much Vitamin C as oranges and cost nothing but labor, I canned one hundred quarts of tomato juice each fall to stow away with the other cold-packed, pickled and preserved bounties of my little piece of earth.

Over and above the satisfaction of producing and preserving

provender were the child-again discoveries that each morning brought. The all-new smell of freshly plowed earth, its nourishment waiting for seed. The seed itself, what scientist could make? I examined one in my hand, to the eye as lifeless as a grain of sand, yet, holding in its secret entity, the mysterious power to bring forth life in its own likeness. Sometimes a spider had spun a web between two twigs, almost invisible except for the opalescent beads the dew had strung along each filament; or ants had discovered a colony of aphids on a new leaf; or a pair of orioles, master builders, were threading a nest on an oak branch at the edge of the garden. These, too, were our neighbors. Without them we could not live.

The tree, itself, its branches reaching ever higher toward the sun, its roots ever deeper into the good earth! Why, when an acorn sprouts, does it not send roots up and branches down? Why does it not have all branches and no roots or all roots and no branches?

I wonder if we don't need to live quietly and serenely like a tree, to grow a little closer to the earth, to look up into the sky and be glad, to take the nourishment God has provided and use it to grow strong and beautiful like a tree. Some experiences give strength and beauty, some sap vital energies. The tree knows how to choose the best. Shouldn't we?

There is peace in the feeling of unity, of oneness with all living things, from the earthworm to the planet, each in the right place in relation to the whole, each a solo voice, unique and indispensable to the great harmonious orchestration of the universe.

On the way to the garden one spring-fresh morning, a collie dog timidly approached me, hesitatingly wagging her tail. Oh, what a beautiful animal, but so thin, so afraid! Memories of another dog flooded my mind as I reached out my hands to her, palms up. She approached slowly, sniffed my fingers and wagged joyously as I petted her silken head and ears. She walked with me to the house and ravenously ate her breakfast. We were friends! We named her Gypsy. As the weeks passed she became sleek-coated and vivacious. She loved us as only a dog that has been starved for love can love. If she were lying, half asleep, near the stove and I looked in her direction, she would wag her tail. If I sat down, she invariably came to rest her head on my knee. If we were out of doors, she was our shadow. Oh, the joy of having a collie dog again!

And how we enjoyed the children next door! George, as part of the family, had lived with them and helped care for them since the day they were born, as dear to him as though they had been his own.

Florence and Walter were ideal parents and the farm an ideal place. The children followed their father and George around as puppies follow children. Both men "had a way" with them and loved them. There was never any whining, "What is there to do?" for on the farm there was always something to do. Walter and George had a close relationship. Their warm sense of humor and love for each other "made the rough places plain."

On the Dopp farm the men did not expect the women to do men's work, nor did they expect to help in the house. I often helped with the haying, though. Since Grandpa's time, the scythe had been replaced by a horse-drawn mower and the wooden hand-rake by a horse-drawn dump rake that gathered the dry hay into windrows. The rest of the operation was much the same. Three-tined forks were still used to gather the hay into cocks. My job was to stand at the front of the wagon and drive the team between the rows of cocks while George and the hired man pitched the cocks to the wagon and Walter built the load, spreading the hay evenly for larger capacity and better balance. One of the most subtle fragrances in the world is that of freshly cut hay, its aroma enhanced by the satisfaction of the harvest, the fruition of a season, and the knowledge that the cattle and horses would be sleek and content with its provender.

When the wagon was loaded, the team hauled it home, up the ramp to the barn floor. Walter stayed on the load to thrust the hay fork in, and I slid down, left the shadowed interior of the barn and went out again into the sunshine to hitch a horse to the end of a rope that reached up to a pulley in the dim rafters and down to the hay fork. At a call from Walter and a cluck to the horse, the rope tightened. How the horse dug in and pulled as the mound of hay rose up and up to the track that carried it over the mow and dumped it there!

A distant neighbor who came to the farm on an errand noticed Gypsy and how beautiful she was. He suggested to George that she and his purebred German shepherd have a litter of puppies. We could have the one of our choice and he would take the rest as soon as they could leave their mother. As George and Walter had been wanting a young dog to train to fetch the cows, that sounded like a good idea. When Gypsy was ready she was taken to the neighbor's to be bred. In due time she had her litter under the porch. We could hear her conversing in the wordless language of motherhood. She ignored all proffers of food. The puppies were two days old when Gypsy crawled out of seclusion, raced across the field until she was a dim speck in the distance and returned to her nest carrying a large bone which she must have buried instinctively for this moment of need.

A few days later she introduced her family to us. She brought them out, one by one, and laid them in a row at our feet—all eight of them. These sightless, bumbling little beings seemed scarcely to merit her pride in them, but as we petted her we lied and told her how beautiful they were. She took them back to their nest, one by one, and the next time we saw them they were roly-poly, romping, rollicking puppies, some golden, some black. We no longer had to lie to Gypsy about their beauty. The one we chose was black, the most frolicsome of all. We named him Tim. A little later he learned his farm duties quickly, herding the cows each morning to pasture and bringing them back for evening milking. But when working hours were over, he was a bouncing bundle of affection and always hungry, as growing boys are hungry.

Dogs were fed table scraps. Who had heard of canned dog food? Gypsy was a delicate eater, nibbling at her food, and Tim gobbled everything available. As they ate at the same dish, we had to train him to wait until his mother was through. He stood back, licking his chops as she ate, then gobbled the rest without taking time to taste it. Gypsy died the next year and Tim, seeming to sense our loss as well as his own, wriggled himself even further into our hearts.

When the chores were done in the evening, there was time to talk with no intrusion from electronic forms of communication. Sitting near the stove, our feet propped up on the chrome foot rest, the lamplight flickering with the drafts that winter brought, George began reminiscing about Topsy. "She was about the smartest little driving horse we ever had. She thought she was people, I guess. Maybe I told you about her before."

Topsy was new to me. I wanted to hear more. "She died several years ago. We missed her for the longest time! Anyway, one rainy night late in the fall—cold then, like it gets just before winter—Dad was roused from sleep by the door rattling. He thought it must be the wind and was nearly asleep again when the noise was repeated. He got up, went to the door, but nothing was there except darkness. He had no sooner gotten back in bed than the sound came again. This time, when he opened the door, Topsy was there. Dad knew, then, something was wrong. She had had her colt and needed help. He put on his rain coat and she led him to the orchard. Sure enough, there on the grass, shivering and wet, was a newborn colt. He picked the little thing up in his arms and carried it to a nest of dry hay on the barn floor, Topsy right beside him. Dad went back to bed, knew Topsy could take over from there."

Those lamplit evenings in our little world were short. Five A. M. came quickly.

There is something basic—fundamental—about the land and those who till it. They are people, rain people, sun people, working with the elements of the universe, learning their secrets, using their gifts. "With quietness they work and eat their own bread."

When the corn was ripe and the stalks still green, Grandpa's cutting sickle, husking pin and shock of corn were replaced by the horse-drawn corn cutter and the gasoline-powered silo filler, owned jointly by the neighbors, who "changed hands" on one farm and the next until the corn harvest was finished. The silo filler, powered by a noisy gasoline engine, chopped the corn, stalks and all, and blew it into the top of the cement silo where it fermented as it waited for winter feeding. Lifting the bundles of stalks onto the wagon and pitching them into the silo-filler was heavy work, but there was camaraderie in it as the neighbors worked together and, at meal time, ate together the meals each farmer's wife, in turn, prepared.

When the crew was working at the Potts farm and I was to be alone, I decided to spend the day with Mama. Backing the little Ford runabout out of the machine shed, I smelled smoke, got out of the car and was terrified to see flames underneath. I ran to the pump house and carried pail after pail of water and, when the fire was finally extinguished, lay exhausted on the grass.

At noon, when Mrs. Potts would be feeding the men their dinner, I phoned to tell George my tale of woe. Jim Potts answered and called George. Immediately I began wailing out the experience of the morning, only to hear in reply, "Why didn't you try pouring on some kerosene?" I am naturally slow to anger, but that mocking response made me furious! My George, so unfeeling! I was incredulous, ready to go home to Mama for good! Jim Potts laughed hilariously, for he had been mimicking George's voice, and it was to him I had told my tale. When George finally got to the phone, he gave the sympathy I had expected.

At grain threshing time, the neighbors "changed hands," went with the threshing machine and ate ravenously the food that the farmer's wife, not knowing just when the crew would arrive, had been preparing for days. Grandpa's cradle and flail were replaced by the horse-drawn binder and the spitting, chugging threshing machine which poured grain into gunny sacks and blew straw onto a growing stack. Some men loaded the bundles on the wagon, others pitched them into the threshing machine while still others carried bags of threshed grain to the granary and emptied them in bins. It was still dusty, tiring work, but the result was a filled granary and a straw stack for bedding the farm animals during the winter.

In spite of the traps and poison which reduced the rodent population, the wily creatures that remained crept into the corn crib and granary and claimed their share of the harvest.

In October when the hills were ablaze and the air was nipped with autumn, there was always a rush to finish the potato harvest before a heavy frost. The children and I, still using a stone boat, picked potatoes following a mechanical digger which tossed the potatoes out of their hills and shook the vines free. It had replaced the six tined fork. A team of horses hauled them, the chief cash crop at that time, to the potato cellar, where in cold weather a wood fire warded off the frost. George and Walter daily scanned the newspaper market report for the best time to sell, then scooped potatoes into gunny sacks, loaded them on the sleigh and hauled them to one of the warehouses in town.

After potato digging, the men butchered two hogs and brought chunks of meat to both houses for processing. After a month in the traditional "pickle," hams, shoulders and slabs of bacon were smoked in an old barrel with a canvas top, our make-do smoke house, the pickled meat suspended from a rod across the top.

Smouldering corn cobs in the bottom of the barrel, replenished every hour, permeated the hams and bacon with the sweet smell of smoke.

Pork fat, cut in small pieces and spread in dripping pans, was "tried" in the oven, as of yore, strained through a white cloth and poured in stone crocks to become the year's supply of lard, the only shortening we had other than cream and butter. Margarine was available, but to a dairy farmer, using it was unthinkable.

In the Plainfield weekly newspaper in March 1930, there was an item which described the attitude of the agricultural community toward margarine. "Farm people coming to Plainfield Evening Institute were greeted with a huge bon fire kindled with oleo licenses and fed with greasy margarine. Fumes from the fire filled the nostrils from the filthy tropical oils."

Usually we had chicken for Sunday dinner. On Saturday George would bring a decapitated rooster to the house where I had spread newspapers on the kitchen floor. Pulling up a chair, I dunked the chicken in a pail of boiling water just long enough to loosen the feathers. The soft feathers were dried for pillows. Wing, tail and pin feathers were of no use and came out the hardest, sometimes one by one. Pungent steam from hot, wet feathers permeated the house—the most unpleasant part of the none-too-pleasant operation. Fine hairs which remained on the bird were singed off at the stove over a torch of rolled newspaper. Then a butcher knife divested the chicken of its "innards" and cut the meat into serving pieces for Sunday dinner.

As the old house in which we lived did not have indoor plumbing, we pumped from the well outside the door all the water for the house and carried out in a slop pail all the water that had been used. We went to the bathroom in the new house and did the laundry in the basement there, a noisy gasoline engine providing power to operate the wooden washer. Clothes were dried outdoors on a line, then starched and sprinkled for ironing the next day while the kitchen fire roared to keep the flatirons hot.

As roads were unimproved, driving a car was not all pleasure. The cheese factory hill was an obstacle course. Deep sand washed to the foot of the long, steep hill, and the snake tracks, which struggling cars produced as they bumped up and down for traction, made it impossible to get a running start for the ascent. Sometimes George and Walter helped the condition briefly by spreading a load of straw over the loose sand. One village business man boasted that his new car could go up cheese factory hill in second, and as everyone knew that was impossibie, he was given the reputation of embroidering the truth.

When winter approached, we asked Mama to spend it with us, but she in her wisdom decided to take Uncle Alanson with her to visit their sister Mary in Tacoma, Washington. Except for that first winter, she spent every winter with us for the thirty remaining years of her life. She and George were fond of each other. I shall always be grateful to him for his kindness to her, but, being George, how could he be otherwise?

Winter changed the pattern of a farmer's life, but the end of the growing and harvesting season did not mean a winter of inactivity. The work went on, but the tools changed. After months at pasture, cows filed into the barn, each in her own stanchion to stay until spring. The silo was opened and the six to fifteen inches of spoilage on the top was thrown out the manhole. Fresh silage was pitched to a hand-drawn cart below and pulled to the barn and along the manger. A three-tined fork still filled the manger with hay and fodder and spread fresh straw in the stalls for bedding. Each morning a scoop shovel was used to clean the barn. Until snow fell, manure was spread on the fields each day to ease the spring work and to assure maximum nutrients leached into the field instead of the barnyard.

In winter there was the sound of axes as the men cut trees, sawed the wood into stove lengths, split it into usable size and stored it in the woodshed for our range and Round Oak heater, and in the basement of the other house for their wood-burning furnace.

The truck and Model T were stored for the winter. Roads were unplowed, and horses were the only means of transportation. As winter progressed, roads looked like crumpled white ribbon with pitch holes which each passing sleigh dug deeper until new trails had to be made through farmers' fields.

There was no social activity. The daily trip to the milk house to wash the separator and pails and the weekly trip across the road to church were my outings. The cold floors of the old house presented me with chilblains, the winter scourge that produced cracked feet that itched and burned and were so swollen it was impossible to wear anything on them but bedroom slippers or overshoes.

Freed from the more arduous tasks of the summer and fall, it was a time for inner growth, for quiet thoughts and dreams. I sewed, crocheted an afghan, made a flower garden quilt from scraps of velvet that had been given Mama by a milliner cousin in Janesville, and showed them with pride to Mama when she returned in the spring.

These winter activities were quite a change from the gay, stimulating days of college and teaching. There was no radio or television, few periodicals and no library. George was working outside most of every day and I am sorry to admit I was lonely. At such times there was solace in getting out the guitar, sitting close to the heater and singing to myself the popular, sometimes rollicking, sometimes questing songs of college. The guitar still shows bubbles in the varnish on the side nearest the stove.

I am glad I had been practicing the positive approach to living, to identifying with life confidently, completely and joyously. To have failed to do so would have been like looking in an imperfect mirror and seeing the distortions of fear, discontent and self pity. Borrowed trouble needs no collateral.

A perfect marriage is not "made in heaven," assuring a story book, happy-ever-after relationship. It has to be developed day after day by two people who are willing to give themselves to it. Its foundation must be, not only love, but respect, trust and understanding.

There were many adjustments to make as two very different people melded their lives together. I was a spinner of dreams. He accepted the miracle of rain. I yearned for a more perfect world. He unquestioningly planted his seeds. But, during the years, he came to share my dreams, and I got a lot of good earth on my shoes, each made more whole by the other's oppositeness.

One sparkling winter morning I went with George to town with a load of potatoes on a sleigh. Sitting on top of the gunny bags of potatoes, a crate of bewildered, complaining chickens on the back of the load, we criss-crossed the useless highway from field to field, the snow glistening and beautiful, the whole white world our highway.

George remembered a time when roads were worse. "That was February 22, 1922. It had snowed all night and was still snowing the next morning when Walter had to go to the Blaine town hall to collect taxes. You know he was town treasurer for years and always went over there because it was near the center of the township.

"Several of the men from the neighborhood went along—couldn't do much at home on such a stormy day. It's a good thing they went! The snow turned to freezing rain, and when we started for home there was a crust of ice on the snow, strong enough to hold us men, but the poor horses broke through every few steps—up to their belly in snow. It was tough going! The sleigh with nobody in it slid along on top of the crust, so we unhitched the horses, and the men pulled the sleigh. Horses had all they could do to take care of themselves. We finally got home—eight miles—but that was an exhausted team."

I remembered that snowstorm too. "Girls from the dormitory hiked out in the country to see a train that was stalled. Some of the cars weren't visible at all and others exposed only their tops to prove that a train was really there. Workmen were shoveling the tracks and excavating the train for a week."

George said, "There was a train stalled near Wild Rose, too. Didn't go out to see it. Had our hands full at home."

"You must have," I commented, "shoveling paths and all the extra work at the barn."

"Not only that," George said. "The next day, John was born and I drove Topsy on the cutter a mile up the road to get Mrs. Potts to help. I thought poor little Topsy would break a leg. Dr. Fisher had a great time getting there too."

He spoke of a woman in the Town of Belmont who was "on the town." In the eyes of everyone who knew it, she was disgraced for receiving $5.00 a month. Folks thought she could have gotten along somehow. "You'll never catch us on the town," they said.

Eventually we reached Wild Rose and, while George went to unload at one of the warehouses on "potato row," I stopped at the store to get some drygoods. Returning, he said the Ladies Aid was serving dinner, so, looking like country bumpkins, we went. For me it was the event of the season.

In spite of the inconveniences that winter brought to the farmer of the nontechnological period, snow was a blessing, a friend, an ally, a part of the natural gift of each season. Buildings were warmer with snow packed against them. Snow buried the fields deep, protecting sleeping roots and little creatures. Snow held in its vast expanse three quarters of the world's fresh water to release in the spring its moisture and nitrates for the bounty of summer.

Snow was beauty to sensitive eyes that saw purple shadows in its drifts, the black exclamation point of an occasional fence post, black lace of bare trees against the sky, and drank in the breathless silence of moonlit nights, a glittering path ribboned across the white expanse. In the country, snow stayed white all winter.

One night George and I got up to go to the barn to see a sow that wasn't doing well, and there we found twelve silky-pink piglets, new born, nudging, tugging in noisy contentment at their mother's teats, their little whirligig tails swiveling. Who taught them how to satisfy their new hunger? Who led them to their source of supply? All was well. Nature had completed its mission.

Outside the air tingled in our nostrils and washed our throats clean. The fullness of each moon brought fresh delight, as though it had never been full before. This new, soft whiteness had never seen a full moon before. The maple's shadow, strong and intricate, was never so real before, and in the sky the constellations, predictable through the centuries, predictable since primitive astronomers first noticed them, Orion in his place and the big dipper pointing to the North, our constant North. George's hand was warm and electric. We walked in silence. The sky was infinite.

In the technological age, snow is an enemy to be plowed from highways, shoveled from sidewalks, hauled from city streets. It stalls automobiles, slows the machinery of a mechanized society, makes sidewalks slippery and disrupts the neat pattern of life, the frenzied rush to the office, the factory, the bridge luncheon. Swirling through the smoke-laden air of cities, snow is dirty before it reaches the ground. Sleighbells no longer ring on Main Street, U. S. A.

At last, in the unchanging pattern of the seasons, spring came, and I flung wide the doors of the house and my heart to let it in. A few brittle brown leaves tried vainly to cover the gnarled nudity of the oaks, but beyond their winter silhouette, in the delphinium blue of the sky and the whiter-than-whiteness of the clouds, it was spring. The first wren saturated the air with song and on every twig of the maple, buds came out to listen. Responding to the blessings of the sun, wild flowers burst forth again. After the rumblings of thunder, the whisper of rain washed the world clean again and swished away the last gray drift that clung to the north edge of the woods.

After the cool cleansing joy of rain, crinkled pink leaflets, new-born, replaced yesterday's brown buds along the bough. A joyous chorus of birds whistled their mating songs, each in his own voice. Squirrels, newly awakened, dug in exploration for last fall's buried acorns, then scurried to a safe branch, peeled off the shell and ate the white meat to satisfy winter's unconscious hunger. As a human might dunk a doughnut, a blackbird dipped a piece of dried crust in a rain puddle. Robins, hopping from clod to clod, listened for earthworms that worked with us in preparation of the soil. The blossoming apple tree could scarcely sustain its aching loveliness, so great was the burden of beauty. The tree was a-buzz with bees, their feathered feet distributing pollen, their searching tongues gathering honey for the honeycomb.

How could one ignore divinity in the pulse and wonder of a Wisconsin spring? The order of it! The bursting glory of it! The sureness of its coming after the "winter is over and gone!" One could almost hear the roots of the trees waking and stretching and the sap surging up to the tipmost twig.

That spring we bought a little radio. A radio! The near horizons were no longer the limit of our world! We were no longer isolated! The marvel of radio brought the outside world to our ears and minds. (In the 1930's there would be Amos and Andy, the Bell Telephone Hour, the Chase and Sanborn Hour! Charlie McCarthy! Fibber McGee and Molly! Jack Benny!)

On the twentieth of May, 1927—I shall always remember the date—the radio brought the exciting news that a young man by the name of Charles Lindbergh had left that morning from New York, flying a single engine plane, his destination Paris! And he was alone! He had none of the scientific trappings that are a necessity in the cockpit panels of modern aircraft—no parachute, no scanner, no wireless. He had faith in himself and the natural laws that supported him, and in his tiny craft. I visualized him up there somewhere, blue sky above, deadly waves below, and at night the darkness and the stars. Telephones began to ring—neighbors asking if we had heard. The nation, the world waited for news.

Since the Wright brothers had flown, in 1903, their homemade plane at 30 miles an hour, other crossings had been made—a German dirigible, a two-man team from the Royal Flying Corps of England, a five-man crew of the U. S. Navy, but somehow those feats had not captured the imagaination of the world as did that of this fairhaired boy who was trying to cross alone.

Unable to sleep, thinking about him, I got up in the night to turn on the radio. There was no news of him. Was his little plane still sailing between earth and sky? Was he going to reach Paris? Could he!

All the next day the radio was turned on at every opportunity but there was no news. When news did come, it was in bits. He had flown low over the Irish coast and shouted down for directions, had been sighted crossing England and that night had landed to a cheering throng at the airport in Paris!

A United States Navy cruiser brought him back to New York to the biggest tickertape parade before or since. When it was over, workmen swept up 1800 tons of paper and the United States—the world—had a hero!

The second winter of our marriage was exciting. The house and farm buildings were wired for electricity! The men bought a milking machine and could finish chores before supper, giving us evenings to share. We did not buy appliances for the house, still using the icebox and carrying water from the well, but now a flip of a switch flooded the house with light. Oil lamps remained on the shelf in case of power shortage, but were seldom needed. We had light! Light!

And in many rural areas of Wisconsin the Community Club movement was implemented! There were several clubs in Waushara and Portage Counties. The one which met in the little church across the road provided cultural and social enjoyment, winter after winter. Soon after its organization, the membership was divided into two groups of equal number and diverse talents, and these groups competed at each meeting in either spelldown, debate, one-act plays, music, oratory. How participants practiced, studied and worked!

Mama and her peers, for whom the spelldown had been an integral part of their education and possible teaching experience, studied together and separately, and on spelldown night were usually the ones left standing when all the rest had been eliminated.

Old talents were revived and new ones discovered. People who hadn't sung or played an instrument in years began to sing again, play again, or debate again or act again. The little church was packed at each meeting, people coming from town and the surrounding area. After the evening program everyone trooped downstairs for refreshments and fellowship.

The notebook I had kept from a dramaturgy course in college, on the techniques of production and notes on literally hundreds of plays I had had to read, was a valuable resource in coaching the one-act plays. We selected those of literary as well as dramatic value, which is probably the reason the local club always won the county contest and went on to Farm and Home Week in Madison to win over plays sent from other communities. What excitement was generated locally!

At the end of each winter season, the losing half of the membership provided a dinner in the church basement for the winners.

Once in a while we had a guest speaker. It was probably an imposition to ask Dr. Silas Evans, President of Ripon College, to drive to our little country church to speak to us country people, but I really believe he was as excited about it as we were. Perhaps it was his introduction to life in a rural community, for he commented again and again on the social and cultural impact of the Community Club movement, ours in particular. Similar compliments are routine with most speakers, but I am sure he meant what he said and I, for one, knew he was right.

When his father died, George succeeded him as secretary of the Wild Rose Creamery Company, and it was his responsibility to figure the amount due each farmer, write the checks and do the bookkeeping. After several years the board of directors decided to hire a full-time manager and urged George to take the job. The offer was intriguing for he was already thirty-five years old and had never had an income of his own. He debated with himself. The long, satisfying years of farming with Walter, his love for the children, did battle with the opportunity to go out on his own, to be wholly his own man. He was sure Walter with his one arm could operate the farm just as successfully with a hired man to do the work George had done for so many years. It was the most difficult decision he ever had to make, but he finally decided to accept the managership.

The creamery built a new little office, and George began his new life. For the first summer he commuted from the farm, but when winter came we turned our house over to the new hired man and his family and moved to town to live temporarily with Mama, who had sold the Etheridge family farm.

In a few days we heard someone at the back door and opened it to find Tim, panting and dancing for joy. He had walked the five miles to town to find us! We were delighted to see our Tim. After feeding him and petting him and having a little visit with him, we took him back to the farm. The next day and each succeeding day he came again—and we took him home. Something had to be done! They needed him at the farm to do the job he was trained to do. The next time he came there were broken hearts—his and ours. We did not invite him in nor feed him nor pet him. Slowly the tail stopped wagging and slowly he turned and walked home, never to come again.

It had been the dream of the Thirteen Club of 1910 that someday Wild Rose would have a library. It took twenty years for it to happen, but the happening, though humble, was momentous.

The date was 1930. The depression had begun and people were hesitant to spend money for such luxuries as books and magazines.

Here was a chance for excitement, for action!

The Woman's Club renewed its interest and joined forces with the PTA to establish a library in the village hall, the only place available rent-free. Volunteers built book cupboards with doors that could be unlocked on Saturday nights when the library was open.

We went from house to house for books and periodicals that citizens were willing to donate. These, though most of them were dogeared, were catalogued and placed on the new shelves.

Mrs. Anna Hoaglin, the first librarian, had a salary of only five dollars a month, but her devotion to duty was as dedicated as though she had received many times that amount.

As there was no money to operate the library (aside from heat, light and salary supplied by the village board) the people earned it. Mrs. Darling, the piano teacher, gave a pupil recital in the hall above Patterson's store, the only auditorium in the village. I directed a slapstick comedy, "The Old Deestrict School" as a library benefit. Admissions for each were 10¢ and 25¢.

Each year there was a donation supper in one of the churches where, after those in attendance were filled and content with the food they had brought and eaten, they gave as generously as their means would permit, to the library fund.

We selected movies from the Visual Education Department of the University of Wisconsin, and showed them one night a week in an otherwise empty building on Main Street. The usual admission of 10¢ and 25¢ totaled $81.14 for the library at the end of the summer.

Thus, in a humble way, library service was begun in Wild Rose.

In the Spring George and I rented a house and had the fun of putting our stamp on it with the old furniture we brought from our first home. We loved the house. It even had a wood-burning furnace!

I worked with George in the office, without pay of course, except in the closeness this new relationship brought.

After a year, our rented home was sold and we went back to Mama, deciding then that the next move would be to a home of our own.

Stop and Shop with Dopp

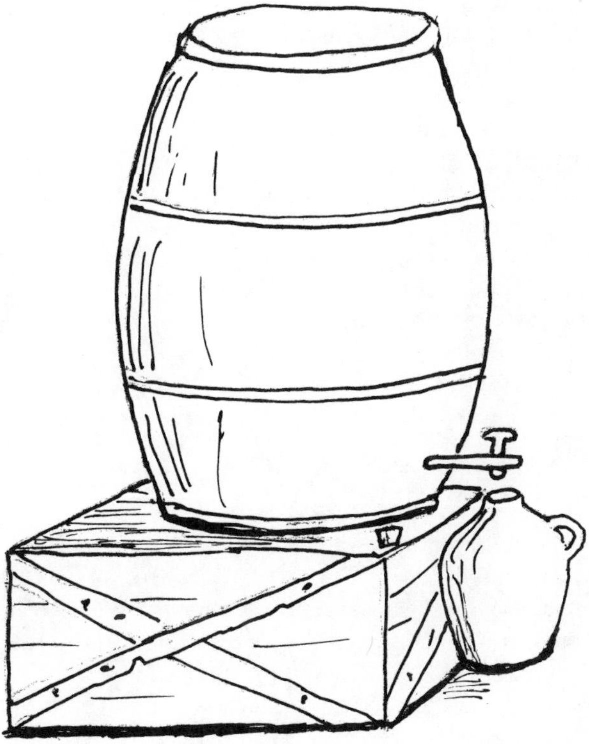

V

George enjoyed the work in the creamery but, subject to the diverse wishes of a board of directors, he was still not his own man. At the death of Fred Clark, the general store was for sale, and George, deciding he wanted his own business, borrowed the money and bought the store. That was in 1931 at the bottom of the great depression. If we sold twenty dollars' worth of merchandise in a day we thought we were doing well and went to the bank to make a payment on our loan. Debt worried us, for we had been brought up on the tradition that one never bought anything without cash to pay for it. Debt was a burden that doubled the weight of the load.

George proved to be a good business man. He was conservative, had integrity and good judgment and was always certain to pay for merchandise in time to deduct the discount. The Wisconsin Traveling Library provided my homework for learning the art of window-decorating and merchandising display. We didn't want our little store to look like the typical country store.

It became my habit to remove from the produce counter everything that was wilted or in less than perfect condition and to take home whatever could be salvaged. Again, as in childhood, we used spotted apples. Many a Saturday night was spent canning peaches, pears, prunes or berries that would not keep until Monday. George and I worked together as a team, through hard times and good, and grew closer through both. If a marriage is a good marriage, struggle in the early years strengthens it.

The great depression was a difficult time for everyone. In the cities particularly, many who had been caught up in the frenzy of prosperity, purchasing stocks on margin, found themselves suddenly destitute, could not face the future without their imagined wealth and took the easy way out. Those out of work stood in bread lines and were issued food stamps, depressed and ashamed at having to accept charity. Country people, though they had little income, could be more self-sufficient by raising their own food.

It wasn't easy being in business during the depression, wondering how we would get the money to pay for the next shipment of goods. It wasn't easy having shelves of groceries and dry goods that our customers, our neighbors and friends, needed but couldn't buy. Many of them, in desperation, asked for credit and received it, and most of them, as money became available, paid it dollar by dollar, expressing gratitude to us for "trusting" them. We found, sadly, in a very few cases, that the best way to lose a customer was to let him have credit.

Papa, at the time of his death, had been president of the Wild Rose State Bank. He and Mama had a little stock which he always told her to hang onto. She did.

She came to us one day with a proposal. "George," she said, "I want you to be a director in the bank. You know I have some stock in it, and I want you there to look after it for me."

"But Mother, I don't know anything about banking!"

"Doesn't matter! You would make a good director!"

"But I don't have any stock. You have to be a stockholder, don't you, to be a director?"

"Yes," she admitted. "I guess you do. And probably nobody wants to sell. Jerry always said it was good security."

I interrupted. "George, you do, too, have stock! Papa left me a few shares in his will. Have you forgotten? What's yours is mine, and what's mine is yours."

Before George had a chance to reply Mama said with finality, "Then it's all settled. I'll get someone to nominate you."

In a few weeks the Wild Rose State Bank had a novice director. Did Mama suspicion that banks were in trouble and hope that George could rescue the one in Wild Rose?

The depression had begun in 1929 with the crash of the stock market. Those who had bought on margin with visions of sudden wealth rushed to sell and sent prices lower and lower until stocks were virtually worthless. Frightened depositors hastened to withdraw their money from the banks until President Roosevelt declared a bank holiday in 1933, closing 4004 of them. Many never opened again.

The banks in Waushara County closed, too, and were reorganized to form the Union State Bank with headquarters in Wautoma and branches in Wild Rose, RedGranite and Plainfield. The bank commissioner appointed two directors from each of the closed banks and George was one of them.

How badly Papa would have felt if he had known that Mama would have to raise $7000, the value of the stock she owned, to pay double liability to the bank. $7000 when there was no money anywhere!

Often George would mention Herman Belter, who was president of the Union State Bank and had his office at the headquarters bank in Wautoma, eight miles away. George would say, "Herman is so good to me, has sort of taken me under his wing. He calls me in his office and we talk and talk. I'm learning more about banking than I realized there was to know—which doesn't mean I know much!"

There was nothing modern about the old store building we rented. Built by Charles Smart, it had been the first general store in the village, the grandest store anywhere. But the intervening years had taken their toll. The building was not only old, it was uninsulated—hot in summer and cold in winter. In the warmest weather George cooled the store somewhat by pumping water from the back yard well and carrying it in pails to pour on the front sidewalk.

In winter we wore snow boots to prevent chilblains. As the wood-burning heatrola was the only source of heat, George had to walk to the store each cold night and several times on Sunday to replenish the stove. The worse the weather, the more often he had to go. "We can't afford to have those groceries freeze," he said. And, winter or summer, the outhouse was near the back door.

Ours was a country store in every sense of the word. In addition to groceries, we stocked yard goods, shoes, notions, wearing apparel and gifts. The people who shopped with us were not only our customers, they were our friends, our neighbors. They shared their lives with us as we shared ours with them.

Though we lived in the village, we were still close to the land. As the farmer was dependent on the weather, so were we. As his needs were met, so were ours. His loss was our loss and his gain our gain.

Having walked in his shoes, we had empathy for him, and in periods of drought we, too, anxiously watched the sky for signs of rain.

Heavy snow in early winter, which gave protection to alfalfa and clover, was also a good omen for us in the store, for it meant that farmers and town people would do their Christmas shopping in the village instead of Oshkosh, Waupaca or Stevens Point. One of our two Christmas windows always had a Christ-centered theme, with no merchandise to distract from the true spirit of the season.

Groceries came in bulk, vinegar in a wooden barrel that had to be hoisted by several men to a platform, where a spigot was hammered in for filling customers' vinegar jugs. Kerosene was brought periodically by the oil man and pumped into our barrel from which customers' five and ten gallon cans could be filled. We had to stock kerosene because it was still burned in the lamps of many homes and a few housewives had the luxury of a kerosene stove. Its oily fumes, though unpleasant, were preferable in summer to the heat generated by a wood-burning range.

All merchandise arrived by freight, and the dray hauled it to the business district from the depot. Cookies came in large cardboard boxes which were fitted with hinged glass covers when they reached the store and placed in a cookie rack. When the customer chose the kind he wanted, the cookies were weighed and he took them home in a brown paper bag.

As most housewives baked their own bread, they bought flour in fifty-pound sacks for 89¢ and bleached the cloth sacks for use as dish towels, aprons, underwear and quilt blocks. Some bought sugar in 100-pound sacks and used the sacks for similar purposes, but for the most part we weighed and brown-bagged white, powdered and brown sugar. The large wooden tea chests from which we dispensed tea in small quantities are now collectors' items.

Each customer who came to the grocery section of the store read his want list to the clerk, who itemized it on a sales slip and brought it to the counter, item by item. It would have been quicker and easier if the clerk could have had the whole list at once, but the customers seemed to prefer to have each item brought to the counter separately, and in our store the customer was always right.

We bought a used ice display case for dairy products and a few sausages that were too salty to spoil anyway. Every few days in summer a wagon pulled up at the back door and the iceman carried chunks to the display case. In the winter the store was so cold that no coolants were necessary. That was the time of year when men cut ice on the millpond and skidded it to the icehouse on the shore to be packed in sawdust until summer.

When electric refrigeration became available, we bought a wooden display case. The old icehouse, having outlived its usefulness, remained for years on the shore of the millpond, the sawdust inside rotting with the roof boards. To the few who noticed it as they passed by, it was a grey and deteriorating shadow from another era.

Bridal showers were such big events that they were usually held in a church basement dining room. Men as well as women came, bearing gifts. Those who did not care to give a personal present joined a gift club at the store. As soon as a shower was announced, we put something practical on the counter—usually a blanket and sheets. People coming to the store added their names to the list of doners, gave 25 cents or 50, and sometimes even a dollar. The night of the shower we totalled the amount in the fund and added merchandise to that amount, wrapped the gifts in white tissue paper tied with narrow crinkled ribbon that could be curled with a scissors, and took it to the shower.

It was the same procedure for baby showers, but men didn't attend. They weren't expected to know about such things.

Although there was very little shoplifting, we knew the few who needed full attention from a clerk. One was a man who taught his young son to conceal pears and other goodies in the pockets of his oversized coat. Another was a woman who carried a large bag, "handy," as she said, "for little things." George caught her stuffing ribbon in her bosom. A telltale end hung from her neckline. As he pulled out yards and yards of ribbon, she rebuked him for undoing the ribbon which tied the yoke of her camisole.

Each night, as there was no night depository at the bank, George emptied the cash register and carried the money home. He always followed the same route, a path across an open field to our house which was on the edge of town. We never locked the house until an irrational patient escaped from the hospital in his nightshirt and woke us from sleep as he wandered through the house. No one ever attempted to take the money George brought home. We never considered the possibility.

The store was robbed once by two culprits who took their time about it, as evidenced by the cookie crumbs and empty beer bottles they had brought with them and left behind a counter the next morning. Most of the merchandise they took was recovered after they were tracked down.

Jennie Woodward, a clerk we had inherited with the store, was dependable, loyal, never had to be told what to do, for having worked in the store for several years, she knew. She had a saucy tongue. Many of the men who patronized our store did so because of the fun they had quarreling with Jenny.

One day she brought George a check for $100 that a stranger wanted to cash. As George didn't recognize the signature, he went next door to ask Richard Hotz, the owner of the hardware store, who had been in business much longer than we. Mr. Hotz was just coming out the back door on his way to the depot to get some freight, but stopped long enough to look at the check and tell George not to cash it.

When Mr. Hotz returned, he found the check in his own cash register. An inexperienced clerk had cashed it while he was gone. It proved to be, as he had suspected, worthless.

Most farm women who came to do their "trading" brought a wooden case of eggs to exchange for household items. The eggs were taken to the back room where a clerk candled them, two at a time, to make sure they were fresh. We had a makeshift candler, a large tin can with a light bulb inside and, on the front, two egg-sized holes against which eggs were examined. When eggs were fresh the yolks were in the center of each egg, while in an aging egg, the yolk had settled to one end. In a spoiled egg, the yolk was distributed throughout.

We candled, even more carefully, the eggs one farm woman brought, for often they contained chicks in various stages of development. Apparently when she found "stolen nests" she robbed the cluck of her partially-incubated family, hoping the eggs hadn't been there too long, or that their condition would not be discovered.

Probably the reason these instances stand out in my mind is that they were so rare. It was an era of innate honesty, when human beings treasured their integrity more than wealth, their ability to "make ends meet," to give "a good day's work for a day's pay." Being able to take care of one's own was a source of pride, even though hands were work-worn and purses thin.

When we bought the store it was customary to stay open several nights a week, but finally that was reduced to two—Tuesday and Saturday.

Every Tuesday night in summer the business men provided a free movie on a grassy slope that overlooked the millpond. In preparation a "bee" had driven posts into the ground to support planks which served as theater seats, one below the other, down the slope to the very edge of the millpond, where they erected a wooden screen and painted it white. People from the village and surrounding area flooded in like a tide. Some brought blankets on which to sit in the aisles if the benches were full. They paid for the gala evening by watching advertising slides projected by a magic lantern, "Stop and Shop with Dopp" among them.

The problem was that farm people waited until after the show to bring in their eggs and do the trading. The sixteen-hour day was too much, even for George, so he asked the farm families to come in before the movie, which they did willingly, making it possible to fall into bed two hours earlier.

We were used to eleven-hour work days, but after Saturday's fifteen-hour day there was no alternative way to spend Sunday. After going to church, we rested. Wild Rose merchants shared the same problem and decided to break the long tradition and stay open Friday nights instead. There was a bit of grumbling from the populace, for whom Saturday night, and coming to town to see friends, had been the highlight of the week, but they soon adjusted to the change and we had a long Sunday—from six o'clock Saturday night to seven Monday morning.

One of the pleasures of operating a store was seeing the people who came to shop. Boyd Clark, who later became county judge was a young boy when we bought the store from his widowed mother. He would come with a penny to spend, his brown eyes shining in anticipation, and stand in front of the candy case trying to decide which kind he most wanted. Then, with his finger on the glass, he would move back and forth across the varieties with "Eeny, meeny, miny, mo—" When he had finished the jingle he would skip several possibilities and choose the one he had wanted in the first place.

Each morning we knew the front door would fly open and two little boys would scamper to the cookie case. The older one would say, "He (meaning himself) wants a cookie." He got his morning cookie and so did his little brother.

We enjoyed, especially, waiting on Spanish American migrants, farm hands from Texas who came each summer to do the agricultural stoop labor. They shopped in family groups and discussed among themselves each possibility before making the final selection. They always appeared pleased with whatever they bought.

One winter morning I had gone to the heatrola to warm my hands when Perry came in the door, his white beard disheveled, his eyes bloodshot. Today he would be considered an alcoholic, but then he was just a drunkard. He lived in part of the old house George's grandparents had built on "the other farm." It was worth no rent, and he paid none. Florence and Walter invited him often to dinner on Sundays and holidays, and he always came cleaned up and sober for the occasion.

Perry staggered down the aisle on this particular morning and weaved his way to the heatrola saying, "Shay, are you George Dopp's wife?" I admitted I was and he grinned, "Shay, if ye ever git to be a widder keep me in mind." When George gets obstreperous I remind him that I have had my chances.

When the Methodist church was remodeled, a lovely old stained glass window was moved to a new location above the altar. As it was round, an arch had to be built around it, requiring the work of a master plasterer. With some misgivings, the job was given to Perry. His work was flawless. Standing back to admire the result and perhaps remember his wasted years, he said, "Well, I wonder what St. Peter will think of that."

Cousin Lelah came often to the store. She spent her life taking care of people—first Grandma Pierce, then her father, her mother and her husband. After his death she became a nurse's aide in the hospital. Whenever I was a patient there, I looked forward to her coming on duty, could recognize her quick steps down the hall and knew that when she entered the room there would be gentle ministrations and laughter.

Each year Lelah had a Christmas party for all the children in her neighborhood. They played games, sang carols, arranged the figures in the creche while listening to the Christmas story. The children, now adults, always remember those happy occasions.

Lelah had a little model T Ford coupe in which she drove merrily around the village. Stop signs meant nothing to Lelah. Nearly every day she would stop in the store to visit a minute, or we would see her driving by. If our eyes didn't tell us it was Lelah, our ears, accustomed to the put-putting of her little car, did. Usually there were children with her, for she herself was "as one of these little ones" in her faith, her joy, her laughter.

A little girl, a newcomer to the village, was among the passengers when Lelah said, "I thought we might drive to New York today." The little stranger wanted to get out, saying, "Oh, I couldn't go as far as New York!"

It was just one more cause for laughter in Lelah's joyous life.

Chosen Children

VI

That night will never be forgotten—the pungent smell of new lumber and fried bacon, the carpenter's great chest and saw horses, yellow shaving curls that lay about us as we sat on the floor before the fire, gray shadows that crept in from the corners of the room to curtain off our world and leave us alone in firelit tranquility.

Nautilus

To build a home!
  Our fondest pencilings
Of plans to rise in wood
  Upon our hill!
To watch the deft hands'
  Patient fashionings
Board to board
  And sash to waiting sill!

To build a home—
  A nautilus to hold
Our treasure of devotion
  Still entire.
To build a home
  And with the hearthstone laid
To come, we two,
  And christen it with fire!

Our new home, for which I had drawn plans during the ten years of our marriage was nearly complete, and we had come to build the first fire in the fireplace and cook our supper there. At last our dreams were wood, plaster and stone, and we were one with the robin in his tree and the chipmunk in his pile of rock. "Even a sparrow finds a home and a swallow a nest for herself where she can lay her young."

We wandered into the kitchen, my dream kitchen. Built-in cupboards! Electric stove! No more wood to carry in and ashes to carry out! Electric refrigerator! No more ice to carry in and drip pans to empty! And at the kitchen sink there would be water at the touch of a faucet! A drain instead of a slop pail! And in the basement an innovative oil furnace that would keep the house warm even when we were gone all day at the store! And an electric washing machine! We could store the boiler and scrub board in Mama's attic and do her washing with ours.

"George, can all this be true?"

Between the kitchen and Mama's bedroom was a lavatory. Indoor plumbing! Standing in the doorway, George told me a yarn from his childhood.

"One fall day Alfred Smart invited me to go with him by train to the County Fair in Wautoma. We left at six o'clock in the morning. We had a great time all day and had supper with the Smart family at the Bean Hotel in Wautoma. I'll never forget the experience. After supper I had to go to the toilet—just had to. I was so embarrassed asking where to find it! After doing my errand, I saw a long chain with a wooden handle on the end. Like most kids, I was curious and pulled the chain. I was never so scared—thought I was flooding the whole hotel! It was my first experience with indoor plumbing." His laughter was always as unrestrained as the bouncing joy of a puppy.

Climbing the stairs, I remarked, "Now we can throw out the little foot tub that has been our bath tub for so many years." And George protested, "Who's going to throw out that tub? We might need that some day!"

We entered the room that would be ours and stood by the window looking down on the river. It was nearly dark, but we could see its silver glinting in the pink light of early evening. We listened to its song, the ancient song of water, the elemental song of the universe.

George said, "Indians used to camp on this spot as they migrated their trail to the big timber for the winter. They came again in the early spring on their way North with a supply of maple sugar."

"I can imagine them, sitting down there in the shadows."

Arm in arm, we went to the smaller room that would be the nursery. With the completion of our home, our years alone would end and we would begin the search for our baby.

With children in mind we had chosen the site for our home on the outskirts of the village between the river and a wood. In a trout stream that flowed across the yard, a child could wade for crayfish and pollywogs and on the bank hunt for cowslips and violets. In the oak grove that came to our very doorstep, a child could find squirrels, birds, wild flowers and the freedom children love. There would be time to dream, to wonder, to discover. We were ready.

I began writing letters to child placement agencies, hoping to be called for immediate interviews. Instead, we received polite form letters regretting that no new applications could be accepted. There were too many would-be parents and not enough children. Then, following a friend's suggestion, I wrote the Kansas City Cradle. We did not ask that the baby have blue eyes, yellow curls and a dimple in the right cheek. We asked only that she be mentally and physically equipped for the larger life we hoped to make possible for her.

Our application was accepted and we settled down to wait. One morning, about a month later, we were awakened by the telephone. I ran down to answer. My heart pounded when a voice said, "This is Mrs. Matthews of the Kansas City Cradle. We have a baby girl we think you might like. Are you interested?"

"Oh, yes!"

She described the child, told something of her background and asked if we could come down.

"Yes, I'm sure we can come. We'll phone you when to expect us."

I nearly fell upstairs to tell George.

"Let's start tomorrow, Sunday!"

Hurriedly I began to assemble the things I had expected to have months to gather. A cousin loaned us a basket and blankets. I packed the kimonos and diapers I had made. We could wait until we reached Kansas City to get the rest.

Mama disapproved of our getting a baby. I don't know why, unless she thought we would be stretching our love too thin if we included another person.

"You are crazy," she said in an effort to clinch her argument, "to bring a four weeks old baby over 700 miles of highway in this July heat!"

We were unconvinced and so blissful in our inexperience that the trip home failed to worry us. As we slid along through the Fourth of July traffic, gaily anticipating the adventure, we decided on a name, Sylvia Delle—Sylvia for the sylvan setting to which we would bring her and for Shakespeare's "Who is Sylvia?" We hummed it as we drove along.

"Who is Sylvia, what is she
That all the swains commend her?
Holy, fair and wise is she.
The heavens such grace did lend her;
That adored she might be."

Blithe as we were, when Kansas City lay spread out before us, we both had the feeling of near suffocation.

We drove directly to the Cradle. The exterior looked like a fine private home, red brick set in cool lawn edged with perennial borders, but the interior was scientifically planned for the care of infants from birth until permanent homes could be found for them.

Mrs. Pearl Matthews greeted us. She was charming and gracious. Her daily contact with human tragedy and suffering had given her sympathy and understanding. In her hands lay the future of hundreds of homeless babies that passed through the Cradle each year. She alone knew the background of each baby and decided into whose care to entrust its future. There is no way to measure the happiness she has brought to countless childless homes.

She took us to the nursery where we looked through glass partitions at the rows of tiny beds and the wee bits of humanity that lay on them. When she was a bit older Sylvia loved this part of the story—how we looked at one baby and then another, saying, "Isn't this one dear? Isn't this one precious? But no, it's not just the one we want for our very own," until we came to the last wee bed on which she lay of whom Mrs. Matthews had written us. Then we knew! "This is the one! This is our baby! Mrs. Matthews, may we have her? Please, may we?"

We went to the reception room. A nurse brought us several babies for me to hold while Mrs. Matthews told us their backgrounds. But we decided we wanted the one she had selected for us. This was our Sylvia, eight pounds big and no longer than my two hands!

That afternoon we went to the Court House to make legal arrangements for the adoption. The July heat was so intense that the blood throbbed in our temples. It was then that we began to realize the full import of what we were about to do.

"George, how can we take a four week old baby out into this blistering sun? The car will be so hot!"

"It kind of scares me. Seven hundred miles is a long way."

"And what do we know about babies anyway? Maybe Mama was right."

Most people's worries are as fruitless as ours. In the morning a cool breeze stirred the curtains at the window. The pavement was wet. The lawn looked freshly washed. The heat had abated.

We went early to The Cradle to get the baby and start for home. After dressing her and feeding her the morning formula, we were ready. We had expected to have to learn to love an adopted baby, but from the moment we carried that precious basket to the car and felt such a surge of emotion sweep over us as we never expect to experience again, she has been our child. I couldn't find my handkerchief. I asked George for his, but he was using it. Blindly we put the basket in the car, conscious all the while that Mrs. Matthews was standing in the doorway to bid us goodbye. Our hearts were too full. We could not say the things we felt. "Goodbye. Thank you! God bless you!" But she had seen people like us before. She didn't need to be told.

Thinking the baby would ride more comfortably on the front seat, we put her basket there. I got in the back and spent most of the miles leaning over the seat to look into that little basket.

We stopped every three hours to buy gas and say to the service man, "Could we plug in the baby's bottle warmer?" The inevitable answer was a smile, a peek at the baby and "The outlet is right over there."

In the hotel that night we put the basket on a chair beside the bed. Tired from the excitement, we retired early. George slept instantly, but I couldn't close my eyes. I must look at the baby every few minutes to make sure she was still breathing.

Sylvia was a good traveler. The miles slid by until at last our home found a baby. A baby found a home. And Mama loved her!

The next morning, George went back to the store and I busied myself adapting our home to a new way of life—even though a storm in the night had left us with a power failure. The phone rang. It was Mary and Arthur, friends from Missouri whom we hadn't seen for several years. "Are you going to be home today? We want to stop by to say hello."

"Oh we'd love to have you! It has been too long. We have so much to catch up on, and we have a surprise for you! Can you get here by noon?"

"Yes, we'll be there. Add a little water to the stew."

"We'll have dinner on the table. See you soon."

"Dinner on the table!" Hanging up the receiver, I realized there was nothing in the house to eat and no way to cook it!"

I prepared the food at home and loaded the baby and the kettles in the car. It wasn't the first time I had cooked a meal on Mama's wood range.

The guests pulled into our yard just as I did, and George was waiting for dinner.

When the meal was over I took the baby upstairs for a nap, put her on our bed and lay down beside her to give her the bottle.

Somewhere, far away, George was calling me. I sat up, bewildered, scarcely knowing where I was. What he said jolted me awake. "It's four o'clock. Mary and Arthur are ready to go."

As I had never been exposed to babies or young children, I was a novice in child care. There must be a way to give Sylvia a shampoo without frightening her. She screamed through the whole process.

I asked a friend, a mother of several, what to do, and I began to understand why mothers are always "talking shop." She said, "Lay her on her back on the kitchen counter with her head over the sink, and tell her stories." It was magic! Preparing for the shampoo, I would ask, "What story would you like today?" Her inevitable answer was, "Tell me about how we got Copper." She wanted the story with no variations.

"We wanted a puppy, a wee cocker spaniel puppy, for Sylvia. They would have such good times together! So—one day our whole family, all three of us, went to Waupaca to a kennel to find one. We looked through the fence at a whole yard full of puppies. Weren't they the cutest things we ever saw? Look at that little black one. He's so roly-poly he waddles when he tries to run."

"Remember the tan one," she interrupted.

"Oh yes, look at that tan one—almost white—playing with himself! Isn't he cunning? See him over there? (And on and on, remembering one puppy after another). How could we choose which one would be Sylvia's? We wanted to take them all home with us. Then a little copper-colored puppy came running to us. He came right to you! He poked his little black nose through the fence and wagged his little fuzzy tail. He loved you right away! He was the one!"

Then, invariably, Sylvia would say, "Now tell me about how we got me." The tale would follow about looking through the glass at the Kansas City Cradle and seeing all the babies, each in its own little bed. She liked one story as well as the other.

It was still a personalized society in small villages, as exemplified by "Central," the telephone operator. She was the distributor of information, the herald of coming events. She would give a general ring on each party line and, after waiting for the click of receivers, announce, "Graduation Friday night at 7:30" or "A donation supper for the library Monday night at 6. Everybody bring a sandwich and a dish to pass. Presbyterian church" or "No school today because of the snow storm" or "Peter Lane's barn is on fire. They need help" or "George Smith has lost his dog, Shep. If anyone finds him, please notify the owner."

When Sylvia was old enough to crawl on a chair, she pushed one under the wall phone, turned the crank and told Central, "I want to talk to Daddy." Central, knowing who on that line had a small child, rang the store, and Sylvia talked to Daddy. Sliding down she would say, "I have the best Daddy in the world. When I was made I wanted him and I got him." On another occasion she placed her father in celestial company. "I love God, da baby Jesus and Daddy."

Oh, joy!

Pearl Dopp
Lullaby to Sylvia
Eleanor Dopp
You swung in your swing with the wind in your
The kit - tens have scamp - ered all o - ver the
The wa-ter li - ly sailed on the sun dap - pled
curls, you chased a brown but - ter - fly. You
lawn, and fro - licked all day in the sun. They have
pool, and gazed all day at the sky, at the
cov - ered mud pies ___ with dan - de - lion swirls ___ and
sharp - ened their nails ___ and chased their own tails ___ and
but - ter - fly wing - ing, the o - ri - oles swing - ing, the
hung a doll's wash - ing to dry ___. But now you are
danced with their sha - dows for fun ___. But now their
birds and the clouds sail - ing by ___. But now the dew
close in my arms ___ my sweet, for a pre - - cious
mo - ther has fed them their sup - per and ten - der - ly
falls ___, the whip - poor - will calls, the sun has gone
mo - ment or two. You are fal - ling a - sleep ___ with your
washed each round cheek. They cud - dle and sigh ___ their
down out of sight. The pink pe - tals close ___ in
head on my cheek ___, while I sing a night song to
mo - ther close by ___, while she purrs ___ and purrs them to
fra - grant re - pose ___, while the eve - ning breeze whis - pers "Good
you, to you, to you, to you.
sleep, to sleep, to sleep, to sleep.
night, good night, good night, good night.
RSC '76

After the coming of Sylvia, I spent more time at home, but when I did work at the store, Sylvia went to her grandma's. Those were happy days for Mama. She would have been glad to have me work full time.

One January night in 1939, the peace of evening had settled on our little house. George seemed secretly animated about something. Finally it came out.

"I heard today that the Niedecken Building is for sale. Don't you think we better snap it up? It's close to the post office, across from the bank—it's a good brick building and a lot bigger than the one we're renting. What do you think?"

I agreed and became enthusiastic. "And we could modernize it before we move in—built-in wall cases for baby things, a swinging rack for curtains . . . a built-in rack for house dresses—a fitting room!"

George added, "All day I have been thinking about arranging the grocery for self service. I bet the guy who dreamed up those wire carts must have worked in an old-fashioned grocery like ours."

"And let's make everything pretty and bright. What about painting all those old counters and showcases off-white and the new walls too?"

George nodded and I went on, "And maybe we could fit some of the counter tops with glass dividers."

The talk went on and on, and in a few days George boarded the early train for Milwaukee, where the owner lived, and came back at night with the deal sealed.

It was exciting modernizing and decorating the new store. The wind no longer sent cold air through the cracks in the floor. The days of stoking the stove and wearing snow boots were over, for we had an oil-burning heatrola, which circulated warm air more adequately.

Nylon stockings were introduced that year and we stocked them in the store. Compared to rayon, they were a luxury, and who could afford silk anyway? Nylon, made from coal and water, was the first of an endless list of synthetics which would soon be taken for granted by the American consumer.

At a meeting of the Woman's Club, one of the members gave a report on a new method of preserving food—freezing. She said electric freezers would soon be available in which the housewife could freeze meat and the produce from her garden and orchard.

They were talking, too, of electric air conditioners which could control the inside temperature of buildings, making year-round thermostatically-controlled temperature possible.

When Sylvia was two we decided it was time to find a baby brother for her. We wanted her to know the companionship of another child, and we wanted to relive the joyous days of her babyhood. It took courage to ask for a son when the dogs of war were at the throats of mankind all over the world. It took faith to believe that a new world could rise from the ashes of the old.

We waited and waited. The agencies were swamped with applications. A year went by without a call. Then a letter came from a dear friend, a college friend, who had gone to Pennsylvania to teach, had married and continued to live there. She and her husband had a foster son, Bobby, aged nine. She wrote in part as follows:

"I can write only a little. This may or may not concern you. Don't let it strike your sympathy and lead you to take a child you don't want. I have one chance in a hundred to get well, only the action of God."

She went on to tell us of Bobby's characteristics, then wrote, "I won't advise you to take him for, after all, he is nine years old and half grown. Don't decide on sympathy, but try to see that in taking him you won't take another you might find still in babyhood. You could have him on trial or 'until Mother gets well,' but if you don't like him I doubt, knowing you, if you would have the heart to send him away when he would have loved Sylvia, the dog and the stream. I know what it is. I am doing it—his dog, the house that he loves as much as we do. It's a terrible thing to send one away! I'm not as hard about this as I sound. The tears have been bitter . . ."

We talked it over and the next day wrote her that we would like to carry on for her in giving him the love she would have given him.

When my letter arrived she said, "Thank God!" She seemed to feel that everything was going to be all right, that she was ready to go. She wired us to come but, while I was packing, another wire came that she was dead.

When we told Mama what we were going to do, she was shocked and disapproving, but remembering how soon Sylvia had won her over, we didn't worry about it.

It was four months before legal arrangements could be completed for transferring Bobby from Pennsylvania to Wisconsin. We drove out to get him in June 1941. As we drove along, looking for the house, an excited voice called, "Hi," and there was Bobby running across the lawn to greet us. He had seen our Wisconsin license.

There was an ache in my throat all the time we were there. Vera was gone! And yet, in everything about her beautiful home and garden we saw her—the curtains she had made, the carpet she had selected, her book of poems on the mantle. The flowers she had planted still bloomed in the dooryard, and Bobby—her Bobby—was sailing boats on the pond. She seemed very near. I like to think that she knew that her last, fondest wish had been granted.

To take Bobby away from everything he knew and loved was hard, and to leave Vera's desolate husband standing there beside his empty house, empty yet saturated with memories . . . Well, there are some things that tear the heart in two.

The adjustment of our home and way of life to a robust nine-year-old was full of problems, but infinitely more difficult was his adjustment to his new environment. The boys at school had to find out what this new fellow with an Eastern accent could take. They let the air out of his bike tires, waylaid him on his way home and knocked him off his bike. Each day he would come home bruised and trying to hold back the tears.

We ministered to his hurts of body and mind as best we could. Even Sylvia would run to get a jar of cold cream to rub on his bumps to "make Bob feel better."

One day when the teacher had left the room, the boys started as usual to tease Bobby, when Gilbert Hadden, a large boy for his years, got up in the aisle and said, "Anybody that picks on that kid is going to get it from me!" The boys sank back in their seats and the room was quiet as Gilbert loomed above them. The persecution was over. I'll always love Gilbert Hadden!

When we were working at the store one day and Bob was home alone, he had callers. People who were renting a cottage at the lake wanted to know if they could have some water from our artesian well for their baby. A few days later the mother of the baby, when she came to shop, told me of the way Bob played host.

"He helped us fill our water jug and then asked us if we would like to see the house. He took us from room to room, upstairs and down, pointing out whatever he thought we would be interested in. He showed us around the yard, introduced us to your cocker, and when we finally got in the car he came running after us to say, 'If you'll come back next week, there will probably be puppies I could show you!"

Bob enjoyed helping in the store, filling shelves, running errands. He liked people and they liked him. He and George built a balcony above the back-room-office—sort of an indoor tree house where Bob could make model aeroplanes undisturbed by a little sister. He liked to answer the phone and would say in a businesslike way, copied from his father, "Dopp store." We all had a laugh on George one noon when it was George's turn to ask the blessing. We bowed our heads and heard him say, absent-mindedly, "Dopp store."

In a little intimate talk one day Bob said to me, "Grandma doesn't like me. She doesn't. I can tell."

I tried to reassure him, "Well, you see, Grandma isn't used to boys. But you are a very likeable person, Bob, and I think you could make her like you. Can you think of ways to do it?"

"By being good to her and doing things for her?"

"That ought to do the trick!"

"Know what?" Bob's brown eyes shone. "I'll go right now and mow her lawn!"

He went, had gone two trips around the outside of her yard, when some boys came by and asked him to go to the school diamond to play ball with them. He went, leaving the lawn mower in its tracks.

Mama never did accept Bob. What a lot both she and he missed! Tension gripped the household. Loving Mama and being so indebted to her, and loving Bob, I wanted so much for them to be happy. I was inadequate. Trying to protect one from annoyance and the other from hurt, body cried out to mind, "Let there be serenity," but there was none.

In retrospect, the problem might have been solved if I had asked George to talk to Mama, to tell her again that we loved her and were happy to have her spend winters with us (which of course she already knew), but that we loved Bob too. He was our son. He was her only grandson. He needed the love of a grandma. For all our sakes, if she couldn't learn to love him, would she try to hide her animosity?

For George she would have tried. But in the stress of each day's living, that approach never occurred to either of us.

I was lay delegate from our little church to the annual conference of Wisconsin Methodism, meeting in Janesville. Mama had gone home for the summer. George urged me to go. "The change will be good for you. Sylvia can stay with her grandma and Bob and I will get along just fine."

I went. In those few days of freedom from stress, in lifting the mind to rarer atmosphere, I felt certain that new insight would come, but the expectant days slipped by, one by one, without the anticipated answer to our need. My heart was heavy. Was there no guidance, after all?

Sunday morning came, the last morning, and the ordination of new ministers dedicated to lives of Christian service. Then the most beautiful contralto voice I had ever heard closed the session with a solo from First Corinthians, and she sang it just for me. "Love never faileth. Love never faileth."

Recalling the pleasure we had had with pets during our own childhood, we wanted our children to have pets too. Copper was the first of a succession of four cocker spaniels. Each time one died, the tears were shed and burial rites spoken and wild flowers left on the new mound, and we went in search of another cocker spaniel. Two were registered as Copper and two as His Nibs, depending on the gender.

One summer we rented a nanny goat and her little kid, the goat to be milked and the kid to be played with. We never had a more fascinating pet than the young goat. Her antics were so merry, so full of exuberance and love of life! She and Copper enjoyed playing with each other as much as the children enjoyed playing with both.

And there was a riding horse, Ginger. Of course I secretly compared all horses to the Colonel of my childhood and none of them measured up; but the children, never having known Colonel, were happy with Ginger.

One winter afternoon Mama and I were in the kitchen making preparations for supper when Sylvia came to us with a sheet of paper and a pen in her hands. She said, "Grandma, will you write your name on this paper—right here?" Grandma did. "Mother, will you put your name here too?" I did.

When George sat down to supper the paper was beside his plate. Bob had added his name, Sylvia hers, and there was Copper's inked paw print. At the bottom of the page in large print was the message, "Daddy, we want a Mercury!" Who could afford a Mercury? Anyway, it was a good try.

Children voice early their dissatisfaction with the status quo. A friend's ten-year-old daughter wrote her mother this letter:

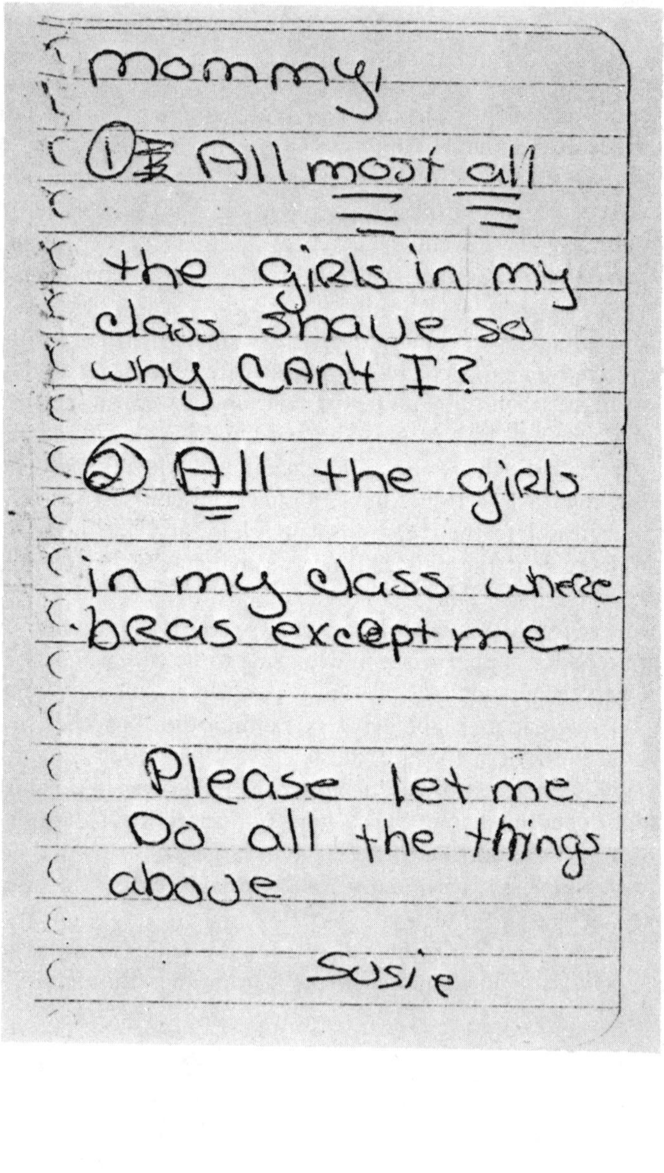
Mommy,

① All most all
the girls in my
class shave so
why CAN't I?

② All the girls
in my class where
bras except me

Please let me
Do all the things
above

Susie

A year later our friend's seven-year-old son issued a warning:

Dear Mommy & Daddy
I'm runing away
from home
because nobody loves
me anymore.
Here are wry:
Susie: Bossis me around.
Mrs. Dickey: Take my things.
Mommy: Yells at me. Wips me.
Daddy: get mad at me.
Mom K.: Yells at me
Mom J.: Nothing
Grandma: Nothing
Uncl Bill: Yells at me.
Uncl Andy: A pest.

Love
Fred

He decided not to run away from home, though, until summer, after he had been to camp.

Parents live through the precious incidents in the lives of their children, the sweet dependency of infancy, the first day of school, the growth of those fine qualities that every child is endowed with—especially our own.

Then came the day when I went upstairs to see what all the commotion was about and found to my amazement that the doll house, doll buggy, doll beds, doll bureau, dolls and their clothes were out in the hall and a very dignified young lady was standing in the doorway saying, "Mother, I don't want those things in my room any more. They are childish. I'm grown up."

So adolescence comes—the most bewildering, the most challenging time for all. The child is now half-child and half-adult, and while being either one, is trying to be the other. She had convinced herself and almost convinced her parents that mother and dad don't know much. They are definitely old fogies who got their ideas way back in the dark ages, way back in 1930. And everybody knows how stingy they are. There isn't a kid in school who doesn't have better clothes. And nobody who is anybody has such a trap of a car. And the stuff in the house is just a pile of junk. And why did we have to bring her up in such a dump of a town anyway? There's nothing to do. Everything is such a bore. And, Mother, why can't you get on the ball?

When a friend told me of the escapades her teenagers were getting into, I said, "Sometimes I wonder how they ever live to grow up." And she said, "Sometimes I wonder if *I* will live till they grow up!"

There seems little parents can do to help. They might as well sit back and rock. In fact, the youth is fortunate whose parents do not become hurt and discouraged but are secure in the belief that early training has been good.

Although Bob had the usual difficulties growing up, he was never as rebellious as Sylvia. The time came when even she could say, "Mother, it's amazing how much you and Daddy learned while I was away at school."

Now our children are themselves parents and have given us grandchildren, our stake in tomorrow. Aren't grandchildren more fun than anything?

The grandchildren, too, have animal friends. A shining black cat came to Sylvia's. Finally, for two reasons, they let him into their house and hearts—the cat insisted, and George and Charles, the two little boys, insisted. Jimmy, they called him.

There was one problem. Often the cat went away, sometimes overnight, and the boys worried that he might not come back. One day their father, the little boys trotting along beside him, was walking down the street when they met the veterinarian and told him, "We have a cat that runs around. Could you give him an operation to change his mind?"

The veterinarian said, "Sure. Bring him over."

The operation was performed, but when Jimmy recovered he still wandered off.

Again they met the veterinarian who asked, "How's the cat?"

"That operation didn't do any good. The cat still runs around."

"Think nothing of it. He's just out canceling appointments."

The boys enjoyed making people laugh, even though the reason for the laughter was a mystery, so they told the kindergarten teacher, the bus driver, the clerk in the hardware store, about Jimmy who had an operation to have his mind changed and then went out to cancel appointments.

House Cat

Pampered cat, on prowl again,
Explores the world through window pane.
On clawless feet, with hunter's eye,
Sees a gopher, stalks a fly.

We have three international children who call us "Grandpa and Grandma." Abdul, through Children Inc., is in a school for the deaf in Salt, Jordan. Dean, in the Philippines, is one of an estimated 100,000 children born to Asian mothers and fathered and deserted by American service men.

In Asian countries, particularly, children belong to the father and when there is no father, the mother and her people reject them, forcing them to be children of the street, sleeping under bridges or in doorways and eating what they can salvage from the streets. The more fortunate ones have been rescued and are in orphanages. The Pearl Buck Foundation tries, when possible, to maintain these Amerasian children with their mother or other relative. Our Dean, for example, is living with her grandmother. Pearl Buck believed that these Amerasian children would be the best hope for binding peace between the two cultures.

In Pearl Buck's own words, "Unknown numbers of these children are in Korea, Japan, Thailand, the Philippines and Okinawa. Everywhere the Amerasian children are growing up without education or hope of a future. Why? Because they are a new group of human beings, a group which Asains do not know how to deal with, illegitimate as well as mixed in race. Asia is still family centered, and without family there is neither education nor jobs. And these Amerasian children have no families. Their mothers, outcast when they give birth to a child out of wedlock, cannot care for them. Therefore they wander the streets, sometimes in packs. In orphanages they are discriminated against because they are of mixed race, lowest among the low. Yet, they are innocent. I cannot believe it is good for American prestige that half-American children grow up ignorant and hopeless, forgotten by their fathers and deserted by their mothers."

The Christian Childrens Fund takes care of Pyung Soon in an orphanage in Korea. She has been our little girl since she was an infant fourteen years ago. She is now entering Middle School, is having music lessons, which she loves, and is looking forward to advanced education which we hope to make possible for her, so she can take her place in a productive way among her own people.

These three children are the byproducts of the cruelty of war. They are but three drops in an ocean of misery. We are so complacent in our comfort that we are unaware of those other thousands who roam the streets and scrounge for food.

I wish the warmongers could hear the words of Socrates ringing in their ears: "Could I climb to the highest place in Athens, I would lift up my voice and proclaim, 'Fellow citizens, why do you turn and scrape every stone to gather wealth and take so little care of your children to whom someday you must relinquish it all?' "

It is inconceivable that mankind still tries to settle international differences with armies and bombs, that so much of the world's productivity is geared to the manufacture of armaments while children starve!

Of late, though, there are encouraging signs in the number of conflagrations that have been averted through arbitration. May that be the trend of the future! Perhaps the two-thousand-year-old promise of peace on earth, good will toward men, will someday become a reality after all.

Heritage

Above the dim, distorted echoings
Of twenty fleeting centuries of time
There floats, distilled and clear,
The song sublime,
As on that hallowed night, still heralding
Man's ancient heritage of peace. A king
And shepherd boy across a cradle smiled,
Were brothers there before a little Child,
As brothers all might be, remembering.

Of late the thunderings of battle cease
And transports tramp the long lanes home again.
But where on the reeling, tear-stained earth is peace?
Above the blatant bickerings of men
Hear the lonely children crying in the cold,
Hungry, homeless children, old, oh ages old!

On a Sunday afternoon in December, 1941, we were decorating the evergreen tree for Christmas. The children were helping hang the ornaments and drape the tree with thin strands of tinsel that we had used each year since my childhood. The little radio was playing Christmas music, and George was popping corn over the firepalce coals, as was our Sunday custom in winter.

Suddenly, the music stopped. A voice interrupted the program to say that Japanese planes had attacked Pearl Harbor and, in less than two hours, had destroyed most of our Pacific fleet, that over two thousand people had been killed—the number only an estimate—and 347 United States planes has been damaged or completely destroyed. George and I stood frozen in disbelief but came back to the reality of home to comfort the frightened children.

The country, once again, mobilized for war across the sea. In a frenzy of hatred for Japanese, Americans of Oriental extraction were herded into camps lest they betray our war effort. American soldiers, 16 million strong, fought in the Pacific and stormed the Normandy beaches.

Thy Child

1941

Look not upon Thy world, O God!
Lest Thou turn back to clay
The man Thy fingers wrought.

Where winter's swirling snow
Turned scarlet as it fell
The spring has come,
And heavy, clodded boots
Tramp over those
Who know the spring
No more.

Is this Thy child,
His eyeballs red with hate,
His music silenced
By exploding shells,
His loftiest dreams
In rubble on the city streets?

O God, let not,
Let not the blinding wind
Blow out the light
Of stars!

While the war went mercilessly on, the atomic bomb was being secretly perfected and shook the whole world when it exploded over Hiroshima and Nagasaki, killing 100,000 Japanese and ending the Second World War. Oh, war! Will mankind never learn! Would this terrible instrument of destruction, too horrible to use, save the world from further wars or would it destroy civilization?

Hitler's Germany was on its knees, her cities in rubble. General Marshall's Plan, the most humane program ever devised to aid fallen enemy, fed the starving, rebuilt the cities and raised the fallen to their feet. We, who had destroyed her cities, rebuilt them and assisted in the most rapid economic recovery in the history of the world. And America became an industrial giant, the munition maker of the world.

The following doggerel verse describes American life in 1944.

Greetings to You

In bed with the flu
I have nothing to do
But write you a holiday letter.
Though it's only a ditty,
To desist were a pity
For I'm always in letters a debtor.

We wish you health,
A little of wealth
And good luck for the new '44;
And at Christmas a thought
For the Young Man Who taught
That peace could abide after war.

George and I, in a dither,
Rush hither and thither.
By doing the work of a dozen
We imagine we're solving
The troubles involving
The national Man Power Commission.

With a stitch here and there,
With a darn for each tear,
And a feeling we're quite patriotic
We are wearing the rags,
The tail ends and tags
I'd been saving for rugs in the attic.

A fellow named Kaiser
Might have a surpriser
If he knew of Bob's aeroplane production.
He peddles his papers,
He cuts all the capers,
He has to know everything's function.

"If God made the tree
And Copper and me
Then who," Sylvia asks, "Who made God?"
She insists like a stickler
God didn't make Hitler.
Her mind is like Pegasus shod.

My mother is here.
(She spoils us, the dear)
We are grateful to be all together.
The V-garden's canned,
There's fuel on hand
And we're all cuddled in from the weather.

But the homeless! the crying!
The wounded! the dying!
To these, O God, give Thy care!
To the young, to the old
Whose hearthstones are cold,
Whose lonely tables are bare.

In 1945 Woodrow Wilson's dream of a League of Nations, for which he had unsuccessfully pleaded after World War I, became a reality when 1400 delegates from 49 countries climaxed a month-long San Francisco Conference by signing the charter of the United Nations.

World War II was nearly over and the Allies were sure of victory—military victory, that is. Ever since World War I, whose hollow victory had brought no peace, they had realized they would have to do more than win World War II. They would have to prevent such a holocaust from exploding again.

The United Nations, though not perfect, is the world's best hope for peace. It provides nations with a sounding board where grievances can be discussed and solutions sought, where attempts can be made to cure the world's economic, social, cultural and humanitarian ills.

After World War II, member countries contributed shiploads of food to the starving, and livestock and agricultural equipment to devastated lands. In 1946 John D. Rockefeller, Jr., gave $8,500,000 to buy six acres of New York City as a site for a permanent home for the United Nations. In 1950, for the first time, member countries of the United Nations sent troops to help South Korea repel aggression.

The peace rose, the loveliest of hybrid teas, is closely related to that period of world history. It had taken the great French hybridist, Francis Milland, twelve years to develop. It was assigned to Robert Pile, a United States rosarian, on the day France fell. He patented it in 1943 and grew 50,000 bushes before it was put on the market.

Enthusiastic rosarians from across the Nation gathered to choose a name. When the news came of the fall of Berlin, the name dawned on them simultaneously—"PEACE!" The Pacific Rose Society christened it in the Rose Bowl in a star-studded ceremony climaxed by the release of two white doves, who flew up and away as though to bring peace to the world.

On momentous V-E Day, each delegate from the 49 nations represented at the United Nations Conference received a peace rose with a card which read, "This is the peace rose, christened at the Pacific Rose Society Exhibition in Pasadena as Berlin fell. We hope that the peace rose will influence men's thoughts for an everlasting peace."

While Bob and Sylvia attended the same Sunday School in which I had been reared, I taught in the junior department. It was so challenging and fruitful that I continued, either as teacher or superintendent, for 25 years and went on to direct children's work in the Watertown district of the Wisconsin conference of the Methodist church, teaching in laboratory and demonstration schools and going from church to church to try to inspire teachers to use better materials and techniques. It was one of the most satisfying periods of my life, for I believed in Christian education and its influence for good.

Long ago, after a hard night, morning dawned on seven tired

and hungry men in a boat on a far-away lake. They had fished all night and had nothing to show for their effort. Then on the shore they saw their Friend and heard Him call to them, "Children, have you any meat?" Or did He say, "The day is before you. What do you have to live on?"

Parents wonder about that. They have seen friends and acquaintances in a day of stress when all their reserves seemed to be exhausted. But how differently they faced it! Some crumbled under adversity, but others went through a day of pain or grief or stress or temptation with purpose firm. What did they have to live on?

Parents think of their children and how soon they will step out into life and all its surging problems. They cannot shield their children long, nor should they want to, for the young must flex their own wings, make their own mistakes and be gratified by their own victories, but they wonder how these children of theirs will meet mornings of stress. What do they have to live on?

For among all the good things we wish for our children the chief, I believe, is the hope that there will be inner resources for abundant lives in any circumstance which faces them.

We use many means to help them reach that goal. From the beginning we are conscious of their need for physical well-being. We give them well-balanced diet, clothe them warmly, immunize them against every possible disease. We believe in health.

We educate them, digging deep in our pockets to give them the best of educational opportunities. Parents are determined that their children will have an opportunity to build up inner resources to meet the unknown world that lies ahead. We believe in education.

And most parents have similar longing that their children may know the enriching experience of religion. How can this be done? Just as health and education do not come by mere wishing, so does the Christian life have to be striven for.

Religion is rooted deep in family life. Right and wrong are like the imaginary symbols in algebra to a child unless he sees them in action in his own home. He sees his parents meeting difficult situations not by seeking the easy answer, but by striving for the right answer. When he becomes old enough to think of honor and justice, those concepts are not new to him for he realizes that his own father and mother have tried to live by them.

There are some shallow soils in which it is nearly impossible for children to develop in a Christian way. One of them is the belief that anything done in the name of religion is good for the child. A little friend of ours came home in mental turmoil, in terror and tears, because she had been told in a Bible story hour that the end of the world would come and bring fire and brimstone to punish her for her sins.

There are mothers so engrossed in routine that they never sense the wonder of the opportunity that is theirs to teach their children that they are not common clay but meant for high destiny.

We recall the priest and the Levite who were so pressed for time in "church affairs" that they did not help a wounded man by the side of the road, too busy with religion to be religious.

Some parents believe they can leave the job to someone else. They say, "The school should teach those kids how to behave," or "That's the preacher's job. What else do we pay him for?"

There is the story of two shieks of Arabia who came to London as guest of Colonel Lawrence. They were housed in the best hotels, given every courtesy, and when they were to leave for home they were asked what they would like to take with them. After considering the offer, they reported, "We would like two hot water faucets, for it would be a great thing for our people if they could turn on hot water whenever they wanted it."

We have known parents as naive, but if religion is to be more than a faucet without a pipe, the family must draw clear, pure water from the mountain top and connect with the great Dynamo before there can be hot water in the faucet.

In some homes there is the poor soil of belief that Christian experience is concerned with some one department of life. One may grow to maturity feeling quite surely saved if he has gone to church or read his Bible or said his prayers or eaten no meat on certain days. Insisting on one phase of religion, however important in itself, is like striving for the little tassels on the fringe of religion without ever sensing the glory and majesty of its core.

But on the other side of the coin, it is refeshing to see families who use the deep, rich soil of Christian living in which to rear their children, where each child is given a sense of security, time to be child-like, friendly companionship and contact with character that can be respected.

Some children, though their parents try to the best of their light to nurture them well, cannot accept guidance, even though gently given. Others, who seem to have little potential, reach for the stars. No one knows why.

Children are fortunate, I believe, who grow up on a farm.

Science and religion are not apt to conflict for one who daily sees God's handiwork in flower, in bird, rainbow, sunset, snowflake, the drifting cloud and the marvelous functions of living creatures. For a child in the country spring is a miracle, the earth bursting into life, the hustling expectant partnership the farmer has with nature, tilling the soil, preparing the seed and sowing it well. If nature is to do her work, he must do his.

And yet, beauty is where one finds it. I recall riding the elevated through the slums of Chicago, through blocks and blocks of rotting tenements and littered dooryards with children crawling through it like ants on an anthill. I felt a deep sickness that children should grow up in such surroundings. No wonder the place breeds crime and disease! Then, suddenly, I saw a tiny garden on a porch roof, a splash of beauty on the drab landscape, and a little child watering the flowers. I knew that inside there was a mother who was determined that her child would have the joy and companionship of growing things and a chance to see the face of God in the beauty that, together, they had made.

Christian attitudes and conduct are never acquired by accident or by inheritance. Those who have them learned them, and they learned them because some person or institution was willing to take the time to teach.

The greatest Teacher who ever lived taught under all conditions and by all means. He taught in conversation, in parables, in miracles, in stories, in sermons. He taught all types of people, rich and poor, literate and illiterate, Scribes and Pharisees, sinners and tax collectors. He taught wherever there were people—in the temple, on the hillside, in a boat, on the road. He taught and taught and taught.

It was difficult teaching in the crowded conditions in the one-room basement of our little church. Classes were so near to each other that the children's attention and participation were distracted. I knew how they felt, for I was secretly amused each Sunday morning when the teacher at the next table began each session with, "What shall we do today to make Clarence be good?" It was a challenge to Clarence, who always outdid himself.

How could it be possible to give children the fundamentals of Christian living in only one hour a week? Many children did not attend regularly, facilities were inadequate, volunteer teachers did not always teach effectively. Public schools could not teach math under those conditions. But, if the Great Teacher could teach under any circumstance, at least we could try.

Often at the end of the session, I wondered if there had been any growth, any development at all. Then something would happen to make it all worthwhile—the hole-in-one that makes the hills worth climbing. One Sunday we were talking about Christmas coming to the people of the world and mentioned that while we were opening our presents there would be children who had no packages to open. A little second grade boy said, "I have a baseball bat I would give to a boy who doesn't have any." I asked, "Don't you use it?"

"Oh yes, I use it. But I would give it."

After operating the store for 22 years we sold it in 1955 and turned over the keys. We had enjoyed it. We would miss seeing the people. But "for everything there is a season and a time for all things under the heavens." We released one season without regret and faced the unknown season with anticipation.

Habits of the years are not easily broken. The first time I shopped for groceries and took them to the opposite side of the check-out counter, the young clerk asked, "Do you really want this spotted apple?"

Last night I dreamed. Bob and Sylvia were grown and gone. Instead of dividing our love they had multiplied it, and we had a lot left to give. So we adopted eight children, all at once, ages 4 to 15.

In the dream we were having a family council and asked the children what kind of a home they would like ours to be. Would they enjoy quarreling and grumbling and having to be scolded, or would they like to live happily together and love each other? They chose the latter. Then they decided on the buddy system, each older child looking after a younger one, and they made a chart, rotating the chores in house and yard. Oh, it was a beautiful dream!

But then, approaching reality, I began to worry. What had we done? Our house wasn't big enough for eight children. Where would they sleep? How could we get enough money to buy food and clothing and education? I woke to the realization that the Great Giver, in His wisdom, gives children to the young, not to great-grandparents.

Spring Again!

Wild geese, homeward bound,
Chorus the advent of spring.

Across the river, hovering
Over the low lands, swaying
On last summer's rushes,
Red winged blackbirds
Chatter, chuckle, chortle
As they hunt secret places
For nesting.
A cat bird chides me from his tree,
Then, in ventriloquist fashion,
Bids me look for oriole and katydid.

Swallows, sailing clear currents of sky,
Sailing,
Sailing,
Gliding on sun-glinted wing,
Swoop low, reflected momently
In mirrored pool.
Somewhere a nest
Cuddling eggs for hatching,
Age-old promise of life,
Life, life again.

Silken bark of birches
Twin reflected whiteness
The stream.
Pussywillow, violet,
Bloodroot, hepatica,
Marsh marigold,
Mandrake,
Jack in the pulpit, fern,
In swift succession
Color the river rim.

Forget-me-nots,
Kin of minute blue stars
Scattered a century ago
By another Johnny Appleseed,
Whisper man's deeds
Live after him.

Oh, My Sister

VII

Through the years there had been no attempt to bridge the miles between Wild Rose and my sisters in the State of Washington. People did not travel then as they do now, and Mama had always seemed reluctant to have me see them. She did correspond, occasionally, with Mira, the oldest sister, whom we had visited briefly when I was seven, but other than that there was no contact.

George and I had been living in our home for several years when Mira and her husband visited us. It had been thirty-three years since I had seen her. She was still a beautiful woman with the large brown eyes and dark hair of our father. She and her husband had worked hard, had reared a large family and were, then, free to do a bit of traveling.

We scarcely knew where to begin to bridge the years since our parents died and I had been brought to Wisconsin. As she lived some distance from the place where we had been born and as she had a houseful of children of her own, she was not as involved in the day-by-day tragedy as the three younger girls were. Having been born in Wisconsin, though, she remembered the felling of trees in the West and the building of the log cabin and the struggle to break the land and make it into a productive farm.

She told me, "In all those hard years our mother worked side-by-side with Father, even in building the new house. She was a talented woman, could do anything she set her mind to. She played the accordian, sometimes for neighborhood dances, rode a horse as though she were part of him—could break a colt, too— she was always working in the church and was interested in everything. She had a camera and developed her own pictures."

I recalled, "I have a faded little picture she took of me when I was about two. She had written on the back, 'Our baby,' and had sent it to Uncle Jerry and Aunt Fanny."

I sat forward, taking in everything Mira said, answers to questions that had been unanswered for so long. "You look like our mother, blond, thin face, long nose—act like her, too, the way you delve into things and work at them, the way you team up with George."

"Was she tall, like me?"

"No, a little woman, full of energy and life."

"And I never knew her." I broke the musing silence, thinking of our father and asking how he contracted tuberculosis.

"Well," she started thoughtfully, "I don't know exactly. He had it for several years. He always worked too hard, way beyond his strength, and got rundown. When he could spare the time, he earned extra money by driving a team and wagon up into the mountains to bring down a load of lumber from the saw mill. It was a long day's travel. One time a terrible rain storm came up and there was no place to find shelter. It turned cold, and he had to ride all those miles, wet and chilled. After that he began to cough and it got worse and worse."

"Wasn't there something that could have been done for him?"

"He did go to Portland to a doctor, but there was no cure for consumption then. He was in the Portland hospital many times, but stayed home as much as he could to be with the family and save expense."

It all swept over me. "The tragedy of it, feeling he could not get well and the anguish of leaving his motherless girls!"

Mira agreed, "It was. He was almost obsessed with the need to find a home for you. Martha, Florence and Elva, he thought they could look after themselves somehow. He knew it would be hard, but they could manage. But you—what would become of you?"

Mira's eyes moistened as she remembered, "And he was worried for fear you might catch consumption if you stayed there to the end. You crawled all over him. They couldn't keep you away from him. You were the only sunshine in that house—too young to know what it was all about."

"How dreadful for the girls!" I wanted to know how they kept things going.

"They worked awfully hard, were grown up before they had a chance to be children. Elva was the farmer. She would ask Father what to do and then do it. She was little for her age, but strong. Florence and Martha did the housework and took care of Father and you."

"Did anyone at home catch it?"

"No one did. Isn't that strange? It was so contagious! The girls didn't know much about sanitation either, like washing their hands after they waited on him."

I wondered, "Do you suppose he had emphysema instead of tuberculosis? Maybe at that time every deterioration of the lungs was called consumption. There was no X-ray laboratory equipment."

"Might be." She had never thought of that possibility.

"What happened to the girls after they were left alone?"

"Father had arranged to have sister Edna and her family stay there with them, but the girls weren't happy with that arrangement, so they went out to work. Not having a home, they married young. Trouble followed them all their lives. Poor Elva knew nothing but hard work and poverty. She had fourteen children, raised ten."

"Fourteen!" I couldn't believe it.

"Yes, fourteen! Her husband was gone most of the time, but came home often enough to make another baby. It was such a struggle for her to keep the family fed and clothed! Sometimes they had nothing but potatoes."

She paused and went on. "She lost one child in such a horrible way! While Elva was out in the barn doing the evening chores, one of the little girls stood on a chair to put a chunk of wood in the heater. She lost her balance and fell in."

I shuddered, "How could Elva live through something like that!"

Mira knew. "She was used to hardship and heartache. Sometimes it makes a person strong. She had all her babies at home, delivered most of them herself. The only time she ever had a doctor the baby died. The doctor told little Alma, who must have been about seven, to come outside with him and hold the lantern while he dug a hole and buried the baby in the yard. That child was terrified and told me later that she was sure the baby moved."

Mira went on, "One time when Elva was expecting, a snow storm came and she had to go out to dig wood out of the snow to keep the baby warm who was about to be born."

I cried, "Where was her husband?"

Mira, in exasperation, said, "Who knows!"

"Couldn't one of the children have brought in the wood?"

Mira spurted, "They were all babies, just babies— a new one every year!"

Thoughtlessly I asked, "Why didn't she leave him!"

"Where would she have gone?" Mira wanted to know. "What would she have done? She couldn't leave those children! She never could! She was trapped!"

"If Papa and Mama hadn't come to Washington to get me, those dreadful things might have happened to me too."

Mira agreed, "Yes, they might."

"All my life," I told her, "I have asked myself why I was lifted out of that hopeless situation and brought here to the love and security of a home while those girls were denied it. Why me? I have wondered, too, but never asked, of course, why Mama and Papa left them there. Why couldn't they have taken all four of us?"

Mira thought a while. "Maybe they thought that the responsibility of taking care of one child, who might be tubercular, was all they could handle. Beside, what would our father have done without them?"

"Anyway, ever since I was old enough to think about it, I have felt guilty that I have had so much and they so little."

Mira protested, "Why should you? There was nothing you could have done about it."

"I suppose not, but just the same I have always felt so indebted to life! Probably that is why I have had such compulsion to do civic work—trying to repay—trying to repay."

Mustard Seeds and Wild Roses

VIII

The Woman's Club had a frustrating time in 1950 when it tried to convert a swamp into a park on highway 22 at the north entrance to the village. As far as natural resources were concerned, it was perfect: Pine River, the possibility of a lagoon, ancient trees along the highway.

Landscape plans were drawn by the State Park Planning Board, and a house-to-house canvas brought volunteer labor, cash, tools and equipment. The agriculture class offered to build a retaining wall for a parking lot and to plant trees from a nearby woodlot.

But when the attempt was made to convert the bog into a lawn, the heavy equipment settled into the muck and had to be pulled out with other heavy equipment. It was impossible! The whole area had to be drained and covered with at least a foot of top soil. This was done, until the $500 appropriated by the Village Board was exhausted. It was a drop in the bucket!

A grading crew was preparing highway 22 for new surfacing. We went to them and asked, "What are you going to do with the soil you are taking from the roadbed?"

"Oh, I guess we'll have to haul it off somewhere."

"Would you be willing to dump it in the park we're building?"

"I guess that would be as convenient a place as any."

Day after day, truckloads of dirt groaned to the edge of the park and dumped the contents there. The mountain grew and grew. As soon as the trucks had finished, volunteers operated bulldozers to spread the dirt over the bogs of the swamp. At last there was a lawn!

The Woman's Club planted 50 rose bushes, and students planted 50 trees and built a retaining wall for a parking lot.

But the broad new highway that made the lawn possible called for cutting the stately trees along the park. The Woman's Club and citizenry pleaded. If the road had to be widened, why couldn't it be done on the other side of the road which was nothing but waste land? We wrote letters, telephoned, made personal contacts, but the loved trees came crashing down.

After all their hard work, the citizenry was so discouraged that the park was abandoned and the lawn grew up to hay. The road to a beautiful town is not always easy!

A few months after we sold the store, George had finished all the odd jobs around home that had been stacked up during those busy years, and was studying for a license in real estate. As a member of the bank loan committee, he found he enjoyed evaluating property and decided real estate would appeal to him.

Then came the shock of Herman Belter's death. George said, "I don't know how we can do without him. He was such a good president, had such good judgment, was so level-headed! There's nobody to fill his shoes."

George came home from a directors' meeting looking as though he was walking in his sleep. "You never could guess what happened to me."

"Then I won't try. Just tell me."

He swept me off my feet. "The board elected me president of the bank and chairman of the board—pending affirmation by the annual meeting, of course." He released me and lifted his hands helplessly, "I'm not capable of doing that!"

"Of course you are, George. Of course you are."

"I can't believe this is happening to me!" He chuckled, "On the way home I remembered a day—I suppose I was about 17—when I was walking behind a cultivator, back and forth, back and forth across the corn field. The sun was hot, and I was sweaty and dirty. I won't say I was tired—never got tired in those days. I had stopped the horse so I could free a hand to wipe my forehead of the sweat that was running in my eyes when Fay Patterson drove by. He was president of the Wild Rose State Bank and was driving a Buick car. He was kicking up a lot of dust that blew my way and I thought, "I wish I could be a bank president and drive a Buick car."

"Well, Mr. President, when are you going to get a Buick?"

Now that George no longer needed me to help in business, there was time to devote to civic problems. Small towns in general were in trouble. The migration away from rural areas was leaving little communities to become deserted villages. That must not happen to Wild Rose!

Mama often called me visionary, and it is not likely that the terminology was intended as a compliment. If visionary means the ability to dream dreams and to BELIEVE that all we dream can be realized, then it was a visionary who invited leading citizens and members of the Village Board to our home one evening in 1956 to discuss civic problems. "If you have faith as a grain of mustard seed, nothing is impossible."

First we enumerated the village assets, the beauty of its natural resources, its little valley surrounded by the rolling hills of central Wisconsin, Pine River flowing through the village, a millpond along Main Street, eleven wooded clear-water lakes within a radius of seven miles of town. Unlike most towns of 600, Wild Rose had a hospital, a high school, a library. But the problems were legion. We talked about them.

"Nobody can make a go of a small farm any more," someone said. "And there aren't any jobs in town either—except for the folks working in the businesses on Main Street and the twenty-five or so in the creamery and saw mill. No wonder kids leave as soon as they are through high school."

A mother in the corner of the room spoke up. "There's no recreation either. Here we are with all these lakes, and most of the children don't even know how to swim. And I'm kind of ashamed of the way the village looks. There's the park that never got finished—and the garbage on the gardens of the back yards! I agree it makes good fertilizer plowed under, but all winter it's just an invitation to rats!"

"And the library"—this from a club woman—"ought to be moved out of the village hall to a bigger place. There must be a building somewhere or even an empty house."

A member of the Village Board agreed that the village had a lot of needs. "But let's quit griping about them and do something about them."

Ideas were tossed back and forth across the room. It seemed as though they were springing up from the floorboards and bouncing off the ceiling.

"That park would be a good introduction to the village for people driving in from the North. Let's finish it! I bet the ag. class would dig up some more trees to take the place of those that were cut. And wouldn't it be nice to have a little park at the south entrance to the village, too?"

"Yes, and maybe we could have a village flower, like Holland, Michigan, does—and lots of other towns."

"There's only one flower that would be appropriate for Wild Rose and that's the rose. 'Village of Roses'—I like the sound of that."

"Guess we never realized what we have in a name. Wild Rose—nice, isn't it?"

"I agree about garbage," added a business man, "and there are a lot of buildings that could stand some paint. I bet folks would cooperate in a clean-up-paint-up-fix-up drive."

"Sure they would. And as far as recreation is concerned—and safety too—what about a Red Cross course in swimming?"

"Maybe some dads would get out there and help the little kids—and older ones too—with baseball."

"I've got an idea! We could make signs reserving fishing for children, especially where the Pine flows through the park. It would be a safe place even for the little ones."

"Good idea! And as far as jobs are concerned, maybe we could get a couple small industries to locate here. We don't want this to be a dirty industrial town, but we do need jobs."

"Something else we need is a new fire truck—one that's up-to-date. And men trained to use it. And what about an information booth? Tourists come to town and don't know where to find the lakes and streams."

"Migrants come to town too in the evening and sit on the curb. They ought to have a place they could get together—sort of a social center."

"I've got three rooms, right on Main Street, that you could have, rent free, for a migrant center."

I remarked that if we were going to accomplish all that, we would need the help of every individual and organization—*everybody*—and we would need a central organization, like a community council to coordinate the effort.

"OK," someone said, "let's meet in a week to organize one. We could send a little newsletter with the paper boys telling people what we want to do and asking them to come to the meeting."

It was agreed.

Sheets of paper were passed around with the suggestion that everybody make a list of the five greatest needs of the village, listing them in the order of their urgency. From these lists a long-range plan could be developed. We would need a few small projects to provide quick satisfaction to keep the momentum going on the large ones. Dreamers need a near view as well as far visions if today's dreams are to become tomorrow's realities.

The lists were collected. The evening was late. As the guests went out into the night they were still exchanging ideas enthusiastically. It was music! It was poetry! The tiny mustard seed was taking root!

The local Woman's Club had just entered the Community Achievement Contest which was sponsored by the General Federation of Woman's Club's and the Sears Roebuck Foundation, the latter providing funds for prizes. It could capitalize on the enthusiasm generated that night.

The next week, as planned, a Community Council was organized. Its function and strength can be visualized by thinking of a wheel, the hub the Community Council, each spoke a local organization, all of them reaching out to every phase of small town life. The Council would be the coordinator. No longer would individual organizations work alone and, too often, ineffectually. Each organization would have a representative on the Council, carrying ideas and suggestions from the Council to the organization and from the organization to the Council. Thus we would move forward together.

I had taken to the meeting a large chart on which were listed the projects that evolved from last week's lists of needs. Those present wrote their names on the chart under the projects that most appealed to them. Committees were thus born.

In our eagerness to climb mountains, whether world-dominating ones or little ones like planting petunias in front of the Post Office (or should I have said "mustard seeds"?), the first step is usually to appoint a committee. Someone has said that if Moses had worked with a committee, the Israelites would never have crossed the Dead Sea.

But these committees were not *appointed*. Members *CHOSE* to work on them, and therein lies the difference.

The committee, the symbol of the republic, does need to agree on objectives, though, or it might find itself in the position of a truck driver who was struggling with a big box on the back of his truck. A friendly passerby offered to help, and the two men puffed and grunted to no avail. "I'm afraid it's no use," panted the passerby. "We'll never get it off! "OFF," yelled the truck driver. "I want to get it ON, not OFF!"

"It's important that a committee know where it is going before it starts," I commented, and there was a chorus of, "We do! We do!"

The Woman's Club Community Achievement Committee and the Community Council worked hand in hand. With everyone working on projects in which he was particularly interested, work progressed rapidly.

The effect of this concerted action on the Village Board was startling. It had been a very conservative group of men because it felt that was what the citizens wanted; but when it began to receive delegations from the various projects, it realized that what the people really wanted was progress. It gave every project its unqualified support.

I went with a fellow clubwoman one day to see the Village President about one of the projects.

He met us at the door and said, "When I see you two coming, I know I have to either roll up my sleeves or put my hand in my pocket." The Wild Rose story is that of a whole community that rolled up its sleeves and put its hand in its pocket.

With new vision and determination, with $300 from the Highway Commission for the lost trees and $200 from a private citizen, with two bake sales and volunteer labor, the park was completed.

The Lions Club put its hand in its pocket for $300 and rolled up its sleeves to build an information booth to publicize the beautiful natural resources of lakes and streams, to help strangers find their way around the resort area and give them help concerning rental and for sale properties. It was part of a three-pronged attack on economic decay through industrial development, soil conservation and tourist attraction.

The information booth was staffed by volunteers nine hours a day, seven days a week, at no cost to the taxpayers. The first summer the booth was operated without information while the Community Council made a survey, cottage to cottage, resort to resort. A five-by-seven foot map of the resort area was drawn and hung on the wall of the booth. Smaller replicas were printed on brochures.

The Lions Club, after several money-making ventures ranging from selling brooms to playing donkey baseball, bought and installed street signs.

Women volunteers with scrub brushes and paint brushes converted the three empty rooms into a brightly clean migrant social center. They made colorful cafe curtains and sent out a plea through the churches for furniture, toys, books, magazines, a sewing machine and a piano. Friends of the project were generous. By midsummer, 1956, the social center for Spanish Americans was opened with a street dance for which the migrants themselves provided an orchestra in the back of a truck, and local businessmen supplied money for refreshments.

That morning, when I went to the center to arrange the refreshment table, three migrant men were sleeping, each on a davenport, and a mother was washing the children's hair with cold water from the tap. Instead of screaming at the cold water, as our children would have done, the little people were smiling. When I went back later, the mother was sweeping the walk in front of the center, and the men, who had driven all the way from Texas without rest, were still sleeping.

Rummage sales at the center provided funds for its operation and inexpensive clothing for the migrants.

When we had a problem we asked help from people who knew the answers. We asked the Wisconsin University Extension for help in a series of classes on community development. Specialists in that field came to conduct meetings in the dining room of the old hotel.

Two young women from Newfoundland, studying for a doctorate in community development, came from Madison for weekends and meetings of our Community Council to gather material for their theses. The community received them with open arms. It was "bread cast on the water," for we had more help from them than we could possibly give.

Instead of planning to rehabilitate delinquents, Wild Rose used the "ounce of prevention." Mr. William Goranson of the State Department of Public Welfare, Department of Children and Youth, was invited to come to study the resources of the Village and to meet with the recreation committee of the Community Council. As a result, a questionnaire, distributed to all the students, asked them how they would like to spend their leisure time. One by one, their wishes were granted.

The chairman of the recreation committee appeared at our door. "Come! I want you to see what the rec. committee did today!" We went to the school yard and saw a slab of concrete, seventy-two by seventy-eight feet. "See," she said, so excited she could scarcely talk. "That's the tennis court and roller skating rink. See that little ridge around the edge? That's to hold the water when we flood it in the winter for figure skating and hockey."

I hugged her. "You're a marvel!"

A skating rink was not new to Wild Rose. For eight winters we had a skating club, a large lighted rink, a warming house with a record player and loud speaker for music to skate by. Each weekend a professional skater came from Milwaukee to give lessons to the village children and to train them in routines for an ice show at the end of the season. Parents took turns supervising the rink, and we mothers spent the winters sewing costumes for the various numbers, elaborate costumes of satin, net and sequins.

One father had an ingenious way of resurfacing the rink whenever it became roughened from much use. He got a tank of hot water from the creamery which dripped on an old rug as he pulled it around the rink with a tractor.

There were throngs of children and youth on the rink after school, in the evening and all weekend, and on the day of the ice show throngs came to watch and applaud from the sloping sidelines. We parents were there, too busy to see much of the show, but applauding louder than anybody when free to watch a number.

And now there would be skating again and music and children in the crisp air doing the swan and the figure eight!

It was decided that the Fourth of July should be a fun time when all could play together, so an old-fashioned celebration was planned, complete with parade and popsickles—"homespun," as Richard Davies called it in a front-page story in the Milwaukee Journal.

Children became enthusiastic and organized an anti-litter campaign. They painted and decorated old garbage cans and distributed them around the village. The idea had come from them, and they were zealots in insisting that the streets and school grounds be kept litterless.

The best way to stimulate interest in rose-planting among adults would be through the children. Hence, slogan and poster contests were sponsored in the elementary school. Every store window up and down the street was filled with colorful posters illustrating how the children thought Wild Rose would look if everyone planted roses. The winning slogan was "Wild Rose—Say it with Roses." Of course the winners in both contests received rose bushes.

In December of 1956 and 1957, the beautification committee of the Community Council went from house to house and business to business taking orders for rose bushes.

A bit more wisdom, though, in the beginning, would have prevented needless disappointment. We should have recommended to the householders that they begin their rose growing by planting only hardy varieties, for many of them knew nothing of rose culture. But in our zeal we let them choose the prettiest roses in the catalogue, which, after the first bitter Wisconsin winter, were dead.

Undaunted, the Community Council continued the "Village of Roses" idea. They established a little park at the south entrance to the Village too. Wild Rose was on its way!

The beautified village was an added inducement to two industries which decided to locate here. (When we see other small communities trying to attract industry, feeling that the coming of an industry would solve all their problems, we could tell them from experience that if the community is first made attractive, industry will come.)

For its outstanding industrial progress, Wild Rose was given a citation by Governor Thompson at the State Fair in August of 1957. Through the State Industrial Corporation, a national agency was engaged to tell the Wild Rose story and that of other Wisconsin communities in ·all all-out effort to attract industry to the state, "not by water, power and land, but by something different in its people," according to an ad in the *Wall Street Journal* and the *U. S. News and World Report.*

To eliminate the necessity for repeated "drives" for various causes, a One Fund Drive was organized. People came from a neighboring town to help us make plans. They said, "Why don't you set the goal for $1200. That would be two dollars from every man, woman and child in the village?"

One of our own, knowing Wild Rose, said, "I think we can do better than that. Why not set the goal for $1500?" Everyone agreed.

A large chart was made with a drawing of a thermometer and placed in a store window, the red mercury rising as the drive progressed. When the 25 canvassers tallied their collections, the red color splashed out of the thermometer with a total of $2593, or $4.50 for every person in the village.

Wild Rose not only distributes funds to all the agencies that originally conducted individual campaigns, but has local funds for health clinics, children's books for the library and other youth activities.

The community safety efforts had five spearheads. (1) Red Cross course in water safety with swimming lessons and training in artificial respiration and life-saving, (2) garbage collection once a week instead of rubbish collection once a year, (3) fire protection with new fire fighting equipment, the cost of which was partially met by serving rural areas, (4) a fire siren which could be blown from the telephone office instead of the previous individual phone calls to the homes of the firemen, and two-way radios for better fire and police protection, and (5) a program of training to make these new safety measures effective.

Although involved with all of these community developments, the one that was most personally gratifying was the building of the Patterson Memorial Library. Mrs. Catherine Patterson had also been one of the founders of the first library in 1930, the makeshift library in the Village Hall. Before going to Florida to live, she had confided in me that she had provided in her will for a new library building and asked that I make sure the money was spent on the type of edifice she would be proud to have provided.

She died in 1956 and the library, which her $10,000 bequest made possible, was the fruition of the Woman's Club's 48-year-old dream.

As far as possible in building the library, local businesses were patronized and local workers employed, and those people gave of themselves in the typical Wild Rosean way, making it possible to complete the building with Mrs. Patterson's bequest and $3500 appropriated by the Village Board.

The beautiful new building deserved new furnishings, but funds were running low. Lest it be equipped with old dining tables and broken-down rockers, a box-holder letter, listing the furnishings needed, was sent to citizens and organizations; and from that one appeal, gifts poured in to the amount of $3000, to completely furnish the library with new, matching furnishings. As we proudly looked at the results we wondered at our lack of faith in hesitating to spend $9.32 for postage.

I remember the momentous day in Wild Rose when the library was moved from the all-purpose room in the Village Hall to the new library building. There was a continuous procession of Camp Fire Girls, Blue Birds and Boy Scouts, each with an armload of books from the shelves of the old library, down the street and around the corner to the shelves of the new. In the procession were two little six-year-old girls. Each had come with a sled and a carton tied on the sled to hold the books. The sleds got in the way of the older children, who finally challenged the two little girls: "You aren't Camp Fire Girls or Boy Scouts or Blue Birds. You don't have any right to help move the library." But the two little girls rose to the full stature of their six years. One said, "I can, too, carry books. My mother is a library trustee!" And the other said, "I can, too, carry books! My sister is a Blue Bird!" They stayed in the procession, making trip after trip until the last book was in its new home.

Library progress in the years since has been spectacular. Ruth Clarke, who became librarian after Mrs. Hoaglin's death, is a trained librarian and gives her all to her work. The Patterson Memorial Library is more than a library. It is a cultural center, the pride of our people and of the State Library Commission.

The spirit of early America was the spirit of the volunteers who rejuvenated their town. No one said, "Let's get a government grant" or "What's in it for me?" or "Why doesn't somebody do something?" Instead, the theme was, "When something needs doing, let's do it ourselves!" There were bake sales, flea markets, home talent shows, plays, book sales. They did it themselves!

And oh! Glorious day! Soon after Wild Rose Woman's Club submitted its scrapbook in the Community Achievement Contest, we received a phone call that our club was among the ten finalists from the 5,500 communities across the nation that had competed. National judges from the General Federation of Women's Clubs and the Sears Roebuck Foundation were on a nation-wide tour of the ten finalist communities, and they were coming to Wild Rose!

The judges spent the day in the new library looking at before-and-after slides and listening as the chairman of each committee proudly narrated its accomplishments. At one of the larger homes, the Woman's Club served a luncheon for the judges, the members and those who had given reports. There was a bus tour to show off the village, but through the rain that poured all day the guests could not see how it had been scrubbed and polished.

A delegation from Wild Rose went to the General Federation of Woman's Clubs convention in Detroit to receive the award. As we entered the auditorium on the evening the awards were to be given, we saw a row of 11 elaborately decorated hat boxes across the front of the stage, ranging in size from small ones on the ends to a large one in the center. During the ceremony each hat box was opened, beginning with the smallest one, and the story it contained of the accomplishments of a club was read to the assemblage.

As box after box was opened, and our club was not described, our excitement could hardly be contained. Finally the box was opened which held our story! We had won $5,000, first place for clubs in towns of less than 100,000 population! My feet scarcely touched the aisle as I went up to receive the award for the local Woman's Club.

We came home to a jubilant village! One of the stipulations in receiving the award was that the money must be spent for further community improvement. As the people had had the vision and performed the tasks, they were given a vote as to how the money should be used. After the tabulation was completed, the fund was divided as follows:

$600 for playground equipment for the school
$300 for a whirlpool bath for the hospital
$400 for a resuscitator for the fire department
$2000 for extended library services
$1700 for village beautification

At last, with $1700 in the beautification treasury, there could be a village rose garden! Two lots on Main Street were given for the garden, the State Park Planning board provided the landscape plans, and we were off on another adventure!

A rose-lover meets so many fascinating people! In the summer of 1958 the Milwaukee Sunday Journal carried a full-page story about Mr. and Mrs. Ervin Kulow of Waukesha, Wisconsin, and their three acres of rose gardens. Scarcely expecting a reply, I wrote Mrs. Kulow telling her of our plans to establish a village rose garden. She replied with many experienced suggestions and invited me to come to see her.

I went and it was a most valuable experience. A member of the Old Rose Committee of the American Rose Society, she suggested that, as we were starting from scratch, we had a wonderful opportunity to plant a garden in historic sequence to which the discriminating rose lover would return again and again. She set me on a fascinating quest with her suggestions of types and classes of old roses, and at the end of the afternoon, served rose hip tea, rose petal jam and home made bread.

Her jam was imported from Turkey, where rose petals and hips have, for centuries, been used for food. After some experimenting, I developed our favorite modernized recipe and have made hundreds of jars, not only for our own table, but to give to the museum gift shop.

Use only freshly opened roses, picked whole. It saves time to hold the rose firmly in the hand while pulling it from the stem and snipping off the white base of the petals. (These are apt to be bitter). It is better to use only old, hardy roses that do not need spraying, and to make jam early in the season before rose beetles appear.

After the rose petals are washed and drained, jam is made as follows:

> 3 cups prepared petals and 3 cups of sugar pressed together for overnight. Add 3 cups water. Boil five minutes. Add 2 tablespoons of lemon juice and 4-1/2 cups additional sugar. When it comes to a rolling boil, add 1/2 bottle of Certo. Boil 1 minute, pour into sterilized jars and seal with paraffin.

I have a tiny china jar of rose pot pourri, which Mama had made in her early womanhood. It still retains the fragrance so treasured through the centuries. In the top of the rose jar is a string of rose petal beads she also made. The petals were cured in an iron kettle to make them black, then beads were shaped in the palms of the hands and dried on fine knitting needles. Mama strung the black beads alternately with tiny gold beads. The fragrance is still lovely.

Mrs. Kulow told me of the House of Roses in St. Augustine, Florida, which was operated by Joan Wickham, and of Jean Gordon, her mother, who is the author of several books about historic roses, "Pageant of the Rose," "Rose Recipes," "Immortal Roses." I wrote them and received inestimable help in securing rose products for sale in the Craft Shop the Wild Rose Woman's Club had opened. When in Florida, we looked up Joan Wickham and Jean Gordon and found them warm and scintillating.

Mrs. Kulow also introduced me to Joseph Kern, a member of the old Rose Committee of the American Rose Society, whose nursery in Mentor, Ohio, specializes in old garden roses. He, too, was generous with help.

This time, after so many achievements, there were those who became "weary in well doing," but the momentum created by the enthusiastic, those indomitable few who had hurdled so many obstacles and given of themselves so unstintingly, carried the Wild Rose Garden to completion, again with volunteer labor. They prepared and seeded the lawn, laid out rose beds, planted a cedar hedge for background, built benches, installed an underground watering system, hauled manure, dug holes and patted the roots of hundreds of rosebushes in the cool earth.

For the first years, the responsibility of the rose garden rested mostly on George and me. We spent countless volunteer hours—and years—caring for it, but in 1976, not having the stamina we once had, we asked the Village Board to hire a gardener, which it agreed to do. Maybe now we can relax and enjoy our own little Eden.

A garden of historic roses would be just another garden without the story of the rose, fossils of which scientists estimate are millions of years old. Wild roses grow in every region of the world, even as far North as Alaska.

It is awe-inspiring to think of the incredible journey of so fragile a thing through the centuries, through fire, flood and earthquake, and then, aided by man, to emerge in all the glory of the hybrid tea rose.

We remember Josephine, Napoleon's Empress, whose emissaries brought to her garden at the palace of Malmaison, five miles from Paris, every known variety in the world, and of Marie Antoinette, who slept on a bed of rose petals that the villagers of Provins had gathered for her, as she stopped for the night on her way to marry the dauphin, who became Louis XIV of France. Undoubtedly her rose-scented dreams that night were oblivious to the dark cloud that hung over her pretty head.

A casual visitor to the garden would enjoy knowing it was the Damask rose that provided Saladin with 511 camel loads of rose water with which to purify the Mosque of Omar in 1187, when he recovered it from the Christians.

One variety of old rose which Josephine grew at Malmaison is the Bourbon. She gave one to the Grand Duke of Russia, one of the distinguished people who visited there. He named it "Empress Josephine" and planted it in the Imperial Gardens at St. Petersburg, Russia.

Even though at that time the English hated the French and Napoleon and sank French ships at every opportunity, if a ship was bearing roses for Josephine, it was allowed to continue on its way.

The Empress Josephine gathered about her at Malmaison not only leading horticulturalists but also poets who wrote about roses, painters who painted them, and musicians who composed music to them. Historians agree that she made a greater impact on future generations by developing the rose than her husband, Napoleon, with all his conquests. But even he, though a warrior and conqueror, loved the roses at Malmaison. The last night, before being banished to Elba, he spent in that garden.

Further back, across the centuries, the Emperor Nero was famous not only for fiddling while Rome burned, but for his lavish banquets. On one occasion, when he ordered showers of rose petals wafted down on his guests from a balcony, some of his inebriated friends were smothered.

The rose of Provins is another Centifolia which was brought to France by Thibaut, a Crusader and grandson of William the Conqueror. Though he failed to recover the Holy Grail, his Provins rose thrived until it became a source of revenue for that whole section of France, where it is still grown to produce perfume. Thibaut entertained notables of the then-known world, among them Eleanor of Aquitaine. After 15 years as Queen of France, she had just been divorced from Louis VII whose piety bored her. She was established in a chamber overlooking Thibaut's famous rose garden. When she refused to marry him, he imprisoned her in her room until she escaped one night, dressed as a servant, to the arms of Henry of Abjou, who in 1154 became England's Henry II and she his queen.

Four Seasons is a Damask rose grown in Turkey, where one-third of the world's rose oil is produced. It takes thousands of pounds of petals to make one pound of rose oil. Women pick the flowers in the early morning when they contain twice as much rose oil as those picked in the afternoon.

The colonists who came to the new world traveled with only their choicest possessions, but many a family carried a rose cutting in a sailing ship across the Atlantic and by prairie schooner across the continent.

Sitigera, the prairie rose, is a native of North America. Its hips are the chief food of prairie chickens. Pioneers whose wagon broke down on the Oregon Trail were saved from starvation by finding and eating rose hips until another group of pioneers rescued them. During World War I, when oranges were not available, rose hips were gathered in the wild areas of the British Isles to supplement the diet of the Allies. A handful of rose hips contains more Vitamin C than twenty oranges.

In our zeal for the Garden of Roses we made many mistakes. For instance, one winter we forgot to put mouse poison under the protective covering of marsh hay. It wasn't really funny, but when the hay was removed in the spring, we could only laugh at the frenzied scurrying of dozens of mice—as they, perhaps, laughed at us and our dismay at the dead rose bushes. "The best laid schemes o' mice an' men gang aft a-gley."

Life in Wild Rose is no proverbial garden of ease. The Wild

Rose Garden, lovely as it is, requires daily tender care. On seeing how easily roses are grown in warmer areas of the world, I sometimes wonder why we try.

When a problem is solved it is a struggle to keep it solved. And new problems continually arise. It saddens us to see the empty buildings along Main Street and the empty spaces in the park where spruce trees were bulldozed out with the coming of the sewer system. In a year of drought the migrants watched cucumber fields parch in the sun. With no income they became resentful, and the furnishings in the social center disappeared one by one until, with heavy hearts, we had to close the center.

After the first great drive, which culminated in winning the $5000 award, we had thought we could coast for a while, dust off the lawn furniture and sip iced tea, but we couldn't. The more we did for our village the more we realized needed to be done. We keep trying to make this the kind of community we would like to move to if we could, but I doubt if we would like Shangri-La if we could find it, for half the fun of living is the challenge of a task that needs doing and the satisfaction of a task accomplished.

Maurice Maeterlinck said years ago, "The real goodness of living is with the journey itself, with the striving and the desire to keep going. I find now that I can look back on eighty-four years with pleasure, and what is more important to me, that I can still look to the future with hope and desire. I have learned to take each inn along the way with a traveler's stride—not as a stopping point, but as a starting point for some new and better endeavor."

Lost River

In the eons, dim eons,
Since you sprang from your mountain
Answering the call
To return to the sea
How many spirits were quicked by your beauty,
How many eyelids lulled by your song,
Oh, far away river of spring?

        Laugh
Your liquid laughter,
        Dance
Your swirling dances,
        Fling
Your diamonds to the sun
Oh far away river
Oh, star sprinkled river
Oh, lovely lost river
Of spring.

Back to the Beginning

IX

Our first flight was thirty years after that momentous day when we teenagers had sat in a tiny plane in a field. George and I soared from Brownsville, Texas, to Mexico City on a small twin-engine propeller plane. The air was bright with warmth and sunshine. We climbed aboard throbbing with excited expectation while others who boarded had the placid faces of those who had flown not once, but often. Could we ever become so accustomed to flight as to be emotionally unmoved?

Passengers settled in their seats, some read the morning paper, others chatted with seatmates and a few looked out the window passively—nothing more interesting to do.

George and I couldn't absorb enough—passengers, people at the gate, airport activity, details of the interior of the plane. Then, suddenly, the whole craft began to shudder, shake and roar for takeoff. The noise was deafening! It seemed as though the craft would disintegrate! My hands interlocked with George's until the knuckles were white. The plane began crawling down the runaway, then faster and faster, louder and louder until the thrust of the wind lifted it off the ground and it sliced the air upward. As the roar subsided and vibration lessened, we dared look out the window.

We were flying low, just over mountain peaks, unspoiled valleys and ribboned streams. We had begun to experience man's long dream of getting above the world and looking down on it—the magnified version of the sensation I had experienced as a child from the top of my secret tree.

On the way home, when we touched down at Tempalo, Mexico, the destination of two passengers, visibility was zero. Thick, white impenetrable fog closed in around the plane and shut us off from the world. There was anxiety; how, we wondered, could the pilot set the plane down on a runaway he could not see, nor lift it off again in the right direction with no landmarks? We learned that the pilot was "flying on the beam." We realized, too, as we broke through the fog and into the sunlight, that above the fog, the ground clutter, the tempests, the wars, the convulsions of earth, always above, the sun is ever shining.

The trip that meant the most to me came in 1956, a few years after Mira's visit. I told George I would like to go West to find my sisters. I had been thinking of it for a long time, but it had seemed impossible. How could we leave the store and the children? The trip itself was a bit frightening. How would we go? What would we find?

George understood my desire to look up my family. "Maybe, early in the spring, before the tourist season, we could go. It would be quicker to go by train than to drive. Sylvia could stay with Grandma and I'll ask Walter if Bob can stay at the farm while we're gone and help with chores before and after school."

The plans complete, the exciting day came, and George and I boarded the train in Wild Rose—destination: Portland, Oregon. Train travel was still luxurious. We had a tiny roomette with miniature lavatory. Though the roomette was a sitting room by day and a bedroom at night, we spent most of our waking hours in one of the dome cars experiencing the grandeur of our native land, the diversity of its landscape, the productivity of its plains, the gold of its deserts, the brooding grandeur of its snowcapped peaks.

The elegance of meals in the dining car! Tables with white cloths and fresh flowers were arranged in front of wide windows! Black waiters in starched white jackets served formally and graciously.

Mira's home looked beautiful as a cousin drove us up the driveway; red brick set in green lawn resplendent with flowers. I wondered if our mother had had flowers in her dooryard, too.

Mira had invited Elva and Martha whom I hadn't seen since I was three—fifty-one years! The four remaining sisters of a family of ten, together again!

Elva had my coloring. Though I was much taller, she still called me "Little Sister." In spite of all she had gone through, she had retained her sense of humor. Care-worn wrinkles criss-crossed her face; her hair was gray and straight, her mouth soft, her eyes sparkling.

Martha was tall and had beautiful brown eyes and dark hair with only a sprinkle of gray. She was gentle, placid, deeply spiritual. I felt that she had accepted life's joys and sorrows in comparative serenity, while Elva had taken life in her own two hands and battled it to victory.

As Elva was working, as always, she had to leave the next morning, but the rest of us drove out to the faded country church in whose burying ground our parents had been interred so long ago. The deserted church, its boarded, sightless windows, the mossed markers, whose legend could scarcely be read, the earth that had received, alike, their bodies and their tears, were lonely reminders of the brevity of their lives and our debt to them for the bounties of America's verdant fields and the gift of life itself. Shoulder to shoulder in death as in life, their spirits were mingling in another time, another where, another Eden.

Springtime birds were singing everywhere. The majestic peak of Mt. Hood was dimly white against the far blue sky, wrapped in the silence and loneliness of the ages, timelessly looking down on their graves as it had on their lives. "The wind blows where it wills, and you hear the sound of it, but you do not know whence it comes or whither it goes."

The soothing warmth of the eternal sun warmed our backs as we leaned forward to read the inscriptions. Grandpa and Grandma Lyon, too, were buried there, those intrepid pioneers whose questing spirit had led them to their promised land. How different Washington must have looked to them when they first saw it in 1881, than it did to us that day—wide fertile fields stretching out across the valley to the foothills beyond, paved roads leading past comfortable farm houses and prosperous farms and orchards to the cities of the West. How indebted we Americans are to them and those other thousands who paved the way for us! If we do not fully appreciate the past, we cannot fully appreciate the present nor recognize our influence on people yet unborn.

We left the cemetery to drive a few miles to the house our parents had built after thirty years in a three-room log cabin. I had been visualizing it for years, sometimes like this:

At last here was the river,
The turbulent, glistening river,
That tumbled out of the mountains
And swirled in foam as it passed.
And here was the weathered bridge,
The arching, mossed green bridge,
Always so dimly remembered,
Oh, here was the bridge at last!

I sensed the fragrance of lilacs,
The pensive pungence of lilacs,
E'er breathlessly climbing the bridge
Their lavender billows I saw,
Lilacs massed in the dooryard,
Lilacs flooding the dooryard—
Who was there now to deny
That possession's nine-tenths of the law?

But when I looked at the house,
Sagging, lonely and gray,
It floated in sudden mist
I could not brush away.

When we reached there, it wasn't like that at all. The house looked loved and cared for, its upright and twin wings freshly painted white, the wide lawns neatly clipped. A pleasant woman answered the knock at the front door. When I told her I had been born there, she invited us to look around the yard and to come in to see the old home. It had been changed very little, she said, since it was built.

I was inspired by the beauty of the landscape, the blue hills on the far horizon, and Cedar Creek, the tumbling mountain stream that, sparkling and glistening in the sunlight, flowed across the back yard. The arched bridge was gone, where Lepha and Veda, two little girls just older than I, had been swept away in a flash flood. The tears our parents must have shed! And flowers were there—wild flowers painting the hillside and splashing their color across the meadow. I had known there would be flowers.

Entering the house our parents had built and occupied so briefly, we wandered from room to room, comfortable, convenient rooms, neat and shining, but not familiar to me. As we entered the little bedroom off the kitchen, Martha said to me, "This is the room where you were born. Pioneering was hard on women—on men, too. It took both our parents." She paused, hesitated, then went on. "And this is where, three years later, our mother got up in the night, as you slept beside her, and ended her life."

At forty-four she had been too old, I told myself, too broken in body and spirit to bear her tenth daughter! I asked myself, "Did giving life to me cause the sacrifice of her own?" My heart prayed, "Oh, God, make me worthy!"

Here in the parlor had been the black box and the tears my infant mind had hazily stored. Here, ten months later, the minister had stood at our father's casket, trying to comfort a family and three dry-eyed orphan girls whose tears had all been shed.

Tomorrow's Yesterdays

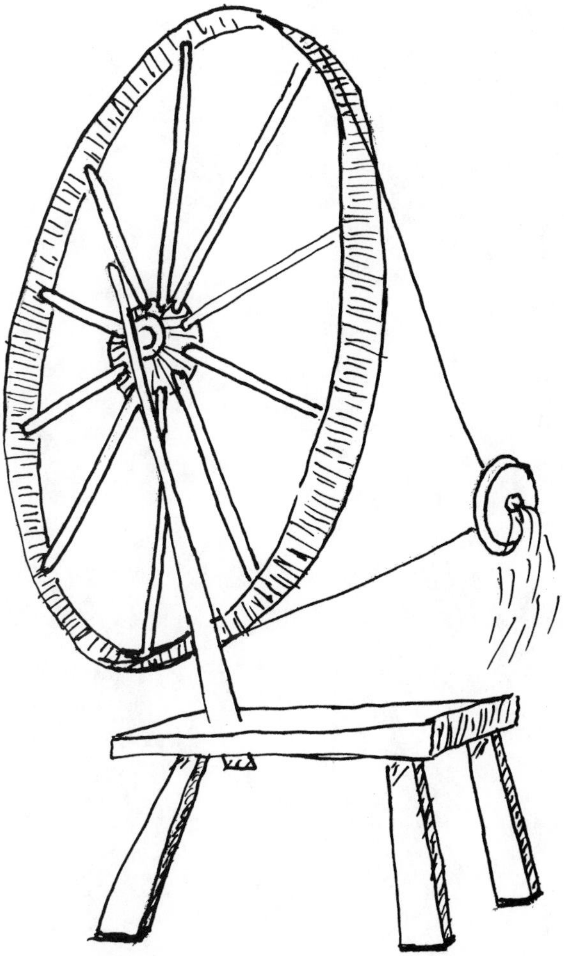

X

In our little town there were many who lived alone and lonely. Mama, a widow for over thirty years, was one of them. In spite of our daily calls and visits, she was often lonely when she was home in the summer. With her and other lonely people in mind, I organized a Senior Citizen Club in 1957, but unfortunately Mama did not live to attend the first meeting.

She had become frail but clung to her independence, always insisting that she keep her own home, which had two stories and a basement—all of which she continued to use. Though we tried to anticipate her needs and desires, she did many things she was not physically able to do.

We decided to build a one-story house for her, a little house without a step to climb. She was happy with the idea, but dreaded parting with the stacked-up "treasures" in her storeroom. Though she no longer drove a car, the solution was to build an attached garage, so she wouldn't have to give up a single feather or ribbon.

George said, "Let's make the shelving out there of orange crates. I've been saving them in the store, you know."

"Yes, I know. George, when did we ever throw anything away?"

"Well, we always find use for it, don't we? I'll never forget that cute dressing table you made out of two crates when we were first married."

"Yes, the skirt was percale. And the doll house from orange crates? That was fun! We papered the inside and painted the outside, and I made little curtains and braided rugs. Guess I had more pleasure from it than Sylvia."

George brought us back to the present. "I think there are enough crates to build shelving down both sides of the garage and a double section down the middle. They should be about shoulder high, don't you think?"

Finally, as the household keepsakes were moved and her perennials transplanted, Mama was transplanted too.

She enjoyed her little house for four years, devoting every hour to some interesting activity, writing letters, braiding a rug, crocheting an afghan.

When she was 89 she had to be hospitalized, the first time she had ever been a hospital patient. She seemed in a coma, lying there so still day after day. The only words she spoke were drawn from long ago, she was teaching again in a one-room school.

"Twinkle twinkle little star,
How I wonder what you are
Up above the world so high . . ."

The hospital was kind to let me bring a chaise lounge from our yard to her room to make the night's long vigil more comfortable as her life ebbed away.

Sylvia came home to see her grandmother. She leaned over the hospital bed and said, "I love you, Grandma." And Mama responded, "I love you, too." That was all.

I grieved that I hadn't tried to penetrate the unconscious during those long still days and nights—to tell her, "I'm here, Mama," and to say one more time, "I love you! Thank you for your gifts to me." But the words I wanted to speak will now never be spoken. I was there, Mama, but you didn't know.

Among Mama's keepsakes were all the letters we had exchanged during the years I was away at school and teaching, neither of us dreaming that they would someday be resource material for a book.

She had also kept "The Annual Calendar and Perspectus" from Evansville Seminary of 1887-8, which she had attended. I quote in part.

"Evansville is 116 miles from Chicago, on the Madison Division of the C and NWR'y. Eight trains pass through daily. Evansville is strictly a temperance town: no license having been granted either for liquor or billiard saloon. The school discipline is such as to develop the power of self government. The importance of strict morality, the value of unswerving integrity, the necessity of courteous conduct toward all, are elements that enter into a thorough education, and these are constantly inculcated both by precept and example.

"Deference to the authority of superiors and to the wishes of equals; neatness, quietness and industry, are insisted upon, as essential characteristics of the scholarly lady and gentleman.

"Board $2.50 per week, payable one-half term in advance, tuition $4.00 a term."

There were three terms a year—fall, winter and spring.

Also among her treasures was a letter written by a young man, a fellow student, June 19, 1887.

"Dear Friend: You will please pardon me for taking this means of asking you something that I ought to have spoken about before you left Evansville.

"I meant to have asked you if I could have the pleasure of corresponding with you, but neglected to do so. Why I can hardly tell. So I take this means of expressing my desire to continue an acquaintance so favorably begun.

"I hope and think that if you give me a favorable reply our correspondence will be both agreeable and profitable to both of us.

"It was quite lonesome here last week but does not seem so much so now. Last week I worked for Prof. That kept me from feeling as lonesome as I otherwise would have felt.

"I meant to write you only a short note, but I see that it is quite lengthy already, and I am not through yet. If you answer this soon (and I expect some kind of an answer) your letter will find me in Evansville. Hoping you will consider my request favorable, I am, truly your friend."

Mama had also kept account books listing all of her expenditures. (I had been required to do that, too, while in college.) In her records for the date August 27, 1905 in Portland, Oregon, was a list of the clothing they had bought for me:

"white dress	1.25
blue gingham dress	.48
lawn for dress	.24
pink gingham for dress	.30
hose supporters	.15
4 pr. stockings	.60
shoes	1.20
mittens	.10"

In the storeroom, among innumerable boxes, was one marked, "Pearl's little clothes." The two smallest dresses she did not make. They were the ones bought in Portland when I was three. All the others were the products of long hours of sewing by an oil lamp after the day's work was done.

I lifted them out, one by one, remembering. The white lawn dress, which I wore as flower girl at Ethel Smart's marriage to Fred Shepherd was a trifle yellow, perhaps, but otherwise showed no sign of its age. I wished Mrs. Shepherd's life could have remained as happy as it was on the day when the little white dress had been first worn.

The marriage had not been successful, and Mrs. Shepherd returned to Wild Rose to rear Fred, Jr., alone. She earned a little money with her hemstitching machine and Fred, as soon as he was old enough, began supporting his mother faithfully for the rest of her life. Even in her old age, "trailing clouds of glory," she would say, when I entered the room, "Here's my little flower girl! She walked down the aisle ahead of me dropping rose buds, just so, one by one!"

Mama had been adept at using two small remnants and combining them tastefully to make a dress. I lifted one of them from the box, a soft red wool plaid with black yoke, belt and covered buttons, remembering how I enjoyed wearing it to Sunday School.

And here were white drawers, petticoats and camisoles with ruffles strategically placed to hide the evidence of approaching puberty.

Here also was a little blue dress that faded. With patient frugality she had unmade it, pulling out the stitching, thread by thread, letting out the tucks and wide hem for lengthening legs, sponging the creases and pressing them with a hot iron, tested for hotness with a wet finger, then sewing the dress together again, seam by seam, inside out.

One of the ways to record the events of history is through the eyes of those who experienced it. These remembrances of establishing the Pioneer Museum in Wild Rose are, of necessity, the events as I saw them and experienced them. Those who worked on other aspects of the project would record the developments as seen through their eyes.

The Senior Citizens project continued and brought pleasure to countless older people, who had trips to historical sites and museums, picnics, parties and programs. How they enjoyed the companionship!

Often someone would say, "I wonder what we could do to benefit the village." "There must be something," someone else would say. "I want to *do* something useful, not just sit and get old!"

They spoke of this thing and that until someone had an idea that pleased them all. "I know something we could do better than anybody. We could tell stories of when we were young and stories our folks told us about their pioneering days. We're the only ones could do it. We're the only ones as lived it."

"I could write about all the schools and churches," came an offer. "My mother had a scrapbook that would tell some things. And I could ask around for what other folks know."

Others chose to write about pioneer families, businesses, historic events, doctors and dentists, how people lived, memories of childhood. Each story, when completed, was typed in duplicate and placed in notebooks with the other reports.

As several of the members did not care to write history, they were tape-recorded. Not knowing the technique of recording local history, we invited William Scherek of the State Historical Society to come to instruct us. The only tape recorder available was kept in the high school office on the second floor of the old building and, as the Senior Citizens found it difficult to climb the stairs, I carried the tape recorder to them (was it heavy!) and spent many hours drawing out their memories.

At the death of Mrs. Lyman Anderson, a lifelong friend of Mama's, her two daughters stayed at our home while they made arrangements for the funeral and burial in Wild Rose. They wanted to give something to the library or history club in memory of their mother.

"Could you use a tape recorder to be kept in the library and used for recording local history?"

"Could we use it!"

The days of carrying a recorder up and down the school stairs were over! Now a priceless collection of recordings is available in the library archives in the voices of scores of people who can no longer tell their story, but whose stories live after them.

We go to the library to hear the late-in-life voices of Uncle Alanson's sons, Jesse and Milford. Jesse was for many years agricultural agent of Oconto County. He said the food of the pioneers consisted of wild berries, turnips, pumpkins, fish, game, wild rice and greens made of dandelions, milkweed, horse radish leaves, pig weed and nettles.

He remembered clearly Grandpa's two-wheeled ox cart which hauled crops from the field and carried the family to meeting. He said. "The box was eight feet long and had to be loaded heavier in front, resting on the oxen's shoulders so it wouldn't tip over backward. Those wheels were five feet high—pulled easier that way—and the tongue was just a long wooden pole."

Milford asked him, "Do you remember that old ox sled, too? It had ten foot poles for runners—no irons at all. Pulled fairly easy in a straight line, but was awkward to turn."

"Couldn't forget that. Of course both the cart and sleigh were handmade with whatever materials were available."

Jesse recalled with emotion a teacher he had in country school. I did the recording and saw his flooded eyes. "She *insisted* that I study for college entrance exams, simply made me do it. And with her help I did and was admitted to the University of Wisconsin. I walked the ninety miles to Madison, earned all the money for my education and give Marie Jones the credit for my full life."

He changed the subject hastily. "Say, Milford, I haven't thought of Harrison and Horton for years. Grandpa always dropped the H's, so he called them 'Arrison and 'Orton." Turning to me, "They were neighbors east and west of Grandpa's farm. For some unknown reason those two old Englishmen hated each other. One carried a revolver wrapped in rags and the other a butcher knife in the end of his cane. Each said he was going to kill the other if he ever got a chance."

I remembered, "Grandpa said he and the neighbors tried to get them to forget their grievances, but neither would go to the home of the other. Finally they shook hands over a fence."

Milford chuckled, "They didn't carry their implements any more, but they never stopped hating each other."

"And there was Binan," Jesse said. "He raised rye and hauled it to Weyauwega to be made into liquor for his own consumption. At testimony meeting at church he would get up and exhort the congregation."

"Yes, he exhorted all right, but he'd slip outdoors every little while to get another swig of rye."

In our family, "Binan's piece" indicated the portion of a pie which was left after enough pieces had been cut to serve each person.

When the pie was passed around the table, Binan, always took the uncut piece that Grandma was saving for another meal."

"Say," Milford said, "There was that old fellow, Mr. Woods. Haven't thought of him for a long time. He used to help Grandpa. One time the ox cart tipped over on him and broke some bones. Grandpa had to walk all the way to Wautoma to get a doctor. Walking was faster than those oxen. It was several hours before the doctor got there to set the bones, and the men had to hold Mr. Woods down 'cause there was no anesthetic. Mrs. Woods couldn't stand it to hear her husband's screams, so she ran out into the field."

Uncle Alanson, the father of Jesse and Milford, had become a mechanic, and after the advent of the automobile, operated a garage. I wish there had been a tape recorder when I spent hours visiting with him in his old age, listening to his tales of childhood and youth. Though we can never hear his taped voice, many of his stories, as I remember them, are incorporated in this book. He seemed to hold no rancor against his father and the strict disciplines of his family, but the vow he made then never to darken the door of a church again was never broken.

Among the tape recordings in the library are those of two brothers, John and Lewis Protheroe, ages 85 and 90, who were involved in law enforcement. John had been village marshal in 1905 when the Post Office and bank were robbed.

Each night," he said, "I had to go to see that the saloons were locked up at eleven o'clock. That night when I got home two men was at my back door talkin' to my wife. They said they was potato diggers and wanted a place to spend the night. That sounded all right, because a lot of potato diggers come to Wild Rose by train in the fall. My wife told them we didn't have room for them, but I said they could sleep in the barn if that would be good enough. They thought that would be OK. That suited them just fine. All they was lookin' for was to keep track of me. You see, they wanted to know where I was.

"About three o'clock in the morning there was a knock at the door. A fella come to tell me the Post Office and bank was bein' robbed, two robbers in each place. The two in the bank had blowed the outside door to the vault and had glycerine to blow the inside door, when they was scared off by a noise outside. The two in the Post Office got their money, and the four of them lit out on foot."

He paused, trying to recall. "There's a lot to it. I remember it all right, but to say it out is hard.

"I. R. Nash and I started to track them. Nash was editor of the *Wild Rose Times,* you know. We knew they went over the bridge, and sure enough, we found their tracks. Each of us had a lantern, and we tracked them as far as the Kaminski school and there the tracks turned and went off across a field toward Idlewild. We followed their tracks all the way to the Hannawalt school, and then we lost them in the grass. We didn't know which way to go and I got to thinkin' we was just two against four and they probably had guns. We better go back to town and get some help—get up a posse. That come to my mind right away, a posse.

"We got a whole bunch of men. I got my rig. They had rigs, too, and those that didn't got rigs from the livery stable, and we went back to Hannawalt school. We hunted all day. It was gettin' toward sundown, and they thought it was no use, they might as well go home, but I said 'There's one more place I'd like to look and if some of you will volunteer to stay we'll surround the woods over there. I'd like some fellows that is good shots.' "

He named some of the men who stayed. "I put the men on each side of the woods, and I went down the middle. There, all of a sudden, I spotted four strangers and I yelled, 'Halt!' They swung around and started shootin'. I got a bead on Old Rambler and knocked his hat off. They ducked into a clump of brush and I lost them for a while, but finally drove them toward the corner where the best shots was. Old Hamlin took a bead on me, put his arm around a saplin' tree. I didn't have nothin' in my gun. I was helpless."

"But he didn't get you."

"No. Somebody got him first. Didn't kill him, just wounded him enough so he was in misery. One robber, Patsy it was, was killed and the other three captured. On the way back to Wild Rose one of them asked me 'How did you find us?' and I said, 'We tracked you.' 'This darn sand is worse than snow,' he said, 'This darn sand is worse than snow.'

"We took them to the hotel to get some supper and then to Wautoma to jail—all but Rambler. He was hurt too bad to be moved."

"Where did you keep him?" we wanted to know.

"In Dick Sage's place. Dick was the undertaker and made coffins—even made his own. Charlie Darling kept a gun on Rambler all night."

Patsy was buried at Oak Hill cemetery in the paupers' field. No one knew who placed a marker at his grave. The other three went to Leavenworth Prison, where Rambler killed himself.

At a special meeting of the Village Board on October 18, 1905, the following bills were allowed:

Dr. Fisher, for professional services on Hanlon, Oct. 6	$ 5.00
Jones and Pierce, casket	20.00
Rough box	3.00
Service	10.00
Drayage of box to cemetery	.50
Livery to take body to the grave	1.00
Digging grave	3.00
Dr. Fuller professional services on Thomas Hanlon, Oct. 7	5.00
Dr. Wilcox, dressing head of Rambler, Oct. 7 and 8	11.00
G. L. Sage for use of room, attendants and bedding	3.00
W. H. Faville, 7 meals for prisoners, Oct. 7, 1905	1.77

George and II did an interview with Lewis Prothereo, John's brother, then 90. He was still a powerful man with strong voice and keen memory. When his daughter-in-law told him to tell what he did for fun as a boy, his booming laugh bounced around the room, "No—No—Turn that thing off if you're going to ask me that!"

When the merriment was over, he told about the piles of freight that arrived at the depot each day when he operated the dray. "Everything arrived by freight then, everything. There were great piles of it on both sides of the depot. There were four passenger trains a day then, and sometimes I had to wait until 1 o'clock in the morning to take the mail to the Post Office. I asked the railroad for a windbreak for the horses—standing out there in the winter was hard on them—but never got it."

For several years he owned and operated the livery barn, sometimes "hiring out" all of his thirty horses at three dollars a day. Salesmen came by train and had a wagon load of trunks to take to Saxeville and Pine River. Sometimes they were gone three days. Some salesmen drove for themselves, but if a driver went along, he got 75¢ a day.

He laughed as he remembered a team of runaways. "Usually I didn't let anybody else drive them. They even took me over the dash board once and dragged me along the ground. Funny I wasn't killed, but I never let go, never let them get away. One day when a couple of men wanted a team, the runaways were the only ones left in the barn. I warned those guys they might have trouble, but they started out anyway. Sure enough, they had a runaway, smashed the buggy all to pieces. They got a milk wagon somewhere and the same thing happened. They paid for the buggy. Probably six or seven dollars was all it was worth."

Again he was consumed with laughter. "A woman beat me out of a horse once. She drove into the livery barn with the prettiest little animal you ever saw. She said, 'I wonder if you would trade horses with me. I'm a little afraid of this one. She's pretty skittish. If her harness catches on some brush along the road, she jumps something awful. (Brush came right up to the wagon tracks then.) Have you got a quieter horse you would trade me?' I told her I had a good steady horse I'd trade. "Do you want me to hitch him up so you can try him out?' She said she wished she could, so I drove with her and she liked the horse. She asked how I wanted to trade and said she thought her horse was younger than mine. I said, 'No, I think mine is the best horse. I've got to have ten dollars." I'd have traded even, but she gave me five dollars.

"The next morning when I went to the barn, that little mare had the heaves something terrible. Well, I could stop the heaves as good as anybody, so when some horse traders came in, I got rid of her. Yes sir! A woman beat me at horse trading!"

George asked, "What businesses were in the village then?"

"Oh, there was a blacksmith shop, a meat market, livery stable, jeweler, dress maker, milliner—harness shop, undertaker—"Wild Rose Times," an attorney, some stores and saloons—a druggist, a dentist—oh, there were lots of businesses here then."

We tape recorded the experiences he had when he was sheriff during prohibition and spent most of his time hunting for and confiscating moonshine stills.

George asked, "What did they make the moonshine of?"

"Oh, flies, swill—really! At one place there was a barrel of mash in the pig pen. You could smell it! The farmer said it was swill and poured a pail full in the pig trough. The pigs wouldn't touch it!"

"Did you find much whiskey all ready to sell?"

"Oh yes, and they hid it in the funniest places. One day I saw a row of three corn cobs sticking up in the snow and dug down around them. There were three five-gallon jugs of moon with corn cob corks."

Armed with a search warrant, he approached another suspect's house and saw "the old lady" and three girls through the window. When he knocked on the door, one of the girls opened it a crack and told him not to come in because her mother was "bad sick." Though unwanted, he entered and saw a bed pushed against a closed door, and on the bed "the old lady" with quilts up to her neck. As he suspected, behind the closed door was a cubbyhole containing mash. When he was taking care of that, the girls disappeared.

Before leaving, he decided to look in the cellar for the "moon." The door was locked. He could hear the girls whispering beyond. Instead of "bustin' the door in" he hunted up the moonshiner and made him unlock it. It was dark in the cellar, so he told him to get a lantern. The moonshiner reached for his gun. After a fight, the sheriff was free to search the cellar, and found the whiskey buried in a bin of potatoes.

Years later, I went to the nursing home to record Mrs. Brown, who had been born near Plainfield and had returned there after the death of her minister husband. She was generous with her memories.

Down the hall someone was playing "Abide With Me" on the piano, and several quavering voices were singing. Mrs. Brown commented, "The Methodists gave us that piano. It just goes 'plinkety, plinkety, plink,' but they like it! We can't take away from them something they like, can we? It goes 'plinkety plink,' but they don't know anything about music, and they like it!"

Although her home in Plainfield had been sold to defray nursing home expenses, she would say to me, "That big outside door is heavy, isn't it? Do you suppose I could get through it? If I could just get outdoors, I'm sure somebody would take me home. All I'd have to do when I got there would be unlock the door, and I'd be home!"

After several taping sessions she remarked to a nurse, after I had gone, "How could anyone so young be so intelligent?" When I need a lift, I remember Mrs. Brown and erase from my mind that she could scarcely see, could scarcely hear and was 101 years old.

People are so generous! A native daughter in the University Extension service gave us the money she received at her retirement party to buy cassette players and tapes for further recordings of senior citizens. How much more convenient to use, is the new cassette player than the heavy old recorder from the school office!

One senior citizen had a hearing problem and was too frail to attend the meetings of the History Club and help establish the museum. Instead she spent years making a card index of all the people who ever lived in the Wild Rose area. She wrote hundreds of letters in her search for historical and family data. The result of her labor is an irreplaceable file in the Patterson Memorial Library. She also researched and wrote a book narrating the history of the Jeffers family.

The Senior Citizens collected and identified old photographs and brought copies of the long-deceased *Wild Rose Times,* whose pages were so brittle they could scarcely be handled. We wrote to a manufacturer of custom note books, a native son, to ask if he could make newspaper-sized notebooks in which each sheet of the old papers could be enclosed in a plastic envelope. Eventually we received ten such notebooks, for which he would accept no pay, saying they were memorials to his parents. The club filed the old newspapers in chronological order, where they can be read at the library without being damaged.

Several of the older people did not like the name Senior Citizens. (It was before there was a federally sponsored program by that name), so the name was changed to Wild Rose History Club. Nearly all the members of that club are now deceased, but their work lives after them.

There was always the realization that written and recorded history was not enough, that some attempt must be made to preserve the artifacts that had played their role in building the community. As older people died, their possessions were scattered, and auction after auction robbed local posterity of the tools of pioneers. The people who bought them were strangers—dealers who cared nothing for the community these artifacts had helped to establish.

As Grandma and Grandpa Etheridge and Mama and Papa never threw anything away, our home contained many primitive tools, pieces of equipment and furniture which they had accumulated through the century. I often said to myself, "Wild Rose should have a museum where these things and the artifacts of other families could be preserved and enjoyed," but one day when I said it to George he shook his finger at me and said, with his usual kindness but without the usual twinkle in his eyes, "*You* are not going to start a museum!"

Charles Bridgeman, in his late eighties, still lived on the family farm between Wild Rose and Wautoma, where he had been born. He had never married, had been County Superintendent of Schools and spent the rest of his life collecting antiques for the county museum he hoped someday would be built, and saving materials for the book he would someday write.

Several times I went to his home, visited with him and asked if I could tape record some of his memories of the county. His answer was, "No, not until I get my book written. If you tape my stories the State Historical Society might get hold of them and publish them first."

Though his knowledge of county history was inexhaustible, there was no likelihood that his book would ever be written, so on a Sunday afternoon I took the recorder with me and tried again. After promising that the State Historical Society would never be given the recording, I was invited in.

The room was piled from floor to ceiling with old newspapers, scrapbooks of clippings, interspersed with antiques he had collected for the someday county museum, leaving a diagonal path through the center of the room. We sat on the only two empty chairs and visited through the long afternoon. The result is a priceless record of county history.

Mr. Bridgeman died a few months later, his book unwritten and his dream of a museum unfulfilled. He left no will. Members of the county historical society identified and salvaged a few artifacts that they were sure belonged to the organization, but the rest of his lifetime effort was sold at auction, scattered to the four winds. He would have wept.

That settled it! Wild Rose was going to have a museum!

In 1963 the Wild Rose Historical Society was organized and affiliated with the State Historical Society. Several charter members gave from $100 to $500 to start the museum fund. I went to the High School files to get the names and addresses of all graduates and sent letters to them explaining the aims of the new organization and requesting memorial funds. The alumni were generous.

There were several old houses for sale. Not knowing which would best lend itself to the development of a museum, we wrote Raymond Sivesind of the State Historical Society, who came and decided that the Keppler property on Main Street would be the best. It consisted of a house of the 1880 period, a little barn and a business building which was originally a cobbler and harness shop. In fact, the breadwinners of each of the three families who had owned the property had all been cobblers.

Elisha Stewart, the first cobbler, who had built the home in 1884, was Justice of the Peace. A ledger was discovered in which he had written the account of the local altercations over which he had presided in that house. Of the many people who brought their disputes to him, two came repeatedly: Dr. Abbot, the local doctor (who was also a dentist) and a patient for whom he had made dentures. Dr. Abbot wanted his pay. The patient refused to pay until he was sure the dentures were satisfactory. Finally the case was settled and Dr. Abbot received his ten dollars.

Jane Stewart, Elisha's wife, helped plat the village. She wore color on her cheeks, which was a daring thing to do, and sang in the Methodist choir—according to tradition, usually off-key.

Until the Stewarts could afford to build the little shop in the back yard, he did his cobbling in the room that would later be the parlor.

Mr. Glover, the second cobbler, who lived there, outgrew the little back yard shop, converted it into a barn for his team and buggy and built a larger building for his harness-making and shoe-making business.

Mr. Keppler, the last cobbler, converted the little back yard shop into a garage for his automobile. The record of a century of change in one little building!

The Keppler descendents were enthusiastic about their old home being used as a museum and offered it to us for $6500. We estimated that it would take $10,000 to buy the property and renovate it for a museum. That was a lot of money! We went to the Village Board to explain our purpose and ask for a grant to acquire the property.

There were those on the Village Board who thought the buildings should be torn down and the land converted to a parking lot. After we suggested they could have parking space around the perimeter of the back yard, the Village decided to buy the property and lease it to us for a nominal sum until we could purchase it. At last the way was clear! We were off on another adventure. I giggled to myself remembering Mama's oft-repeated comment, "The only reason you get all these jobs is that nobody else is so foolish." Well, Mama, here we go again.

With money we had raised, we began repairing the old buildings, a never-ending process. After we advertised for artifacts, they began to pour in—on loan, of course, because few thought a museum could be successful in so small a town.

One day George was helping a woman carry in dishes that had belonged to her mother. Somehow, he dropped a plate and stood there aghast looking at the shattered pieces on the floor. Bless her heart, she laughed and teased him repeatedly about breaking her mother's dishes.

Jennie, hobbling around with arthritis, said, "Trouble is, we don't get interested in antiques until we are too old to do anything about it." But she did something about it, and for ten years operated the little gift shop which helped support our efforts.

The Elisha Stewart House, named for the first cobbler, was restored and furnished first. Everything that was not needed there was taken to the harness shop—farm implements, carpenter's tools, spinning and weaving equipment, dishes, costumes and on and on. What a hodge-podge! It was a herculean and frustrating task, trying to arrange these heterogeneous materials in presentable and interesting displays until the out-buildings were ready to receive them for permanent exhibits.

Ready or not, the Pioneer Museum was open to the public on the evening of July 18, 1964, with a candlelight tour for the Village Board and local citizens. Beginning that evening and continuing ever since, the tours have been personalized by trained volunteer guides. In fact, all the work of developing and operating the museum has been done by volunteers. One of the most difficult disciplines in writing this story was to eliminate the names of those who gave of themselves, their labor, their resources, their heirlooms. It would take volumes to list them all, and that is not what books are made of. As all could not be mentioned, none must be—those hordes of volunteers who were an inspiration as they worked together at a common task.

I accepted the responsibility of developing the grounds, the out-buildings and the old harness and cobbler shop. There was lots of help. Interested people cleaned, polished, scrubbed, lugged, planted, restored and hauled. It was an exhausting experience for all of us, but an exhilarating one, too, working together on such an interesting and worthwhile project. One volunteer said, "After all we have gone through together, it's a wonder we are all on speaking terms."

The old harness shop was used as a second hand store, when the village bought the property for the local historical society, and the back yard was strewn with everything from tin cans to broken bed springs. Two truck loads of rubbish and brush were hauled away from the back yard.

Puny little rose bushes were struggling to survive in the sod where the parking lot would be—roses Jane Stewart had planted when the house was built, undoubtedly the descendants of slips she had brought when she came from York State. Volunteers dug the roses and reestablished them in a hedge around the perimeter of the back yard. She would be pleased if she knew that her roses bloom again.

There was a brick smoke house, ten feet square, behind Kimball's Store in Pine River, about ten miles from Wild Rose, where custom smoking had been done for the early settlers. It was of late years unused, a beautiful brick building with little portholes under the eaves through which smoke could escape. It looked like something from Williamsburg. The inside was black and pungent from a century of smoldering fires. In the beams were handmade hooks and nails from which the hams, bacon and sausages had been suspended. Every time we drove by I said, "We just have to have that for the museum."

Sid Lewis, whom I had met in several community development meetings elsewhere, was a landscape architect working for the state. He came to advise the best way to develop the grounds. I told him of my dream of adding that little smoke house and a blacksmith shop, and he incorporated them in his plan, connecting them with curved walks, hopefully of old red brick.

We contacted the owner of the smoke house, who agreed to give it to the museum if we could move it. There lay the problem. Professional movers said, "That can't be moved. The soft, handmade brick would disintegrate." The sidewalk superintendents and most of the Historical Society agreed with them.

One day, when telling a friend of the difficulty of getting the smoke house moved, she said, "I think my father could do it. Why don't you ask him?"

So I went to Waupaca to find Mr. Bonikowske. An old gentleman opened the door. I introduced myself and told him the purpose of the visit. Though eighty years old, he still had a twinkling smile and the old-fashioned farmer belief that whatever needed to be done could be accomplished. He was a bit hesitant about moving the smoke house but finally said, "I guess I could do it."

In a few days he went to Pine River with tools and a flatbed wagon. After reinforcing the little building inside and out, he excavated under it, jacked it up and hauled it on his wagon to the museum grounds with a tractor. The smoke house was too heavy for the wagon, which broke down when it reached the museum, but the treasured old building was unharmed. Every time I open the smokehouse door and smell that pungent goodness, I think of Mr. Bonikowske and say a mental thank you to a resourceful gentleman, long since gone.

The desire to build a blacksmith shop in the back yard of the museum in memory of Grandpa became a reality. With help from the Historical Society and our own funds, George and I found a mason and a carpenter who built a stone lean-to on the end of the barn for a blacksmith shop.

A friend from those long ago days at Ripon College often came from Chevy Chase, Maryland, to visit her mother who still lived on the family farm near Coloma. On one of many trips to Coloma to get the things they offered for the museum, I asked, "Do you know of anyone in this area who has equipment to furnish the museum blacksmith shop?"

"There's a couple who have a blacksmith shop, still intact, on their farm near Coloma Corners. Maybe they would be interested."

I went there, introduced myself and told them about the museum. They were dear, gracious people whom I visited often, always coming away with things they were glad to give. She said, again and again, "It's a real satisfaction to us to have the equipment in our old blacksmith shop go to a museum. We have wondered and wondered what would become of it. It hasn't been used for many years."

"And you can't guess how grateful we are! Think of all the people who will see a blacksmith shop for the first time and realize how important it was in the pioneer settlement."

"There's just one request. We've decided we'd like to have it called 'The Coloma Corner blacksmith shop.' "

"It will be. You can depend on it. And as soon as it is all finished, I'm coming over and take you to see it. You come to our house to lunch and then we'll tour the museum."

Unfortunately, neither lived to see the completed project.

In 1960 the old Kimball Store, a general store in Pine River, was discontinued, and we bought the fixtures at auction, old counters, shelving and showcases which had been used there for over 100 years.

I went one day with the proprietor of the Wild Rose drug-variety store to his back room to look for something—old wallpaper, as I recall—and there, under packing boxes, cartons and stored supplies, was the original apothecary chest which had been used in Smart's Store, the first large general store in the village!

"Oh! Oh! Oh! What are you going to do with this? Would you sell it to the museum? Look! Some of the old powders and crystals that the druggist used are still in these little drawers!" I turned around to look at him and saw a prescription counter—oak with ornate superstructure. What a find! "Would you sell this too?"

He was amused at my excitement but said, "I don't know that I want to sell them, but you can move them over there and use them."

What a task it was to move those two heavy pieces from the back room of the drug store to the museum! It was accomplished by volunteers, as always—those unsung people who developed the museum from inception to completion.

With patent medicines from three old drug stores, a realistic apothecary shop developed. It is amusing to read the labels on the patent medicine bottles. "For diseases of the stomach, liver and kidneys" or "A cure for consumption." Was there anything that camphor was not good for? The Indians said, "No smart, no cure," the proof of which was to rub some on the forehead for a headache and accidentally get some in the eye.

We were given a large handmade loom, which was assembled in the old cobbler's shop, now a spinning and weaving room. The loom was put together with pegs, not only because handmade nails were expensive, but because the one-room cabins in which such looms were used were too small to accommodate a loom for longer than the weaving season. With pegs removed, the wooden frame was tied in bundles and stored under the bed or in the loft until weaving time again. With the addition of spinning wheels, yarn winders and implements, raw wool and flax and woven coverlets, the whole textile-making process is demonstrated in tours of the museum.

As the property we were developing had always been the home of a cobbler, we must somehow find cobbler's tools and equipment! We made several trips to surrounding towns to try to locate materials used by the early cobblers. It was a discouraging search, ending in nothing.

One day a stranger who was visiting the museum asked me, "Could you use a cobbler's bench?"

"A cobbler's bench! Could we use it! We have been looking for one for years!"

"Well, the last cobbler in Poy Sippi just died and nobody knows what to do with his things."

"My husband and I will come over this very night."

George and I were delighted with what we found, a quaint bench with a round leather indentation where the cobbler had sat, tools, shoe lasts and drawers of supplies. It was just what we had been looking for! It fitted nicely in the corner of the room that had been used as a cobbler shop for so long. Above it we hung the shoe lasts that Grandpa had carved and used for making shoes for his children before there was any other means of getting shoes.

As you may have guessed, George became enthusiastic about the museum and spent countless hours working there, hauling, lugging repairing, gardening.

With the buildings in place, renovated and furnished, we concentrated on developing the grounds. A solid board fence with a picket top was built to encircle the back yard, forming a background for the hedge of old roses and closing off the parking area and the twentieth century.

We agreed that the paths from building to building should be built of old brick, preferably red, but where to find brick? Wherever we went during the years the museum was being developed, we scanned farm dooryards, hoping somewhere there might be a pile of used brick. Then someone said, "The old jail in Waupaca has been torn down. They're building a new one. Guess the bricks are in the city dump."

Volunteers with a truck drove to Waupaca and dug bricks out of the other rubble in the dump, but as no effort had been made to preserve them, there were not enough whole bricks to do the job.

To the misfortune of the owner, but to our good fortune, the bricks fell away from the wall of a store building in Plainfield. George and a crew of boys found enough bricks in the dump there to complete the paths. Three sixth grade boys, members of Junior Historians, and I laid the curved brick walks in a checkerboard pattern. The boys worked diligently, spurred on by praise and an occasional Coke or ice cream bar, and were as proud as I when it was finished.

One of the members, in his eighties and with a malfunctioning heart, assumed the task of planting gardens in the yard. How hard he worked and how happy he was at the beauty he and God created! In his enthusiasm for the project and his happiness in it, he ignored his frail heart. Too soon it stopped beating.

At last the long-range plans were brought to fruition, bit by bit, piece by piece, like parts of a jigsaw puzzle. It was a lifetime satisfaction to the volunteers. As I look around the museum, remembering what it was like when we started, I can't believe what I see. I just can't believe it!

To cap its satisfaction, the Wild Rose Historical Society was awarded the Reuben Gold Thwaites trophy from the State Historical Society for its outstanding museum.

In addition to the museum and the materials on local history in the library, there were other efforts to develop pride in ethnic background and appreciation for the pioneers who had settled in the wilderness of Waushara County.

The first of a series of Heritage Nights was presented in the gymnasium in 1969. The Woman's Club sponsored it and invited the public to a program representative of the three nationalities that had settled the area in about 1850, the Welsh with Welsh singing, the Norwegians with a game, ringen gaar, played by descendants of Norwegian pioneers in native costume, and the English with a one-act play, "They Came Singing," which I had written about the pioneer days of Grandpa and Grandma Etheridge.

Another Heritage Night, sponsored by the Woman's Club, presented costumed Norwegian dancers from Stoughton High School, and still another featured a folk dancing group from the University at Stevens Point, with Polish and Russian traditional dances.

Each summer the Horeb Church hosts a gymanfa ganu to which persons of Welsh descent come from all over the state to sing their loved Welsh hymns. There is an afternoon songfest, a church supper and an evening song fest with everyone in the congregation singing. Two organs accompany, a new electronic organ and the large reed organ from the Caersalem church. Thus the ethnic heritage lives on into the twentieth century.

In 1973, as part of the Wild Rose Centennial, my three-act play, "Glory Hallelujah," was presented to the public. It was the story of Grandpa Etheridge and his family in 1873, a sequel to "They Came Singing." For the nation's bicentennial I wrote another play, "Edna," about life during the years of the Civil War. Profits from the production and sale of each play were used for civic improvement.

As we step into the village's second century, we hope that the local history we have made available will continue to instill appreciation for our great American heritage. Although we "see through a glass darkly" as we look to the future, we are sure of one thing. The artifacts of the courageous pioneers who came to the wilderness so long ago are now preserved. Children of the future will glimpse in the Pioneer Museum a way of life that they could, in no other way, visualize or appreciate. As the pioneer ancestors made history for us, we are preserving history for the generations to come.

Snow Blindness

Drifting snow whitens the air,
Frosts marshes, glitters the hills,
Winter branches filigree
Inks black lace across the sky,
Twigs sparkle, vapors rise
To dance the river in fairy ballet.
But we'll retreat to our heated lair
And hibernate till the first of May.

Woman

XI

Leo Tolstoy said, "When I have one foot in the grave, I shall tell the truth about women. I shall tell it, pull the lid over me and say, 'Do what you like now.' "

I don't want to wait that long to tell the truth about women. One truth is that they have come a long way since the beginning of the twentieth century. With the "woman's lib movement" sometimes one wonders if they are going forward or backward, but they are on the march.

It seems only a few years ago when women had no voice in a man's world, no labor-saving devices in her home, no way to keep in touch with the world beyond the horizon, no vote, little education. While her sisters in the city worked in sweat shops, farm women were spinning, weaving, knitting, making from flax in the field and from the wool on the sheep's back all the clothing for her family, and from the garden, field and barn, gleaming the raw materials for nearly all the food her family consumed. Her work was never done for there was not time between daybreak and bedtime to do all that was required of her. Divorce was out of the question. She had to stay with her husband. Where else could she go? What else could she do? Her husband needed her as much as she needed him. There was no alternative.

It was in the early 1800's that Women's Clubs began springing up in isolated villages across the country. Men were nearly unanimous in their belief that no organization of women could last long or be of any significance. But the women, who belonged to those scattered groups were not about to give them up. They found the windows of their minds open to a wide new world. Through studying together they became aware of the world's problems and opportunities. They began to appreciate art, music, literature and the cultural development of the ages.

They really studied. I still have the "Mentor" magazines and the "Bay View" magazines that Mama, who was a charter member of the Wild Rose Woman's Club, used in those early days of the Wisconsin Federation. As these women worked and studied together they began to see the needs of their own communities and the world beyond the horizon and realized that by improving themselves and uniting their efforts, they could build a better world for their children to inhabit. Instead of fading away, the Woman's Club movement spread until now eleven million women in fifty-three countries belong.

The public image of club women has not always been flattering. They have been described as "Dumpy little gossips in fantastic hats," "Corset-girded do-gooders," "Ample dowagers with time hanging heavy on their dimpled hands, who carry more weight physically than intellectually." But despite that, the Womans Club movement has grown and grown, banding women together for everything that is worthwhile—the largest and most influential organization of women the world has ever known, The General Federation of Women's Clubs.

The Female Benevolent Society of Beaumont, S. C., was organized in 1814 and is still functioning. The Ladies Society of Detroit was organized in 1816.

Jacksonville, Illinois, was already an educational center, even though it was just emerging from the frontier. It had the Illinois College for Men and the Jacksonville Female Academy. There the Ladies Association for Educating Females began raising funds for the education of women as teachers. Though the name was changed to the Ladies Education Society, the purpose remained the same and resulted in the education of thousands of young women at a time when few women were educated. Yet this club began as many others did, yielding to the custom which dictated that no "lady" should take part in any public meeting. Therefore, the early officers of the club were men chosen from the community.

It is hard to realize now that there was a time when women's skirts swept the ground. Everyone walked more then. That was the way to get there! But streets were unpaved and there were no sidewalks. Skirts dragged through mud and tobacco juice and took the filthy conglomeration into the homes to spread dirt, disease and infection. The "Rainy Day Club" of New York City was organized for the sole purpose of raising the hemline four inches, even if the ankles did show! Any woman who had dared do it alone would have been considered a hussy, but several women, doing it simultaneously, started a trend.

There was also an Elderberry Club to bring together widows over 65 years of age.

The story of the General Federation of Women's Clubs is that of innumerable individual women who have given themselves to it. In 1859 Constance Owen Fontleroy, who had spent years abroad, returned to the United States and found the little frontier community in Indiana stifling. She brought together the young women of the community for reading and literary pursuits and named the club Minerva because Minerva was the Goddess of Wisdom. Miss Fontleroy gave the club a five-room house, which had been built in 1815, as a club house. It has been preserved with all the original furnishings and all the club records and was purchased by the Indiana Federation of Women's Clubs as a national shrine.

Jane Cunningham Croly was a newspaper woman whose pen name was Jenny June. When Charles Dickens was on a reading tour of the United States, and was to be the speaker at a meeting of the New York Press Club, she was refused admission. Furious, she decided to organize a group of women who could band together in friendship and be free of male domination. The Club, which was named Sorosis ("an aggregation, a sweet flavor of many fruits") flourished and, twenty-one years later, invited every known Woman's Club to send a delegate to a convention at Madison Square Theatre, New York. There the General Federation of Women's Clubs was born.

During the construction of the Panama Canal, the morale of the workers was low, due in part to the unhappiness of the workers' wives. There was class distinction between the clerical ladies, the army ladies and the steam shovel ladies. William Howard Taft, Secretary of War, sent a New York woman, Miss Helen Boswell, to the Canal Zone to organize a Woman's Club in each of the six largest towns. This she did and brought them together to form the Canal Zone Federation. On getting to know each other, the women found they had a lot in common, were far from home and needed each other, raising the morale of both wives and husbands.

Carrie Chapman Catt went to the Philippines in 1921, when she learned that no group was working there for women's suffrage. She organized a Woman's Club, the first of 826 clubs in the Islands. Together they fought for and won suffrage for women. During World War II, Philippine club women helped to feed, clothe and protect American citizens and service men in Japanese prisons. The Federation president, Mrs. Josefa Escoda, and her husband were imprisoned for their efforts and presumably were executed, for they were never heard from again. The Philippine Federation Club house was burned but has been rebuilt.

Mrs. Mary Sherman and her family moved to Estes Park, Colorado, hoping to improve the health of their only child. Looking out at Long's Peak day after day she determined to spend her life saving such unspoiled beauty for generations to come. As Conservation Chairman, she enlisted the influence of the General Federation so successfully that six National Parks were established and the National Park Service.

Mary Sherman's other great interest was the improvement of home life, and through her efforts the General Federation established the Home Life Department to raise the standards of homemaking and initiated the teaching of Home Economics as part of the school curriculum. Home agents began teaching rural women the basics of homemaking. With the help of the National Demonstration for Better Homes in America, a model home was constructed on the White House lawn. One hundred thousand people visited it the first year. When it had served its purpose, the Federation gave it to the Girl Scouts of America for their permanent headquarters. It was moved to a new location in Washington, D. C., where the gift was formally received by Mrs. Herbert Hoover, the Scouts' national president.

The list of women with significant accomplishments for good is endless. Banded together, each clubwoman has a strong arm and an influential voice in national and international affairs. She is one woman made international.

One of the most effective ways to reach out to another person is to call him by name. This I am finding very difficult to do! Perhaps this lazy memory began during the fourteen years of service on the State Board of the Wisconsin Federation of Women's Clubs, crisscrossing the state to encourage women to make the most of themselves and their communities. Meeting so many people, I never expected to see again, and concentrating so earnestly on what I wanted to leave with them, there was no effort to memorize names.

I have since tried all sorts of gimmicks to remedy the situation, but to no avail, and then decided to try association. Yes, association would be the answer!

Some time ago, having to go to Ripon to give a program for the Woman's Club there, I left early to take a nostalgia trip out to South Woods. It was autumn. The air was laden with yellow leaves floating down, some of them settling on me as I sat on a fallen log. The sun poured down on red oaks and yellow maples and dappled the waves of spent leaves that covered the ground. The rivulet was scarcely discernable because of the fallen leaves that bridged it. Over all, far in the tops of the tall, tall trees, the wind whispered, like the sigh of all mankind as it drifts from here to there remembering.

One must not stay too long with yesterday lest the present slip by unobserved. With reluctance I walked back to the car and drove to the home of Mrs. Marigold, the program chairman, who had invited me to have lunch with her before going to the club. Her name, Mrs. Marigold, was firmly fixed in mind. Association, that was the answer.

On reaching home, I wrote her a note to thank her for her hospitality. Not knowing her husband's first name or initials, and thinking, "Well, in that size town, she will get it anyway," the letter was dropped in the mailbox. In a few days it came back—"Person unknown." I sighed, put it in the desk and thought, "Someday I'll learn her husband's first name and send the letter on its way."

One night of insomnia, I got up to read the area paper and there before my eyes was his name. Walter! Walter Marigold! I went to the desk, found the letter and discovered I had addressed it to Mrs. Primrose! Association is not always the answer.

Janie Reed, past president of the Wisconsin Federation of Women's Clubs, had, as a theme for her administration, a Chinese proverb which says, "Anyone can count the seeds in an apple, but not even the wisest man can count the apples in a seed."

Working with the Wisconsin Federation of Women's Clubs awakened my awareness of the contribution the General Federation of Women's Clubs had made, and how far those first "apple seeds" have spread.

We take so many things for granted! We have enjoyed life as it is for so long that we forget there was a time when there was no Pure Food Law, no Home Economics in the school, no compulsory school attendance, few libraries, no National Gallery of Art—when even in large cities there was no public water supply or sewage system. There were no national parks and no attempt to preserve the natural beauty of the country. Children worked in mines and mills and shared the same prison cells with hardened criminals. The American Indian was not a citizen of the United States. Alaska was not a state. There was no United Nations, no U. S. Children's Bureau or child labor legislation. In one instance after another, the GFWC was responsible in whole or in part for the remedying of these conditions, beginning with each woman in her own community, the action point of democracy. There Democracy is made and there it will be kept.

A phase of life about which the General Federation of Women's Clubs has been deeply concerned during the last two decades is the shift of population from rural areas to the cities. Everywhere cities were ill-equipped to cope with the influx. With overcrowding, even good neighborhoods soon deteriorated, and school, health and crime problems grew. In rural areas and villages the shift of population left a dying economy, vacant buildings and deteriorating homes.

The General Federation of Women's Clubs began urging every community to study its resources and needs and develop a long-range plan of action. There were other organizations and many of them: Chambers of Commerce, religious orders, service clubs, labor organizations, farmers co'ops, professional societies—an endless list. At no time in history have more people belonged to more organizations. Each organization is dedicated to performing a certain task, a specific civic service. This is the bulwark of democracy, for ever since the first colonists stepped ashore on this new continent, Americans have believed that they, as ordinary citizens, could with their own hands build the kind of community they wished to live in.

But other organizations concentrate their efforts on their own special interest—gardening, homemaking, farming, laboring, whatever—and are more or less oblivious to the needs of the community as a whole. The General Federation of Women's Clubs realized that if human beings are to develop better places for enriched living, they would have to study and work on the whole community, looking at it through a wide-angle lens that sees all of life from the hearthside, to the community, to the wide reaches of the whole world of which each community is a part.

Enlisting co-sponsorship from the Sears Roebuck Foundation, the Community Improvement Program was initiated, in which villages and cities around the world studied their needs and began the process of solving their problems, through the work of local volunteers. For this effort the General Federation of Women's Clubs supplied the organization and the work, and the Sears Roebuck Foundation supplied funds for the awards. Every two years a team of judges from Sears and the General Federation inspects the best of the efforts and awards substantial prizes for further community improvement. As a result, tens of thousands of communities became better human environments, and Wild Rose won a $5000 award.

When the time came to decline to serve longer on the state board of the Wisconsin Federation of Women's Clubs, it was because the years were slipping by and I wanted to spend more time with George. I missed, though, the exhilaration, the challenge, the companionship of stimulating women of vision and outreach, and the funny things, too, that happened to us. Some, I still giggle about.

One year the State convention was in a northern Wisconsin city in a hotel that had seen better days and has since been replaced. A committee meeting was scheduled for my room one morning at eight, before the general session began. When the hour approached, I unlocked the door and sat down to go over an agenda. There was a knock and I called, "Come in." No one came. I sang out again, "Come in." When there was no response, I thought, "Must be they can't hear me" and opened the door. Across the narrow hall a man was knocking on another door. He turned toward me, smiling, "I'd like to, but—" He will never again see such an astonished woman.

It is a great challenge to be a woman in the twentieth century. It is also a great privilege. Through the Divine provision of motherhood, woman cradles the human race, and as she sews little garments and sings lullabies she dreams long dreams of the kind of an adult this child shall be and of the kind of world he will inherit. Perhaps this very closeness to the essence of human life, as she develops an awareness of the needs of her children, makes her more sensitive to the needs of people everywhere.

The beauty of a woman is not in the line of her nose or the curve of her figure, as so many advertisers would have us believe, but in the depth of her love for people and the understanding of their potentialities, the breadth of her vision and the tenderness of her compassion. Perhaps her influence reaches only a few people, but they in turn reach others, and they others. Like the pulses that are set in motion when a pebble is dropped in the sea, her influence reaches out and out into the infinite. It is almost a frightening responsibility, when we stop to think of it.

The saddest thing in the world is that so many human beings live so far below the level of their potentialities. It is easy for individuals to be so preoccupied with trivialities or consumed by petty annoyances that they cannot see the big things of life. They put personal desires above public good.

Why the present accent on youth? It is not because youth is more mature. Spiritual maturity, emotional maturity, even mental maturity, increase with the years. But too often maturity brings apathy, the deadly poison to a full life. Uselessness courts disaster. The great gift of youth is that it is concerned, alive, alert, aware! The pebble does not yet hide the mountain.

Too many people pray for mountains of adversity to be removed when they should be praying for courage to climb them.

And there are mountains to climb! The dark mountain of illiteracy, the black mountain of poverty, the long, steep mountain up which the colored masses are struggling toward freedom and equality, the vicious mountain of greed where dope distributors, beer barons and pornography peddlers are corrupting children and youth for private gain, and the dangerous mountain of moral laxity.

There is the insidious mountain of casual acceptance of infidelity. A college friend and her husband stopped to visit us this summer on their way home from a trip. He remarked that on the previous night, when they stopped at a prestigious motel, the desk clerk asked him if he wanted the room for the whole night.

Arnold Toynbee, the great historian, expresses the opinion that of the twenty-two great civilizations of the world, nineteen collapsed when they reached the moral condition in which the United States is now.

Perhaps the most difficult mountain to climb is a very personal one. We saw the symbol of that struggle in Frogner Park in Oslo, Norway, where on a 56-foot shaft of marble, the great sculptor, Vigeland, chiseled 121 human figures, each figure struggling upward toward a better life. Since the dim beginnings of time, man has been reaching upward and upward toward greater nobility of spirit, and in his search, woman has led the way. Somehow made of more sensitive clay, she has held the lamp for her husband and children.

But the late Peter Marshall, revered chaplain of the U. S. Senate, said that with the coming of the twentieth century, woman has demanded equality, the right to dress like men, to act like men, to have an alcoholic breath, to hold the jobs of men, to have the vices of men. And in becoming equal, she has stepped down. He concluded, "Today they call it 'progress.' But it is not progress when purity is not so sweet. It is not progress when womanhood has lost its fragrance. Whatever it is, it is not progress!"

Now her family eats commercially prepared foods which she stores in the freezer and cooks instantly in the electronic oven. Wearing clothes from a fashionable dress shop, she has taken her place in the industrial and professional world and in the councils of government. She can live with whom she pleases, bear children or not, as she pleases. She is liberated by the technological advances which have enabled her to do her housework quickly and with little effort. She has time on her hands. She is bored, feels useless. Her wants are limitless. To satisfy these desires and to fill her empty hours she gets a job. Children, running home from school, no longer fling open the door and call, "Mother, what is there to eat? I'm starved!" Or, "Mother, Bobby hit me. See the bump?" The house is empty. The child turns on the television and sits passively and alone watching trivia or crime or sex or violence.

Through the millenia of trial and error, the family has evolved as the highest form of human relationship. Contemporary women should worry about anything that weakens or cheapens that relationship. The Woman's Liberation Movement has brought about one of greatest changes in this century of change. It should be applauded for its efforts to help women realize their own worth. One hopes it will not be at the price of moral laxity and the destruction of the family unit. Free love is not love and it is not free.

Our grandchildren are now in high school and university, soon will take their places in shaping a new world. We wrap our lives around them. Through them we shall go on into a future which we cannot see.

Bob and his family are not near enough to be with us often, but do come home for his summer vacation. Barbara and Debbie are high schoolers, and David is at the university, reaching for a degree in metalurgical engineering. He is doing it the hard way—working while going to school and supporting a wife and baby.

When I was in college, students waited until after graduation to marry. If a young man was assured of a job, he and his sweetheart might join others in the rush to the altar during commencement weekend, but usually they waited until he had money in the bank and was sure he could provide for a family. But David and his little family live in student housing, built especially for married students. They belong to the Mates Club for married students, and she to the Dames Club for wives of married students, and they are having all these memorable experiences together. Who can say which is the better way?

As they live nearby, Sylvia and her family breeze in often. One day she announced, "Mother, I'm going to Chicago and get a job."

"You have said you wanted to work, but Chicago is so far away! Chicago—"

"Yes," with finality. "Chicago!"

"But what about your family?"

"Well, this is my plan. I'll go to Chicago, get a four-day job and be home for a three-day weekend."

"Do you realize," I wanted to know, "that Chicago is five hours' driving time away?"

"Of course. But I'm young and strong. I can do it! Anyway, my family doesn't need me any more."

"Don't tell me that."

"Well, they don't! They are completely self-sufficient. They cook as well as I do. The boys and their father are gone all the time." She enumerated on her fingers. "Basketball practice, football practice, all the athletic events, hunting, fishing—." She ran out of fingers and began on the other hand. "Boy Scouting, camping, back-packing in the mountains every summer . . . No boys ever had a better father, but I'm not going to wait and vegetate! Not any longer, I'm not!"

"A casual observer would think you had everything—an indulgent husband, two great sons, a beautiful home on a lake. You are educated, are blessed with talent. Seems as though that ought to be enough, but I guess it isn't. What does your family say about this?"

"They say, 'Go ahead. Do your thing!' "

"How would you and Bob and your father have felt if I had gone away to work?"

Without hesitation she said, "We'd have hated it if you had gone away, but you worked all the time anyway. After you were through with the store you worked full time on the village. Sometimes we hated that."

"But I had to make my contribution to life where I was, in the here and now. You always wanted some other time, some other place."

"But," she protested, "I can't build libraries and rose gardens and museums. I wouldn't get any satisfaction out of that AT ALL!"

"You have a Masters Degree in art, Sylvia. Why don't you paint? You could do that at home."

"I can't paint in a vacuum! Who would want my work anyway? Everybody's painting. It's good, bad and indifferent, and there aren't many who know the difference. As far as teaching it is concerned, the market is flooded with art teachers who end up selling peanuts!"

"What will you do?"

"I don't know, but I'll find something. My life is half over, Mother! I have to get away by myself and decide what I want to do with the rest of it! Don't you understand?"

"Yes, I understand."

An anxious look crept over her face. "Will Daddy be disappointed in me?"

"He may wonder why you aren't content. He'll be concerned about you, as I will, but he'll admire your courage and he'll always love you."

I have spent my whole life making mole hills out of mountains, but this really looked like a mountain. Grandpa would have said, "Woman's Lib is an instrument of the Devil!" Mama would have said "Such works! All I could say was, "I understand. Yes, I understand."

Today

Capsule of time
In man's mind, midnight to midnight,
In God's, arc of sun across sky.
    Today
Grain of sand on beach,
One breath in a million life spans,
Microcosm in macrocosm.
    Today
Hyphen between yesterday and tomorrow,
Whole, unique, complete,
A circle.
    Yet, today
Is part of every day
That ever was
Or ever will be.
    This fragment of time,
    Today,
Like a single pearl,
On an endless strand,
I hold in the hollow
Of my hand.

Elva

XII

A few years ago, when Elva was 80 and Martha 78, George and I wrote them that their Christmas present was to be round-trip air tickets to visit us. They had never been in Wisconsin, had never left the West Coast. The days flew by as we anticipated a reply. Finally a letter from Elva assured us that she would come, but that Martha didn't want to travel so far.

On a sunny autumn day, Sylvia, her little boy and I went to Milwaukee to meet the plane on which Elva would arrive. She came down the corridor, her arms loaded with a flight bag, purse and a shopping bag of California pears. Although I towered above her, she whispered "little sister" as we embraced.

As we stepped on the escalator to go to the ground floor, she lost her balance and fell on her back, head first, across the unyielding edges of those steel steps. We couldn't get her on her feet from that awkward position! Oh, why hadn't I anticipated that she was unfamiliar with escalators! Why hadn't I supported her! Her body would be broken! A police officer below saw the confusion and ran to the foot of the escalator to flip the switch that stopped it. He ran up the steps to help. And she got up laughing! Although I am sure her back must have been severely bruised, she insisted repeatedly that she wasn't hurt, that she was "just fine, sweet pea!"

Elva stayed several weeks, fitting into the new environment as though it had always been hers, busy every minute. She helped pot dozens of daffodil bulbs to take to residents of the nursing home. Whenever she wasn't doing household chores or exploring the yard and woods, she was thirstily reading our magazines. She said repeatedly, "These are the happiest days of my life!"

Not having a home, Elva had married, at 16, a man eleven years her senior. They went into the mountains to live on a homestead he had "proved." She said, "I didn't get off that mountain for 19 years, kept pretty busy, had seven children the first nine years, seven more after that, not quite so close together, raised ten. Once I came close to dying, so close I don't know why I didn't. I had a miscarriage, and peritonitis set in. Oh, I was sick and got weaker and weaker. My husband knew something had to be done, but somebody had to stay up there with those little children. He lifted me onto a horse, propped me up so I wouldn't fall off, and I rode 16 miles down that mountain trail to the nearest doctor, a Chinese doctor. He examined me and shook his head, said it was too late. He gave me some herbs anyway and somehow I found a room for the night.

"I don't know how many days I lay on that bed. I was delirious and heard the most beautiful music, sô sweet and peaceful! I knew I was going, and I wanted to. Then, in the back of my mind, came the picture of those babies at home. They needed me. I had to go back to take care of them. Over and over I said, 'I've got to get well. I've got to get well and take care of those babies. I *will* live! I WILL! I WILL!' And I did."

"Oh, Elva, how courageous you are!"

Trying to direct the conversation to more pleasant things, I asked, "When you were a child what did you wish for most?"

Without hesitation she said, "For our father to get well. I wanted that more than anything else in the world. Next to that, I wanted to be a teacher, always dreamed of being a teacher."

"You would have made a good one."

"I don't know about that, but if WANTING to be one would have made me a good one, I would have been a dandy. But, life doesn't always bring the things we wish for most. Of course we three girls had to stay home the year our father was so sick—and then, when Edna and her family came to live with us, her husband wouldn't let me burn kerosene to study. Oh, I didn't like that man!

"When I got my work done and sat down to study, it would be his bedtime, and he would make everybody go to bed. I took the lamp up stairs with me, but if he saw a light under the door he would yell, 'Blow out that lamp!' I can hear him yet. I'd lie awake until I was sure he was asleep, then light the lamp and study. If I was going to be a teacher I had to learn all I could.

"But—it wasn't to be. When I couldn't stand it any longer I left home and hired out picking prunes or anything else I could find to do. I guess that's why I married so young, just wanted a real home again."

"How you deserved one!"

After a reflective silence she said cheerily, "We lived four and a half miles from the country school, too far for little children to walk alone, so we waited to start them until there were three to go together. The oldest was eleven and the younger two were eight and nine when they started. Then we waited to send the next three until they were big enough to walk that far.

"They always walked the railroad track because it was much shorter than around the road. I can see them yet, hopping along from one tie to the next. They had to cross quite a few high trestles, which worried me, but the train crew always looked out for them and started blowing the whistle a long ways away."

That morning she seemed to feel like talking about her experiences, and I sat back and listened.

"We were fourteen miles from a town, but had to go once in a while with a team and wagon to take our crops to market and get supplies. It was an all-day trip. I always let one of the children go with me, so each one got to town about once a year.

My husband was gone a lot. Guess he should never have been a farmer. One time he wrote me to meet him in town at the depot on a certain day. Don't know where he had been, didn't seem to like work very well, so I set out with the team and wagon, did the trading when I got to town and loaded the wagon with heavy stuff we needed on the farm. Well, when the train pulled in, he wasn't on it. I started back up the mountain toward home. Miles from anywhere the wagon tipped over on the trail."

"What did you do?" I visualized her there alone on a mountain trail.

"Oh," she said nonchalantly, as though it were all in a day's work, "I jumped on one of the horses, rode home, and in the morning came back with a long rope. Some of the things on the wagon were too heavy for me to lift into it my myself, so I tied it all on the wagon box, threw a rope over a tree limb, and the horses pulled the whole thing upright, just as easy as that," waving her hand.

She laughed, "A lot of funny things happened up there. Once, when I had gone to town, some men stopped the children on their way home from school to tell them to go straight home, that there was a mountain lion up that way. Told them to do their chores early, go in the house and lock the door and not go out after dark. That's what they did.

"Well, the children had been teasing for a dog, and in town I found a great big shaggy one that someone wanted to get rid of. It was way past dark when I got home. I thought I would surprise the children, so I crept up to the house and scratched on the door. I had heard them inside running around, but when I scratched on the door they were still—not a sound. I scratched again. Finally I opened the door a crack and pushed the big old dog in without their seeing me. You never heard such screaming and racing around in your life. I wondered why they would be scared of a big old dog. When I went in, Billy, the oldest, was crouched at the top of the stairs with an axe, while the smaller ones were hiding behind the furniture. Funniest thing I ever saw! I laughed and laughed. But the children didn't think it was funny, for they thought the big old dog was the mountain lion."

She spoke of how hard she and the children had worked keeping the farm going and food on the table and clothes on their backs. A lot of the time there wasn't much of either. If she spoke of her late husband at all, it was always with compassion, never with criticism. She said, "His father died when he was five years old." There was a wistful glow on her face. "Maybe, if he had had a father . . ."

For many years after the children were grown and gone, she had cared for elderly people. Her last patient had just died, leaving her free to come to Wisconsin. "I had taken care of that old couple for years and stayed on after the wife died. Poor old man was so feeble! He used to get terrible cramps in his legs and feet, and I would rub them. Didn't know what else to do. Felt sorry for him. One night he said, 'Did you find that twenty dollar bill?' I said, 'No, what twenty dollar bill?' He pointed to the dresser. I went over and picked it up and asked, 'What's this for?' He motioned me closer. 'It's for you to get in bed with me.' I burst out laughing, took the money, stuck my nose in the air and said, as I went out the door, 'Thanks for the twenty dollars. I'll give it to the church.' I guess men never get too old to have funny ideas."

When she had finished laughing about the incident, she said, "I have an old pickup truck. It works just fine. One day I got arrested for speeding. Now the grandkids call me their 'hot-roddin' grandma.' "

Suddenly she was serious, deep in her thoughts, the shadow of sadness on her face. Going back to her childhood, she said, "Those were awful days when our father was so sick! Oh, how I loved him! He was the kindest man I ever knew. It was such a relief to him when he got that letter from Uncle Jerry that they would take you to live with them! But, oh, when they came and took you away, I went down by the river and bawled all day. Guess I was a coward. I should have stayed there to comfort him because he must have felt worse than I did, for he knew he would never see you again. And here I am, in my little sister's house!"

Tears came to her eyes, and I went over to hold her close.

When we took her to the plane we stayed together until the last minute. Then, as she disappeared with a jaunty wave, I wiped the mist from my eyes, sensing we might not meet again.

The next year she died—that courageous, indomitable, laughing woman, to whom life had given so little and she so much!

Earthlings

Earth
Seed
Sheaf of wheat
Bread,
Earth
Cradle
Abiding place
Sepulcher.
Yet something there is
Earth cannot hold.
Mind
In tune with MIND
Travels trackless highways
To the stars,
Bears the flag of freedom
To the moon,
Shouts a whisper
To infinity,
Bursts forth as April
To joyous Thou art!

Paying the Piper

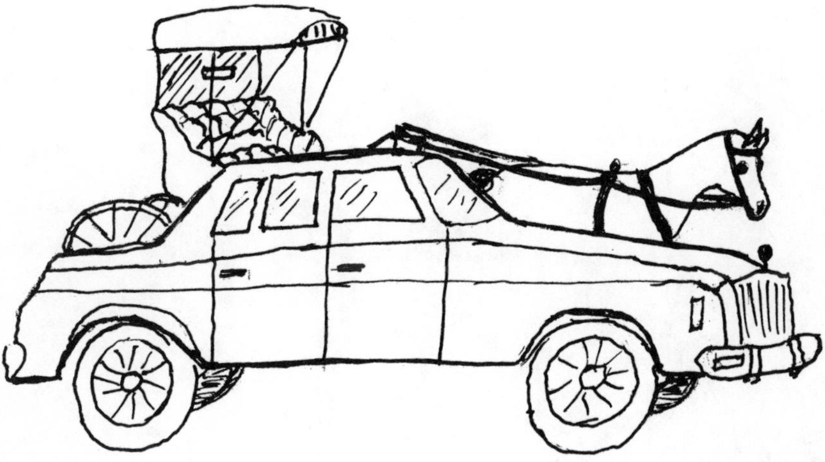

XIII

Our insidious involvement in Viet Nam began innocently in 1954 when 300 advisors were sent to assist the French in governing the little country. President Eisenhower sent 300 more. President Kennedy sent 16,000 Americans, some of them military, and President Johnson, trapped in a situation he did not know how to solve, engaged 543,000 American military men in an effort to save South Viet Nam from Communist domination. The effort was futile and cost him his political career.

The United States was in turmoil. Seething resentment in the black ghettos erupted in violence. College students across the country demonstrated and rioted to protest American involvement in Viet Nam. Many of them were attending college not because they wanted education, but because it excused them from military service. Thousands of other young men chose desertion or imprisonment rather than participation. There was an angry American outcry against a war that could not be won.

This, President Nixon inherited. Determining to end the war, even though in defeat, he brought the soldiers home, the thousands who were still whole, 304,000 who were wounded—many disabled for life—and in flag-draped coffins the 54,000 who had given their all. In addition to the human tragedy, the episode had cost the United States $150 billion, dishonor in the eyes of the world, and had left in ruins the South Viet Nam it tried to save.

Gradually the rioting and bitterness at home subsided. After decades of tinderbox situations in Russia and China, President Nixon diffused the tension.

And then came Watergate! It is impossible to imagine anything more inane! It was, and still is, the greatest human tragedy in the history of the nation. The assassinations of President Kennedy, Robert Kennedy and Martin Luther King were tragedies, but these men died in the fullness of their productive years. They were heroes. They were martyrs. Their memory is held sacred. But for the most powerful and influential man in the world to have been caught up in such a senseless involvement, to have disgraced his position and exiled himself in the self-made prison of San Clemente is tragedy indeed! And tragedy, too, for his loved ones and the men and families who had fallen with him!

And Mrs. Nixon, who had been a First Lady of grace and dignity and had radiated good will wherever in the world she traveled! Each night after going to bed, I placed her in subconscious as a little girl, took her on my lap and rocked and patted her until her sobbing ceased and she fell asleep.

Though the Watergate scandal tore the American people apart and made them cynical toward all public officials, it accomplished one good thing. Through television, Americans and the world saw the republic in action.

Television is the new master of the household. It governs the time of working, eating, entertaining, sleeping, playing. For mothers it is a dependable baby sitter, an insidious tranquilizer given to her children in order that she might receive the effect herself.

Television occupies more than one third of a pre-schooler's waking hours. Many children spend more time watching it than they spend in the classroom. It shapes their attitudes and produces a non-reading, non-participating generation of classical and Biblical illiterates.

Though much in television programming is an insult to human intelligence and degrading to the highest concepts of living, its potential is limitless for elevating the intellectual, cultural and ethical standards of the human race. There is now the possibility of a children's channel without sex, violence and offensive advertising, and of a fine arts channel for the discriminating viewer. Instead of reflecting the sordid, violent and vulgar, the time may come when it will reflect the constructive qualities of life, which, though unheralded, are the bulwark of America.

Through television, people are made simultaneously aware. They can begin to understand the miracles of the universe, from the microscopic division of cells in human reproduction to the exploration of space and the landing on the moon.

The armored tank which was being developed in England during the First World War, was a closely guarded military secret until forty seven of them in 1916 overran the trenches in France and routed the German army. By 1917 there were 400 in operation, deciding the outcome of the war.

Since then the strides in the ability to exterminate have outstripped the moral development to control it. War and its rush to human destruction is as mindless as the lemmings and their mysterious rush to the sea, but preparation for war and the development of more devastating military equipment go on and on. As nations struggle for arms superiority, there is only a balance of terror. There can be no peace when each nation fears its neighbor's intentions.

I wonder if Alfred Nobel would have invented dynamite if he could have imagined the wreckage, both material and human, that his genius would produce. The Swiss millionaire, unmarried and lonely, was influenced by Bertha von Sullner, a pacifist, who worked one week as his secretary, to do something great for mankind to compensate for the destructive effect of his invention of dynamite. He said to her, "Perhaps my high explosive factories will end war sooner than your peace movement. When two armies are able to annihilate each other, all civilized nations will recoil in horror and disband their armies." Though his rationalization proved untrue, the Nobel Peace Prize brought recognition to those throughout the world who have given themselves to the promotion of peace, literature and science.

In 1964 there was applause in our living room when the announcement was made on television's evening news that the Nobel Peace Prize had been awarded to an American black, Dr. Martin Luther King, for his non-violent crusade for civil rights.

After a courageous seamstress, Rosa Parks, refused to give up her seat in the front of a bus in Montgomery, Alabama, to a white passenger, blacks, led by Dr. King, boycotted busses for a year until the Supreme Court outlawed bus segregation.

At about the same time, Oliver Brown in Topeka, Kansas, insisted that his daughter be permitted to attend a school in which there were only white students, and, three years later, nine children in Little Rock, Arkansas, were escorted by Federal paratroppers to a white school in defiance of Governor Faubus and his National Guard. The Supreme Court outlawed school segregation.

For ten years Dr. King led non-violent marches throughout the South to call attention of the United States and the world to the need for racial equality. But the Peace Prize did not shield him from an assassin's bullet. If he had lived, the racial strife of the next few years might have been avoided.

Though progress has been painful and, in many areas, too slow, blacks have come a long way in the twentieth century, from Jim Crow isolation to Civil rights, from hopelessness to the possibility of self-fulfillment.

One would hope that before the century ends there might be an Emanicipation Proclamation for the American Indians, those forgotten people whose lands are gone, whose ancient way of life is gone and who have found in alcohol the easy release from despair.

Andrew Carnegie, an immigrant from Sweden, amassed millions in the steel industry and, in gratitude, gave millions away during his lifetime building libraries, endowing education and the arts and giving organs to churches. The Carnegie Corporation continued his philanthropies after the benefactor's death and became the model for thousands of other foundations which benefit mankind. Americans are the most generous, the most humanitarian people in the world. Each year individuals and foundations give an average of twenty-five billion dollars to improve the quality of life around the world.

Though the first successful oil well had been drilled in Titusville, Pennsylvania, in 1859 and the Eastern part of the country used oil for industrial lubricant, the rest of the country was aware of it only when the evening lamps were lit. Even in 1901, when drilling started on the Gulf coast of Texas, or in 1914 in Oklahoma, and 1920 in California, no one dreamed how oil would revolutionize American industry and way of life.

Seas of convertible power in the secret recesses of the earth would grease the wheels of commerce and industry, replace wood for heat, make the manufacture of automobiles feasible, revolutionize farming and power ships at sea and planes in the air. The uses were limitless and everyone thought the supply inexhaustible.

Extravagant use would culminate in the alarming energy shortage of the 1970's and the necessity to develop power from tides, sun and wind. Perhaps the old mill in Wild Rose and the thousands of mills across the country, around whose millpond and waterwheel small pioneer villages had clustered, may someday have to be reactivated, and perhaps windmills will again whirl and cry in the wind.

The building of the Alaskan Pipe Line was one of the costliest and most daring feats of the twentieth century. From the oil fields in Prudhoe Bay the 798 miles of pipe line to Valdez Harbor crossed three mountain ranges and 350 rivers. Fourteen thousand laborers defied the brittle cold and the fifty-six days each winter of sunless darkness. The ecologists' protests fell on deaf ears when the urgency of the fuel shortage made itself felt. Alaska's fragile permafrost environment may never be the same again.

When Teddy Roosevelt, lover of the out-of-doors, was president, he added 150 million acres to the public domain and awakened in Americans the awareness of the bounties and beauties of their country's natural resources and the necessity to conserve them for future generations.

Since then, while environmentalists struggle to save the land and its creatures, developers spread suburbia across the countryside, and highway builders, instead of widening and improving existing roads and rejuvenating the railroads, cut wide highways across millions of acres of farm land. The great interstate system, though not yet completed, attracts tourism and trucking. As small towns died when bypassed by the railroad, so small towns die when bypassed by the superhighways.

Though we hear that resources are never destroyed, only out of place, unrealized, it is hard to find them when they are buried under incalculable acres of concrete.

The advances in the techniques of health care are incomprehensible to the non-scientific mind—organ transplants, open heart surgery, pacemakers, the equipment for monitoring a patient's heart—not only in his hospital room, but simultaneously at the nurse's station and that of a cardiologist many miles away! And the development of serums which have eliminated scarlet fever, diphtheria, typhoid, smallpox, measles, tuberculosis, whooping cough and polio, the merciless crippler of children!

Five years ago George had an agonizing pain in his leg. He was rushed to a large hospital fifty miles away, his leg cold and turning dark. The doctor warned it might have to be amputated. He said,

"Immediate surgery is necessary to remove a blood clot in the groin that blocks the artery. But first I have to do a blood dye X-ray to locate the clot. It will be risky because it might cause the clot to move to a vital organ."

I pleaded, "Oh, do you have to do that, Doctor?" His reply was, "Lady, if I'm going to cut into that artery, I'm not going to guess where the clot is! I'm going to know!"

Because of the X-ray and the blood dye technique, the surgery was successful and George walks on his own two feet. Thank you, skilled staff, thank you Marie and Pierre Curie and the countless other scientists who discovered and perfected radium and the X-ray. There are new and unbelievable uses for the X-ray—the scanner, the mammograph and a camera that takes an instantly-developed motion picture X-ray of a physical function.

In the Fort Myers, Florida, area where we winter, an ambulance, fully-equipped for emergency care en route to the hospital, can be summoned instantly. During hours of heavy traffic, a helicopter, unhampered by highway congestion, descends in the dooryard. We had taken these services for granted until George's heart attack last winter shocked us into gratitude.

In a little waiting room I sat alone in the night while a cardiologist inserted through George's arm an emergency temporary pacemaker. The enveloping stillness was pierced by the cry of a siren which grew louder in the street below. There was the rumble of a cart down the hall followed by hurried footsteps. Someone else needed help. I knew their anxiety. The long minutes stretched into hours. The surgeon came to the waiting room, took my cold hands and spoke words of encouragement, then returned to the operating room with another cardiologist who had been summoned.

In trying to keep my mind busy with other things, I thought of Wild Rose and the little building, no bigger than this room, where Dr. Fisher practiced medicine with little more equipment than an examining table and a stethescope. Mama might not have been a widow for thirty-three years if the technology in use in this hospital this night had been available then. What a difference that would have made in her life and, in consequence, in ours! Now, in little Wild Rose, there is a hospital, a clinic, a nursing home and federally-sponsored migrant health center.

I thought of others who had sat in this room alone through the night, waiting, waiting as the long minutes passed, perhaps trying to summon again childhood's faith. I knew those people, their strained faces and the anxious silence that enveloped them.

It was encouraging to think of the human body and its powers of recovery. The great Life Giver had built it well. When a child cuts his finger, the mother cleanses the wound, uses a Band-Aid to keep out dirt, and in a few days the body has joined the two sides of the cut. The finger is healed. The doctor sets a broken arm, puts it in a cast, and Nature does the rest.

After a busy day sometimes the body is so weary that it cries out for rest. The moon, looking down, might think, "What a pity that Johnny is so tired! He'll never be the same again." The moon doesn't know that while Johnny sleeps, his body is rebuilding itself and will be as strong as ever in the morning.

Winter must be a great shock to a tree. When the cold winds come, it loses its leaves and looks gray and dead. But in the spring, recovery!

When winter comes to a lake, the sparkling water is congealed in ice. But spring comes, the lake begins to stir and toss; ice is hurled on the shore in great blocks. Water breaks its bonds. It has recovered! It is free!

I wondered if something like that happens when a person dies. Life has been bound in the body, and when death comes it is released. It is free! But, oh, George must not die! "Please, God, not now! At some later time, of course, but not now!"

It was 2 A. M. when George was wheeled to "Intensive Care" and I took a cab home. Later a permanent pacemaker was installed, which functions automatically when his heart does not. Life at our home is normal again.

I am forever grateful, too, to Dr. Werner Forssmann, a German scientist who pioneered the intravenous use of catheters in heart exploration and treatment. After using the new technique on cadavers, he was sure of its feasibility. As he could not bring himself to ask a living person to submit to the experimentation, he inserted a catheter in his own arm and watched through a fluoroscope as it entered his own heart. This he did on nine occasions until he was sure it was a safe medical procedure.

Two American doctors, Dickenson W. Richards, Jr., and Andre F. Cournand, continued the work and shared with Dr. Forssmann the Nobel Prize in medicine.

Oh scientists! In discovering the Great Giver's limitless bounties, you can make a body whole again!

When spending a week at the School of Arts in Rhinelander, I was fortunate to be a member of a class, "Writing the Wisconsin Story," taught by Professor Robert Gard of the University of Wisconsin, who perhaps better than anyone else knows and appreciates our heritage. It was fascinating to hear him spin yarns about the people, customs and legends associated with the ethnic growth of the state. I sat in the back row, completely absorbed. He inspired us all to add our bit to the written record. This book is the result.

The members of the class were not introduced. He used the first name of those he called on. Near the end of the week he said, "Pearl, would you come up and tell us your ideas for a book on the Wisconsin story?"

I went up, sat in the chair he had vacated facing the class, and began telling early incidents as I remembered them. A pretty little woman in the front row said, as though to herself, "My brother used to go with a girl named Pearl."

Concentrating, I went on with my story. When I finished she looked up and asked, "Was your maiden name Pierce?" I nodded and took my seat.

When the class was dismissed, she was waiting in the hall and it dawned on me who she was. I asked, "Are you Margaret?" She nodded and smiled, "After fifty years!" She had been a high school girl in Ripon when I was attending college there.

We went to a quiet place to talk. The first thing she said was, "I've always wondered. You and my brother were friends in Ripon College. Why didn't you marry him?"

I was surprised at her forthrightness, but told her several reasons—the chief one, of course, that I loved George. "There was another reason, a purely selfish one. Your father insisted that his son return home after college to operate the family general store. I didn't want to live in an isolated village and be the wife of a country storekeeper! I'd rather marry a farmer!"

Margaret was amused. "My brother was so unhappy that our father relented and let him go to medical school, which he had wanted to do all along. He was a doctor in Illinois the rest of his life."

It was my turn to be amused. "And George and I bought a country store and spent twenty-two years behind the counter!"

"Served you right!" was her response.

Anyone passing would wonder what those two white-haired women were laughing about.

We drive out to the farm often. George is interested in watching developments there, as Walter's grandsons carry on the work begun so long ago.

A truckload of eggs, bound for the city, is leaving the egg ranch, which was once a farm. Chickens no longer have free range of the farm yards. They spend their lives in large metal buildings where they are scientifically fed until their prime producing days are over and they become Sunday dinners for America.

We pass the State Fish Hatchery, established in 1907, when fishing was becoming a sport instead of a necessity. Trout and game fish are raised there to put in streams and lakes so the sportsmen will have the fun of pulling them out.

One old farm we pass is now an auto graveyard where salvageable parts are retrieved from rusting automobiles, lined up in neat rows across the fields. A fledgling evergreen hedge will someday screen them from the highway.

Other than these three businesses, there are residences along the first two miles of the road from town. There is no evidence that the land was ever cultivated. As we glide up cheese factory hill without reducing speed, I remember the dusty road and dreaded sand-traps at the foot of the hill.

Since the advent of the power mower, farm yards are green and spacious. In a field, a long arm of irrigation, fed from a deep well, sweeps in a circle around a forty-acre field, producing rainbows as it goes.

A school bus stops ahead of us, and two children get off, one carrying a transistor radio and the other a calculator, no lunch pail and few books. The little Dopp school down the road stands empty. Ragweed and brush grow where, at recess, children played.

The little Dopp Methodist Church across the road is still in use though the Wild Rose church, served by the same minister and only five miles away, could be reached easily by automobile. The little country church is the heart of the community, binding the neighborhood together in labor and love.

With the coming of combine, chopper, conveyor belt, baler and loader, the camaraderie of the harvest season is gone, and so are the small independent farmers who once comprised ninety percent of the population of the United States. Where the pioneer farmer cut one and a half acres of hay a day with a scythe, five percent of the population now feeds America and much of the world.

During the 1960's, one third of the farmers gave up and sold to farmers with larger acreage who were clamoring for more land. Little farms along the country roads of Wisconsin have deserted dooryards, bare stone foundations and clumps of lilac bushes to speak of the people who once lived there, the proud, independent, hard-working, self-sufficient people who were the foundation of America. Their horse-drawn plows, drags, cultivators, mowers, and rakes have rusted away. The few remaining wagons, buggies, sleighs and cutters are used now only in parades to bring nostalgia to the elderly and, to the young, a glimpse of a life style they never knew and can scarcely imagine.

The family farm has doubled in size since we lived there, for only farmers with large acreage can afford the machinery of the technological age. There are three little children in the big brick house now, the fifth generation on that family farm. Their future looks bright, for though land and equipment are costly, they will probably inherit agribusiness.

In this mobile generation, it is ballast to a floundering society to know there are rural families that have lived on the same piece of land, enlarging it of course to suit changing methods, even unto the fifth generation.

The cow dog no longer takes the cattle to roam the green hillsides and brings them back, night and morning, in time for milking. Cows are confined in the barnyard, where they have access to the new lounging barn and at chore time file into the milking parlor to be milked, eight at a time. The milk they produce is conveyed from the cows through glass tubing to a stainless steel refrigeration tank. Where is the milking stool of yesterday?

The feeding trought which stretches across the barnyard is automatically supplied by conveyor belt direct from the silo. Compared to the five great glazed tile Harvestore silos and the new lounging barn, the cement silo and red barn that George and Walter were so proud of look like toys.

We open the door to that old barn. The six horse stalls are gone now, the harnesses hanging forgotten, the bits and buckles rusted, the leather cracked and stiff. The old barn is a maternity ward, where cows are artificially inseminated and calves are born.

On the way home George became nostalgic. "We had an organization we called Lodge when I was a kid. The boys in the neighborhood came on winter evenings to our engine house. It was always warm in there around the stove. We wrestled and boxed and pulled sticks—"

"What's 'pulled sticks'?"

"Oh, two fellows would sit on the floor facing each other, their feet touching. They'd have a broom stick crosswise between them and pull to see which could get the other fellow off balance. And we played games and memorized crazy verses and recited them like orators."

From the days when tented circuses had side shows, George bawled out the following, which his grandchildren love to hear:

"Right this way, lad-ees and gentlemen, and see Hy Ky, the wild man, captured on the northern bound coast of Africa after thirteen years of hardship and star-va-shun. He is covered with hair two and three quarters inches in length, has two sets of lower teeth, feeds upon venomous reptiles, *bites* the heads off and *peels* the skin down as you and I would eat a ban-an-ah.

"Over here we have Lillie, the fat gal, the bay-bee won-dah. Only six years of age she weighs the enormous amount of 749 pounds, measuring *68* inches around the calf of her leg and *49* inches around her right forearm. Only costs you a dime—ten cents—"

He chuckled, "We really had fun."

"Don't stop now. Go on with your hawking Lay Hunt and the rest."

He protested, "You've heard that a hundred times."

"The one hundred and first time will be the best of all."

"Well, remember you asked for it. Over on yonder platform we have Lay Hunt, the living skeleton, the only human being that does not cast a shad—ow. Walk right up to the platform, and if you can't see him, ask him to turn around. It's FREE!

"I'm Buffalo Bill. I don't work and I never will. I was born in the shade of the Rocky Mountains, drove together with thunder and lightening, part horse, part man and the other part boa constrict—ah. I was never licked, skinned, scared or laid on my back, but I can lick, skin, scare, and lay on his back any man, wild, woolly and full of fleeeeze.

"Then there are the three won-dahs of the world, the white Alabama coon, the horned toad and the African snake. The horned toad was discovered 170 feet below the surface of the earth in solid rock by two Chinamen by the light of a little diamond. It neither eats, drinks nor sleeps, but still is in constant motion. Only cost you five half dimes, *two* dimes and a half, 25 cents or a qua-tah of a doll-ah.

"Be astonished and amazed! The greatest, most stupendous aggregation ever set before the American public!"

In a quieter vein, he quoted a verse from Whittier's "The Huskers."

> *"And all that quiet afternoon*
> *Slow sloping to the night*
> *He wove with golden shuttle*
> *A haze of yellow light."*

Last winter the Wild Rose depot burned. Arson was suspected. The slate shingles of its roof, the bricks of its chimney, part of the landscape of my childhood, lie in black rubble where for three-quarters of a century the red hub of travel and commerce stood. The coal chutes and water tower had been torn down when the diesel engine replaced the chugging, puffing steam locomotive. Passenger trains had been discontinued when Americans began their love affair with the automobile. Two freight trains a week still use the rusting rails, but even these are scheduled for extinction.

Mail, which was once sorted in the mail car, en route, comes by plane and truck and though a letter costs six and a half times as much to mail, it usually takes longer to deliver. Trucks, bearing freight the trains once carried, thunder along the highways.

Recently the fire department set fire to the last potato warehouse on potato row to make way for modern business places. We watched as the last symbol of another era burst into red flame and settled into its own ashes.

As each civic project on which I had worked through the years attracted other enthusiasts, it was a pleasure to step aside and watch other hands carry it forward. It was time, now, to withdraw from the library. Of the five founders, I was the only one living. I had been 28 years old then and am now 75, a trustee for 47 years. The library had been part of my life, but it was time I stepped aside and sat on the sidelines.

At the annual meeting I said, "I have reached the point in my life when I can no longer serve as trustee and chairman. It has been a treasured experience, but . . ." My voice broke, and I had to lower my head lest they see my drenched eyes. I couldn't believe what was happening to me! Where was my "cool"?

The trustees were cornered. They said the kind thing. "We won't accept your resignation." I was in no condition to argue. Before the next meeting, though, I'm going to sharpen my resolve, take a tranquilizer and finish the job.

One "cause" on which I spent ten years of concentrated effort did not bring about the hoped-for results. The implementation of a statewide organization, Citizens for 21, had as its sole purpose raising from 18 to 21 the legal minimum age for drinking beer in Wisconsin. Although teen-age drinking multiplies the possibility of alcoholism and is related to crime and illicit sex (as Ogden Nash quipped, "Candy is dandy, but liquor is quicker") we chose to attack the problem on the premise that it was responsible for Wisconsin's too large proportion of highway fatalities. With records from the State Department of Transportation that would be easy to prove—the "right to drink" versus the "right to live."

The need was urgent, for Wisconsin had nearly twice as many highway deaths among 18-to-21-year-olds as any of the bordering states, in all of which 21 was the legal minimum age for drinking. Wisconsin teen-agers had three times as many highway deaths as their proportion of the population. These were not impersonal statistics. These nearly 300 fatalities a year had been living, breathing young men and women with zest for life and plans for the future. All the profit from all the beer ever sold is not worth the life of one of these!

One wishes that those who think that teen drinking is an acceptable phase of growing up had gone with the ambulance to pick up one of the broken bodies, had stood by the doctor when he pronounced him dead, or had gone with the minister to notify his mother and father.

The board of directors of Citizens for 21 was comprised of the heads of state-side organizations—not only church-related groups, but the Wisconsin Congress of Parents and Teachers, the Wisconsin Federation of Womans Clubs, The Farm Bureau, District Attorneys Association, etc. It was a well-organized, influential group with backing from the Governor that flooded legislators with mail, attended hearings, publicized facts. But the Wisconsin Goliath, the beer lobby, is the most powerful force in the halls of government, invulnerable to all the slingshots that were ever directed toward it. For many years it had not lost a single piece of legislation, whether it be the hour of closing, the minimum age for drinking, staying open on election day (which only two other states permit) and on and on. While the tax on everything else has continued to rise, the tax on beer has been raised only once in forty-four years. It is a serious thing, when the policies of a State are controlled by any one industry.

The breweries employ skilled lobbyists who make it worthwhile for legislators to vote with them. When one of our Citizens for 21 lobbyists, who asked no pay for his services and had no money to spend, attended a hearing on the "21" issue, he and one of the beer lobbyists were chatting by the elevator afterward. As each legislator came to get on the elevator, the beer lobbyist gave him a prolonged hand shake, then turned to our volunteer and laughed as he opened his hand to reveal a roll of twenty-dollar bills, commenting, "You can't beat that!"

One legislator told me his political life depends on his voting with the lobby. "If I don't," he said, "the word goes out through the distributors to the taverns and across the bar to the customers that I am not cooperating, that So-and-So should be elected to take my place. When the votes were counted, I'd be out of a job."

All bills dealing with alcoholic beverages are sent automatically to either the Veterans Affairs committee or the Excise and Fees committee, whose membership is reputed to be approved by the members of the lobby. When, finally, one of our bills to raise the drinking age reached the floor, it lost by one vote. Such a bill was never released from committee again.

I nearly lost faith in the democratic process. I thought to myself, "Why not cut taxes by disbanding the legislature and letting the breweries run the state above the table instead of below it?"

When 18 became the legal age for voting, there was one more verse to the old refrain, "If they're old enough to fight, they're old enough to drink." It became, "If they're old enough to vote, they're old enough to drink." Our effort was hopeless. We folded our tents.

The Food and Drug Administration has been the watchdog of the nation's health for many years. Its work is vital to our physical well-being. However, it is wearing blindfolds in spending time and resources on red food coloring and saccharin and their miniscule danger to human life, if it does not see in the nation's ten million alcoholics the real problem substance. These ten million Americans have not only burned up their own bodies but have left a wake of broken homes, broken hearts, dependent children and highways strewn with innocent people whose lives have been snuffed out by the automobiles of intoxicated drivers.

Hospitals, homes for the indigent, prisons, orphanages, homes for the mentally handicapped are overflowing because of the misuse of alcohol. And now we have detoxification centers, rehabilitation centers, half-way houses, higher auto and health insurance, larger police forces—for the same reason. And who pays the annual fifteen billion dollar bill for alcoholism? The taxpayer. We could justify the cost of and emphasis on rehabilitation if an equal amount were spent on prevention.

Would intensive alcohol education in the schools reduce the problem? Or would a movie taken of the young inebriate and shown to him when he was sober convince him that he was not the cleverest, the wittiest, the life-of-the-party he imagined himself to be?

It is difficult enough for young men and women to grow up clean and strong in this complex society without giving them a crutch which only multiplies their problems.

There are stately homes where Ginger, the horse, once pastured. The tiny barn in the woods is no longer the home of animal friends. There, storm windows and a riding lawn mower give no joyous greeting. Our house is quieter and our lives more serene, and the river flows timelessly by.

In the village people still walk to the Post Office to pick up the morning mail and stop to visit with each other a few minutes. Some go on down the street to sit on a bench in front of the garage to watch folks go by. They know everybody's car, know where they have been and where they are probably headed. And those who are being watched don't mind because they have nothing to hide.

Most people in a small town are volunteers in the hospital, the museum, the nursing home, wherever help is needed that doesn't have to be paid for, and the volunteers feel possessive about the organizations and civic causes they work for. They say to their children, "See that red brick walk at the museum? I helped lay that when I was just a kid." When a neighbor needs a helping hand, he gets ten.

In small towns, people still take cookies to the nursing home. Peggy and Harold, Christian Scientists, were our neighbors for a while. They were always doing something for someone. The other night I dreamed about her. I was in the woods between our homes, looking for the clump of violets that always grew there, when Peggy came toward me with a large plate of cookies she was taking to the nursing home. Her phone rang and she ran back home, telling me to give the cookies to the residents. I started toward the nursing home, but stopped to eat a cookie. It tasted so good I ate another, and another and another until half of them were gone. Then Peggy and her little grandson, Kevin, came toward me and, not wanting her to see how few cookies were left, I started to run, only to stub my toe and fall, scattering cookies on the ground. Little Kevin reached me first. As I lay there groaning, he asked, "Isn't there a pill or something you could take to stop the hurting?"

"Kevin! You're a Christian Scientist!" That shock woke me.

Rural and village life is not all joy. Many tried it for a few years and left—educators who had had a compulsion to try farming or a small business, doctors who had longed for quiet and country air but left for more lucrative practices, families who lived in the parsonage for a few years and were transferred to larger fields of service, parents who wanted greater cultural opportunities for themselves and their children—the concerts, lectures and theater that the city offered.

These were our loved friends. As they moved away, one after another, there was the aching throat, the feeling of being bereft, the secret loneliness. I missed the kinship of spirit, shared ideas, stimulating conversation. A Chinese proverb admonishes people to enjoy completely all of life's gifts, but to be prepared to part with them at any moment. Enjoying friends is easy, but I have not yet reached the philosophical maturity to lose them freely.

Mama and Papa used to speak of their enjoyment of T. S. Roberts of Chicago, who boarded with them as he came and went, buying right-of-way for the coming railroad. He brought news of the outside world. He was a fresh breeze from beyond their restricted horizon. But they also said, "You have to continually make new friends or you will find yourself without any."

And new friends came. People of retirement age fled the city and settled in the Wild Rose area. They were free of the necessity to earn a living and had time to enjoy the rolling wooded hills, the lakes and streams, the clean air and quiet countryside. Free of the commitments of their productive years, they joined local volunteers in the hospital, nursing home and museum. And many who had left during their productive years came back to retire and joined the others in volunteer work.

And there were those who never left, those stable, dependable people who are the continuity upon which village life depends, whose roots are wrapped around the bedrock of their native area, who remember the struggles of their forebears to wrest the land from the wilderness and pass it on to their children.

The technology of the twentieth century has brought motorized transportation on hard-surfaced roads in cars with inside-controlled temperature and a self-starter instead of a crank. It has brought the all-electric home, freedom from household drudgery, a new knowledge of outer space and inner space, instant communication and the computer that not only reshapes business procedures but formulates political letters and speeches designed to please the majority of the voters. It has shifted warfare from the foot soldier to the bomb and guided missile with the capacity to destroy all life. It has taken the practice of medicine from the horse and buggy and the doctor's satchel to the laboratory and the hospital.

With technology came air pollution, water pollution, soil pollution and the pollution of noise and pornography. There is the social acceptance of alcohol and the acceptance, without embarrassment, of food stamps and the welfare check.

The Great Depression incubated the welfare state and the wide reaching social reforms of Social Security, Medicare, nursing homes, aid to dependent children and the labor reforms of vacation with pay, retirement insurance, unemployment insurance, health insurance, the minimum wage. Then came the black revolution, the "woman's lib" movement, the pill, planned parenthood and demands for equality for women in education, marriage, jobs and pay.

These social reforms, however much needed, must not go so far as to destroy personal incentive and make workers dependent on the ever-growing size and dominance of government, rather than on their own skills. Dinosaur bones speak of a creature who died of his own weight. we must not be deluded into thinking that bigger and faster is necessarily better.

James Thurber, in his inimitable wit said, "Man is moving too fast for a world that is round. Soon he will catch up with himself in a great rear-end collision and man will never know that what hit him from behind was man."

One hopes public officials will consider the direction in which we are going, rather than the size of the vehicle and the speed with which we get there. It is folly to believe that the more a consumer consumes the better off he will be, that the more pay he receives the happier he will be. An abundance of things often leads to poverty of spirit.

The richness of American life is dependent on one's attitude toward it, from the idealism of American youth who joined the Peace Corps, 15,000 strong in 1961, to state employees who, this year, left the aged and handicapped in their beds in a walk-out strike. One of the strikers in an interview on television said, "You gotta have dough! If you ain't got dough, you ain't nobody!"

It takes more than "dough" to make a person somebody, or to bring him happiness.

One wishes that workers found more satisfaction in their jobs. I asked a hospital porter who was wheeling a recovered patient to a waiting car, "Do you enjoy your work?" His reply was, "It's a job, that's all." That is undoubtedly the attitude of those caught in the treadmill of mass production. Somewhere along the way, pride in workmanship has deteriorated in the scramble to look for something for nothing, to turn to "big daddy" in red and white striped pants for the good things of life.

In this materialistic, impersonal society, the time may come when the human hands of the assembly line may be replaced by artificial intelligence and the automation of the computer—when the effort to produce a super race through genetic experimentation may produce robots, for real "super" persons are those who have struggled to perfect themselves and measure their success by the quality of their concern for fellow man.

There is the casual attitude toward debt. Each year tens of thousands of Americans take bankruptcy as the easy way out, seeming to ignore the fact that someone else has to pay. The United States Office of Education has lost $400 million in bad student loans.

Our country is well fed, but many are undernourished. It has the finest homes, but too often poor family relations; the biggest autos but the largest highway tragedies. Our people are the most protected, have the greatest security, but are engulfed by fears. It is a land of abundance, but there is moral poverty. It has been a long road from the darkness of poverty to the darkness of excess.

The clash between nineteenth century romanticism and twentieth century materialism goes on, as does the race between decadence and vitality. How much of the world's resources are we going to leave for future generations? Are we going to "get our share" and, in times of shortage, hoard what we want for ourselves?

Jesus defied the tradition of "eye for an eye and tooth for a tooth" and taught a new system of values that lightens the step and sparkles the eyes. "Love your enemies, turn the cheek, go another mile, give more freely, love more deeply."

Will the munition makers, the fist-and-muscle materialists, the exploiters turn art, beauty, thought and woodlands into things to be possessed and, in so doing, become themselves possessed? Or will America be led by the aspirations and dreams of a free, a gentler people for whom the greatest abundance is non-material, who feel the responsibility of a trusteeship over that which can be experienced for the short span of a lifetime but can never by possessed?

Scientists climbing the mountains of the mind, trying to discover and give to mankind the secrets of the universe, brought about the technological development of the century. But scientists are not creating. They are not inventing. They merely use the elements that have been available since the beginning of time, waiting for the mind of man to find them and make use of them. MIND waiting for minds!

With the telescope and space exploration, earthlings are trying to learn about the rest of the universe and to find man's place in its vastness. Of all the creatures on the planet Earth, only man can look to the future, can control his own destiny. As only man can defile himself, so only he can purify himself, the air he breathes, the soil he cultivates, the water he drinks and the thoughts he thinks. Only man has the intelligence to discover the laws of the Great Giver and, in using them, walk the hills and valleys of the Moon; and he only, by destroying the ecological balance, can make the earth uninhabitable and thus destroy himself.

Whether our nation, built on the principles of work, faith and service, can survive leisure, wealth and moral laxity, remains for future historians to record. Through the last seventy-five years I have seen the transformation from that culture to this, America can endure only if her people return to the basic principles of integrity, sobriety and morality. Many civilizations have perished when in this they failed. "Whatsoever a man soweth, that shall he also reap."

Fulfilled

A blizzard of leaves floats through the sun-dappled air
And with a sigh settles in brown drifts across our hill,
Color of chipmunks
That burrow among them
And scurry with heavy cheeks
Through holes in the stone wall.
Hornets dance in rhapsody
Along the sun-warmed house,
Drinking with us the last sweet drop of autumn
Before the cold.

And I wonder in the long, still years ahead
Who will love our autumn woods
And make the hearth fire glow,
Who will bed the roses warm against the wind
And plant the bulbs
For springtime's sweet awakening.

Oh, that there might be returning
On some sun-swept azure day
To hear the sibilance of oak leaves falling,
To smell their fragrant pungence,
To see them sail the stream adventuring,
To hold again a long-loved hand!

The Gift

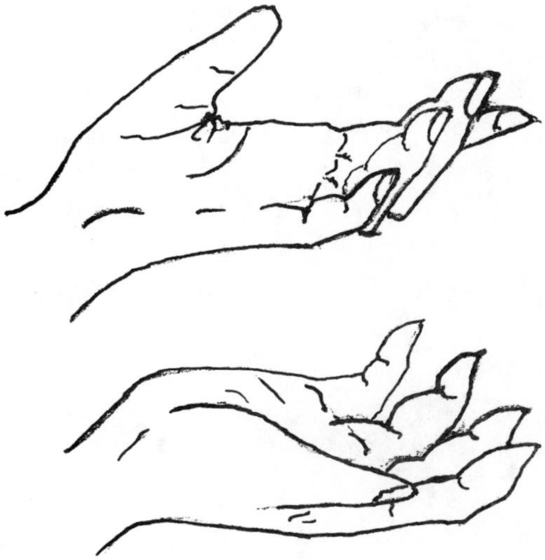

XIV

The surest way to find out what a person is really like is to study the stubs of his checkbook, for what a person gives his money to is a proof of whether or not he is willing to give of himself.

Thoreau said, "My only fear is that I may not be extravagant enough, for love is spendthrift, it is seen in what it gives; it never ceases to give; it never can give enough . . ." His words challenge us to give instead of get, to climb instead of coast, to follow a high dream, to use the gift of life for high and loving purposes. The more we give of ourselves and our resources, of our love, the more we have. It returns multiplied. If we don't reach out we fade out, for the path to happiness comes with losing oneself in something greater than self.

Many believe there has to be reciprocity in human relationships if they are to be meaningful. That is the spirit of the Christmas exchange. But to give to someone who has nothing to give in return is the real essence of the Christian way.

If the thought of return motivates the giving, it loses its effectiveness. It is no gift at all. The gift of self must be given with open hand and heart, with love for people and a sincere desire to improve their environment and potential.

Centrifugal

An ego-centered person has
No more friends than a hermit has:
Reigning king
Without a kingdom,
Starling wing
Without a wingdom.

If the secret desire to receive gratitude or recognition is the motive for trying to improve the community, the whole joy of the work itself is missed, of seeing the dream materialize, step by step, of watching others catch the spirit of the dream and work together for a common goal. Perhaps it is the child's delight in building a house with wooden blocks or a bridge or windmill with Tinkertoys. Whatever it is, it is the warp and woof of happiness.

Those whose goal is recognition and praise are doomed to disappointment, for with the wrong motive they miss the joy of the task and find that while a few may appreciate the effort, there will be a multitude of detractors.

After Wild Rose received the Community Achievement Award, a friend gave me the copy of an advertisement which had appeared years before in the Saturday Evening Post. The following is a partial quote:

"In every field of human endeavor, he that is first must perpetually live in the white light of publicity. Whether the leadership is vested in a man or a manufactured product, emulation and envy are ever at work. If the work is merely mediocre he will be left severely alone. If he achieves a masterpiece, it will set a million tongues wagging. Long after a good work has been done, those who are disappointed or envious continue to cry out that it cannot be done. The little world continued to protest Fulton could never build a steamboat, while the big world flocked to the river bank to see his steamboat float by.

"There is nothing new in this. It is as old as human passions. And it all avails nothing. If a leader truly leads he remains the leader. Master-poet, master-workman, each holds his laurels through the ages. That which is good or great makes itself known. That which deserves to live, lives."

In spite of the above, I am convinced that a leader never functions in a vacuum, does not function on presitge or ability, but in relation to the group and the need. Leaders are not born. Social situations automatically produce them.

Years ago I read of two men who were cutting wood with a crosscut saw, one man on one end of the saw and the other on the opposite. One of the men was doing less than his share and was finally reprimanded, "I don't resent your not doing your share of the pushing and pulling, I don't even mind when you ride on the saw, but I really get mad when you drag your feet!" How much people miss who treat life like a slot machine, putting in as little as possible, always hoping for the jackpot!

Although there are always a few, a very few, who drag their feet, if there is a civic need and a jointly and carefully-evolved plan, the task will go forward to completion, and it is interesting to note that the people whose eyes reflect the joy of life are those who worked toward that end. They have no personal axes to grind; their only satisfaction is the well-being of the whole.

Public servants who are dedicated to the task at hand learn to go calmly about it, listening to constructive suggestions and unruffled by the less than enthusiastic.

Only one person—a friend I treasure— left a mental scar. In her fondness for me, she chided me for working so hard and said, "This dumpy little town isn't worth working for! Why don't you quit?"

Taken aback, I blurted, "I believe in this little town and see its potential. This is our home, our community, the place where our friends live and our children are educated. It provides us with livelihood, security, happiness, sympathy and the rights of free-born Americans! I don't want to quit! I can't quit!"

The conversation ended with her rejoinder, "You aren't working this way for the sake of the town, but because you need to do it for yourself. Everything anyone does is ultimately for himself."

She left, this loved friend whose concept of community was so divergent from ours, and my eyes smarted with unshed tears. For the first time, discouragement consumed my spirit. I had poured my life into this little village. If it had been to no avail, I had lived in vain.

Time heals even scars of the spirit, and in a few moments I could see Wild Rose in perspective again, from the tip of my secret tree—the drab, decaying village of thirty years ago hidden by the fog of time, and a new village sparkling in the sunshine, transformed because countless selfless people with no thought of personal gain had given of themselves and their resources for the public good.

I saw a library where the wisdom of the ages is available to anyone who can read; a Pioneer Museum where the past is preserved for the future; the Garden of Historic Roses, weedless and in full bloom; the newly-deepened millpond shining in the sun, around its shoreline a nature trail, at its base a restored mill, and little Pine River babbling on its way, as clean and clear, since the installation of sewers, as it was before the white man found it. I saw the new elementary and high school, a lighted athletic field and tennis courts, a new convalescent home, a new apartment building for the elderly, a hospital, a clinic, a migrant health center, a park with Pine River sparkling beside it and the four white church spires that still pierced the sky. They existed because of the civic zeal of its citizens. These things I saw, and they were good and worth working for. This was Wild Rose! This was home!

It has been said that the work of the world is done by willing people, those who are willing and those who are willing to let them. But I have found that once people catch the vision and become enthusiastic, nearly everyone finds joy in working toward a common goal.

I am continually impressed by the extraordinary greatness of ordinary people, each playing his own instrument, his own special note, in the orchestration of community. The whole is always more important than any one of its parts, but each is necessary for complete harmony.

In going on a listening walk along a country lane, the music is that of bird, cricket, worm, grasshopper, wind, pine bough, leaf—each voice unique, each voice needed if the ecological chorus is to produce harmony. In seeing, smelling, hearing, listening, feeling, one senses the vibration of countless forms of being, each essential to the well-being of the whole, the oneness of the universe. The mastery of life depends on the mastery of self, and the humility to recognize that we are dependent on the universe and its creatures, on our fellow man and the Creator of all.

We stand in awe at the realization of the interdependence and interaction of all things in the universe, but nothing can compare with the magnificence of the human body; the millions of cells in the human brain; the little muscle of the heart that pumps ten pints of blood through the 60,000 miles of vessels one thousand times a day, year after year as long as life lasts; the hundreds of muscles and bones; the marvels of the five senses that register sight, sound, fragrance, taste and touch. No assembly line production this! Each human being is endowed with his own unique self!

We can scarcely comprehend the marvels of the human body, but, oh, the limitless scope of the human mind! The high potential of the human spirit! The enfolding oneness of Universal Love!

In the years of public service there have been awards and commendations. Of course it is pleasant to hear, "Well done." I do not wish to seem ungrateful. But how much more gratifying are the elation of the dream, the exhilaration of the task, the companionship of the shared goal and the glow of fruition!

During the years I have wanted so much to reciprocate for the debt I owe for life, love and opportunity, to lay some precious gift at the feet of mankind, a spring of cold water in a desert place, a glimpse of light in the brooding dark—something that would say, "I love you, world! I love you, God! Thank you for your gifts to me." But if the opportunity ever came, it passed without my knowing, and now at 75, the gift I wanted to give may never be given.

I have come, at last, to realize that the debt to life can never, never, never be paid. It reaches not only to the recent past but, each generation giving its gifts to the future, back and back to the beginnings of time and the greatest Giver of all, who gave and gave and gives and gives.

Borrowed Light

Moonlight drips
From plum tree tips
And splashes over the grass.
Moonlight lies
In dream-lit eyes
Of the boy and girl who pass.
Do lovers guess,
Does night confess
That the burnished beams of the moon
Are reflected rays
From the glowing face
Of a greater light, the sun?

From the brimming bowl
Of a singing soul
I give my song to the night.
Aroused from sleep
Two robins peep
In the plum tree hung with light.
But if the two
In the plum tree knew
Would they, alike, rejoice
That life-long
My every song
Is an echo of your voice?

On the Eve of a Golden Wedding

XV

The hearthfire burns nightly on these fresh spring evenings when the sun's warmth goes with its setting. How many hundreds of fires have we lit on this hearth since that first one, forty years ago when, our new house nearly completed, we came to sit among the shavings and cook our supper over the first-lit flame?

On the floor between us are shoeboxes of letters we had written to each other before our marriage and since, when one had to be away from the other. We take turns reading them aloud, reliving the young dreams that wrapped themselves around our little world. We smile at the naive visions of the years ahead—hard work, of course, but always tempered with sunlight and laughter, never by dark days that would make us strong. Evening after evening we had taken turns reading aloud, his letters to me and mine to him, until the last letter was enjoyed and replaced in its box.

We sit looking into the flames, thinking the serene, unhurried thoughts of those who have lived long, the world far away in our oneness.

Rising slowly, he leans over to kiss me goodnight. He looks back from the foot of the stairs. "It has been good, hasn't it!"

"Yes, George, it has been good!" He goes to bed early now.

I hear overhead his preparations for bed. Warmed through and through, the hypnotism of the dancing flames binds my mind and body. The house is still. I am alone but not alone.

The lifelong bond between a man and a woman is too precious to share with others, except perhaps as its light shines through to those who tread their pathway. All else we give to the future, the little treasures we have accumulated through the years—our work, our home, our all—but not the secrets of the heart. These we cannot share.

From the pile of yellowed letters I take one and lay it on the embers, watch the edges ignite in yellow flame and feel the warmth on my face that opening the envelope for the first time brought. This is not like closing the door at the end of summer, but locking in our hearts alone the joys the summer gave. I yield another letter to the flames and feel its warmth again, another and another, one by one, until all have been consumed and lie in a silver cloud over the coals.

I look at my watch. (I have always thought it would be pleasant to have a large clock that chimed the hours away, bonging softly and in harmony throughout the house, but that is one of the few minor desires life has not brought.) It is now five minutes of twelve. The house is alive with stillness. I listen raptly, but not long, for tomorrow friends will come to greet us on our golden wedding day, share the festive cake and wish us well. Tomorrow—our golden wedding day!

Though I climb the stairs slowly, a hymn of gratitude wells up within me. Life, how sweet, but LIFE, the perfect WHOLE, how magnificent! Tomorrow is today!

Entering the bedroom, the open window draws me, as it has so many times before to the secret-tree view of the river, the shadowed lawn and the far blue hills which are still the boundary of our world. But the horizon that encircles the valley cannot encircle the mind or the questing spirit, nor quench the dreams that are larger than reality nor the love that reaches out to people everywhere.

I listen to the voice of the river, our loved and lovely river. Tonight the stream is twinkled by moonlight. In the shadows of the birch trees, lacing across the lawn, I see in fancy the quiet forms of the Indians who camped on this little piece of earth we call our own, and the shadows, too, of those other peoples whom the future will bring to the river, those others who will live here until their generation joins the generations of history in the ebb and flow of the centuries.

But as people come and go, live out their lives and pass on to other dimensions of being, the river will remain, flowing on through time, as it boils from the dark depths of resurgent springs—liquid music, eddies bedecked with stars, ever old, ever new. Always a river.

Epilogue

From earth's dark caverns
Crystal springs bubble
Birthing a river, glinting and free.
Thirsty sun stores it in cumulous cisterns
To spill back to earth when the sky overflows,
Filling the caverns, greening the valley,
Eternal cycle that flows past our door.
　　Birch leaves, now yellow, embark on the river,
　　In turn with the river, slowly glide by.
　　Tiny galleons
　　With cargoes
　　Of summer sun
　　Wind whispers
　　Bird song.
　　Where will they harbor, these spent gifts of summer,
　　To become the black goodness purple violets dwell upon?
Soon we who have savored
The essence of living,
People, dawnings, the dew,
Soon we, like leaves, will be free of anchor
On another adventure to where and when.
　　Where do we go then
　　In what form and space,
　　Where will our harbor be?
　　Or could we, like the river,
　　Our ever-new river,
　　May we, like the river,
　　Traverse this valley again?